# MEN
# Who Believe in
# FEMINISM

# MEN
# Who Believe in
# FEMINISM

Amanda Goldrick-Jones



PRAEGER

Westport, Connecticut
London

**Library of Congress Cataloging-in-Publication Data**

Goldrick-Jones, Amanda, 1956–
Men who believe in feminism / Amanda Goldrick-Jones.
p. cm.
Includes bibliographical references and index.
ISBN 0–275–96822–7 (alk. paper)
1. Women's rights. 2. Men—Attitudes. 3. Feminism. I. Title.
HQ1236.G57 2002
305.42—dc21 2001054589

British Library Cataloguing in Publication Data is available.



Library of Congress Catalog Card Number: 2001054589
ISBN: 0–275–96822–7

First published in 2002

Praeger Publishers, 88 Post Road West, Westport, CT 06881
An imprint of Greenwood Publishing Group, Inc.
www.praeger.com

Printed in the United States of America

The paper used in this book complies with the Permanent Paper Standard issued by the National Information Standards Organization (Z39.48–1984).

10 9 8 7 6 5 4 3 2 1

**Copyright Acknowledgments**

Grateful acknowledgment is given to the following sources for permission to quote from: Mick Cooper, *A History of the Men's Movement* (London: Achilles Heel Publications, 1991), pp. 6–9; Bob Pease, personal interview, May 6, 1999, in Melbourne, regarding MASA; Michael Kaufman, personal interview, December 3, 1993; Jack Layton, personal interview, August 31, 1993.

# Contents


Acknowledgments vii

Abbreviations ix

Introduction: "Profeminist" Men: Who and Why? 1

1 Women's Struggles for Change: A Brief History 11

2 "There Was Liberation in the Air . . ." 31

3 "An Idea Whose Time Has Finally Come" 51

4 Trials and Errors: Being Accountable to Feminism 67

5 Profeminism and Inclusivity: Vexed Questions 87

6 "The Ongoing Female Holocaust" 111

7 "Breaking the Silence to End Men's Violence" 131

8 Politics and "the" Antisexist Male 157

Appendix A: Profeminism on the World Wide Web 177

Appendix B: A Method of Analyzing Profeminist Men's Motives 185

References 189

Index 203

# Acknowledgments

I did not realize that men were doing feminist work until late 1992, when—as a graduate student studying in the United States—I first heard about the Canadian White Ribbon Campaign. Since then, my awareness of profeminism has increased a hundredfold, and for that I owe a large debt of gratitude to the men and women who have talked with me, suggested resources, and provided access to documents. Any errors or omissions in this book are my fault, not theirs.

For information about and perspectives on the White Ribbon Campaign, my thanks to Richard Barry, Craig Jones, Michael Kaufman, Jack Layton, Mike McGee, Liam Romalis, and Ron Sluser. I received much early encouragement and information about Canadian profeminist and men's movement issues from Chris Bullock, Stuart McKinnon, and Randy Harris. As well, my thanks to Susan McCrae Van der Voght, a Toronto feminist activist, and to artist Joss MacLennan, who designed the striking "red rose" symbol used by the YWCA to commemorate the December 6, 1989, massacre of fourteen young women in Montréal. I am also grateful to David Rice-Lampert and Marty Dornkervoort, who expressed their perspectives about men's antiviolence activism at a feminist conference in Winnipeg in 1997.

I want to thank Simon Pratt for introducing me to the members of the *Achilles Heel* editorial collective in London, putting me in touch with a number of people, and inviting me to publish in *Achilles Heel*. Warmest thanks to Paul Wolf-Light for his hospitality and insights, and to Mick Cooper, whose comments and materials proved invaluable. Thanks also to

Robin Tuddenham, to Calvin Bell and Jo Trelfa of the Ahimsa (Everyman) Centre, and to Chris Shelley and John Head, both of King's College at the University of London.

Many thanks to Bob Pease of the Royal Melbourne Institute of Technology, who was exceptionally helpful and hospitable and allowed me access to his collection of articles and clippings. I also want to thank Bob Fuller, Chris Dawson, and Andrew Compton for their insights. I'm grateful also to Marnie Daphne and Robyn Henrickson, who spent time with me and shared their experiences and research. My thanks to Gerry Orkin for his perspectives. I also owe Michael Flood in Canberra a great deal of gratitude, not only for allowing me to go through his files and back issues of *XY* magazine, but for graciously putting up with me as a houseguest while I was suffering from Australian flu.

This book would have been incomplete without access to the materials about the American men's movement gathered in the Changing Men Collections at the Michigan State University Libraries. I am grateful to the former curator of this collection, Edward Read Barton, who not only helped me navigate this impressive collection but continued to show a lively interest in my project. He suggested, among other things, that I propose a paper on profeminist men for the American Men's Studies Association. My thanks also to Jim Doyle, editor of the *Journal of Men's Studies*, for his encouragement.

An opportunity in 1998 to visit the University of British Columbia's Centre for Research in Women's Studies and Gender Relations allowed me time to start conceptualizing this project, for which I am very grateful. I would also like to thank the University of Winnipeg's Women's Studies Program and the Centre for Academic Writing for their encouragement, as well as the University of Winnipeg for funding some aspects of this project. Many, many thanks as well to my three research assistants, Sarah Buhler, Leita Kalinowski, and Mary Ann Keane, of the University of Winnipeg.

Finally, a big thank you to my family—Joneses, Goldricks, and Rosengartens—and especially to my husband, Herbert. You have constantly supported this work and encouraged me to keep at it. I might have been able to do it without you, but only just.

# Abbreviations

| | |
|---|---|
| AAUW | American Association of University Women |
| ANZAC | Australian and New Zealand Army Corps |
| CAMP | California Anti-Sexual Men's Political Caucus |
| CEW | Committee for Equality for Women |
| *CM* | *Changing Men* |
| CR | consciousness-raising |
| EMV | Ending Men's Violence |
| IASOM | International Association for Studies of Men |
| M & M | Men and Masculinity(ies) Conference |
| MAN for ERA | Men Allied Nationally for Equal Rights Amendment |
| MAS | Men against Sexism |
| MASA | Men against Sexual Assault (Australia) |
| MLAs | members of the legislative assembly |
| MNC | Men's Network for Change |
| NAC | National Abortion Campaign (1970s)<br>National Action Committee on the Status of Women (Canada) |
| NAMBLA | North American Man-Boy Love Association |
| NCADV | National Coalition against Domestic Violence |
| NOMAS | National Organization for Men against Sexism |
| NOCM | National Organization for Changing Men |
| RAVEN | Rape and Violence End Now |
| RCSW | Royal Commission on the Status of Women |

| | |
|---|---|
| SUV | Sport utility vehicle |
| VOCA | Victims of Crime Act |
| WAP | Women against Pornography |
| WAVAW | Women against Violence against Women |
| WEL | Women's Electoral Lobby |
| WLM | Women's Liberation Movement |
| WRC | White Ribbon Campaign |
| YWCA | Young Women's Christian Association |

# Introduction: "Profeminist" Men: Who and Why?

> [t]he struggle for women's liberation *is* the struggle for men's liberation as whole and feeling persons capable of equal relationships. We say flatly: the women's movement is the best thing that has ever happened for men. It has given women the support to bring us challenges. The challenges have lead [sic] to insight and personal growth. This growth has enriched our lives as men.
>
> Statement issued at a public demonstration, December 30, 1978, at the 5th National Conference on Men and Masculinity, Los Angeles, California

Over the three to four years it took me to write this book, I lost count of the times people said to me: "You're writing a book about men who believe in feminism? *Are* there any?" The answer is yes. Enough men in this world have believed in feminism to fill libraries with documents and books, create numerous web sites, and lead me to create dozens of files and hundreds of pages of research materials. All this is quite aside from the many men around the world who incorporate feminism in their teaching and daily lives, study men and masculinity from feminist perspectives, and engage in a variety of public and private activities to help bring about gender justice and equality. This book explores the motives and tells the stories of antisexist men's groups in North America, Britain, and Australia from the early 1970s through the end of the 1990s. Though diverse, these groups shared a common goal of inviting men to support feminist principles and do feminist work.

We are supposedly living in a "postfeminist" age in which white middle-class women are taking over from men and running the world. Yet sexual stereotyping seems once again to be on the rise in North America, and appalling numbers of women live in poverty worldwide. In North America, Europe, and other First World countries, women have secured a considerable number of rights. Yet macho values are celebrated each time a new SUV rolls off the assembly line or a new fight breaks out on the hockey rink. It seems almost quaint to be invoking a time when men's liberation was a subject for books, magazine articles, and public discussion.

Why should a man or group of men support feminism today? After all, isn't "feminism" hostile to men? It's true that the question of men's relations with feminism—what it has been, what it is, and what it should be—has generated mixed feelings among feminist women. In 1973, Mary Daly cautioned that "it is important to be aware of the ways in which men can and do avoid hearing women's new words while appearing to listen."[1] In 1974, a feminist collective in Portland, Oregon, put together a committee exploring "the role of men in the women's movement" and argued that women would *be* able to do feminist work more effectively without men's political involvement.[2] In the April 1978 issue of *Ms.*, a collection of articles looked at "Secrets of the New Male Sexuality" from women's perspectives. "Is this the year of the man?" asked Carol Tavris in this issue after attending a conference on masculinity at which "participants busily assured each other of their liberated credentials" and a "Professional Male Feminist" propositioned her.[3] Carol Kleiman wondered whether it was yet time to say "Goodbye, John Wayne" after spending three days at a men's conference. "I realized," she concluded, "[that] while I was supportive, and often enthusiastic at the convention, I still didn't like *my* rhetoric co-opted by 'the enemy,' who often benefits from my oppression."[4] During the mid-1980s through the early 1990s, academic feminists debated whether men should be "in" feminism and whether the new field of men's studies might, in fact, undermine feminism while claiming to do otherwise.[5]

While still wanting to hold men accountable, many feminists believe that men are good for feminism and welcome their support and initiatives. Among them, Gloria Steinem is on record for calling on men to join feminist women in their struggle for gender justice. "Make no mistake about it: Women want a men's movement. We are literally dying for it." For bell hooks, a black feminist writer and academic, men's involvement in feminism is "a necessary movement. . . . When feminism is defined as a movement to end sexism and sexist oppression, it is clear that everyone has a role to play."[6] Lynne Segal asserts in her book *Slow Motion: Changing Masculinities, Changing Men* that feminism has had positive effects on men, and she applauds men's anti-sexist initiatives such as Canada's White Ribbon Campaign, whose goal is opposing violence against women.[7]

In the early- to mid-nineteenth century, respectable middle-class feminist reformers were discouraged from speaking publicly. These first feminist reformers acknowledged that men needed to add their voices to the forum of discussion about women's rights. Since then, men have played a supportive role in women's struggle to secure the vote and access to higher education. Men have also helped women fight for reproductive choices, pay equity and workplace rights, and an end to male violence against women.

It seems difficult to believe that for many men in the 1970s and early 1980s, feminism was one of the most exciting social movements they had ever experienced, full of possibilities for both sexes to become "liberated." Nor was it unusual, at least in the United States, for supportive men and feminists to create and sustain good working relations. In 1970, Steinem wrote an article for the *Washington Post* called " 'Women's Liberation' Aims to Free Men, Too."[8] The National Organization for Women formed a committee during the 1970s on the male mystique, chaired by none other than Warren Farrell. During that decade, *Ms.* magazine ran a semiregular "Men" department, featuring a different guest male writer each time. In the early 1980s, feminist women were part of the planning and executive groups that formed the National Organization for Changing Men. Feminist women also attended the annual Men & Masculinity conferences. In August 1984, *Ms.* published a special issue on "What Men Haven't Said to Women." Almost all the articles were written by men and expressed men's perspectives on such issues as power, anger, housework, listening, and birth control. As Steinem noted in her introduction to this landmark issue, "we decided to turn this month's 'Ms.' into a free place where a variety of men could tell the truth about themselves and about their feelings toward changes in the female/male balance of power."[9]

Then and now, men who believe in feminism have often been inspired by female partners, friends, or family members.[10] In his study of British antisexist men in the early 1980s, sociologist Harry Christian confirms the significant influence of feminism as a motive for doing profeminist work: "nearly all the men who had become motivated to join an anti-sexist men's group said their earlier experiences had been reinforced and further developed by the influence of feminism . . . in most cases by a close relationship with a particular woman who had a feminist outlook."[11] Some men have learned about feminism from working alongside feminist women in academe, government, or in sociopolitical movements such as environmentalism. Some men, influenced as children by strong women, grew up sympathetic to feminism. One Australian profeminist I spoke with said he remembers standing up for women's issues even as a child, inspired in part by his social worker mother. Some younger men, born in the 1970s or later, have been brought up in feminist households. A small minority of men today are learning about feminism from women's studies courses or programs, in some ways paralleling the experiences of men in the 1970s who learned about feminism by reading the literature and "rapping" with feminist women.

A strong sense of social justice, the presence of feminist women in their lives, a feeling of being trapped by traditional masculinity, and/or a sense of "the inherent rightness"[12] of the women's movement have been among the main reasons some men have supported feminist causes and done feminist work. The rise of men's liberation and men's antisexist activism in the 1970s through the 1990s has been the latest and most active period for profeminist work. In Britain and in North America during the 1970s, thousands of men were inspired by the women's liberation movement to form consciousness-raising groups and speak publicly against sexism. In the early 1980s, the first national profeminist men's organization was formed in the United States, and mainstream media coverage of the new sensitive man was not rare. In 1991, the all-male White Ribbon Campaign called on men across Canada to end men's violence against women. Dozens of similar, if smaller, men's antiviolence and anti-rape groups still exist in North America, Europe, Australia, and New Zealand.

I use the term "profeminist" throughout this book in deference to the fact that most men who believe in feminism today prefer describing themselves as "profeminists" rather than "feminists." Broadly, profeminist, spelled with or without a hyphen, refers to men who ground their personal lives or political acts on feminist principles. Australian profeminist Michael Flood explains: "The term "pro-feminist" is almost equivalent to "anti-sexist," and I often use the two terms interchangeably. But I like the term pro-feminism because it suggests an explicit and ongoing commitment to support feminism. Without this, men may drift towards an understanding of sexism that neglects men's power over women."[13] According to American profeminist Harry Brod, the hyphenated term is favored by supportive men "who believe feminism to be essentially of, by, and for women."[14] While Brod respects this viewpoint, he himself prefers profeminism, which speaks of "a developing feminist politics of, by, and for men" and a willingness to "*fully* commit ourselves to eliminating patriarchy."[15]

Profeminist activism has a rich pedigree and is associated with a growing body of academic literature. Much of this has been produced by men currently or formerly involved in profeminist work; some of these men are academics involved in gender studies or in men's or masculinity studies. Yet relatively few feminists—let alone members of the general population—know about men's feminist work: its history, motives, challenges, benefits, failures, or future possibilities. This is partly because the number of men who actively support feminism and gender equality is limited. Also, organizations like the U.S.–based National Organization for Men against Sexism, Canada's Men's Network for Change, or Australia's Men against Sexual Assault have disbanded or shrunk considerably. While some profeminists who have dropped out of the larger campaigns or organizations are still doing profeminist work, this is often on a small or local scale, enriching the lives of a few but escaping the awareness of the many. Even most students of women's studies are startled to hear that men have played a role, at times significant, in redressing gender injustice.

Of those familiar with profeminist work, some are pessimistic about the current state and future of what Segal calls collective antisexist initiatives. Such initiatives "still occupy only a small space in the cultural landscape . . . all the more embattled in the tough, individualistic climate encouraged by conservative governments."[16] Many feminists are also worried that the once heavily antisexist men's movement has become more concerned with men's emotions, issues, and rights than with helping women fight sexism. While at least one U.S. conference per year still attracts an antisexist contingent, other types of men's gatherings have drawn larger crowds: warrior weekends, mythopoetic groups drawing on masculine archetypes described in Robert Bly's *Iron John*, the evangelistic rallies of the Christian Promise Keepers, and in 1995, the all-black Million Man march. Kay Leigh Hagan's 1992 collection *Women Respond to the Men's Movement* is perhaps the best-known example of feminists critiquing the motives behind men's gatherings, especially those inspired by Bly.

It may indeed seem that men have lost interest in working for gender equality and that feminist women are once again on their own. Yet, argues Gloria Steinem, if any of these men's groups can help men "reject male privilege" and encourage them to "share the struggle" with women, then there is still hope.[17] In my own cautiously optimistic view, now may be just the right time to tell stories about men who believe in feminism and why they decided to act on their principles.

It hasn't been easy forming profeminist groups or keeping them together. Men who believe in feminism are also faced with what Susan Faludi, in her book *Stiffed: The Betrayal of the American Man*, calls a "bedeviling paradox, and the source of male inaction."[18] If feminists can organize against patriarchy, which many have equated with masculinity, against what enemy can men mobilize? Patriarchy literally means "the rule of the fathers," but is understood within contemporary feminist thought to encompass any practices and systems that oppress, control, or dominate women. For feminists, patriarchy creates and perpetuates an interlocking system of inequalities or, if you will, creates an endless series of uneven playing fields. Among other goals, feminism seeks to name, critique, and transform the ways patriarchy operates within family relations, economic systems, and institutions globally (see chapter 1).

But as Faludi puts it, "The solution for women has proved the problem for men." In order to support the feminist goal of dismantling patriarchy, profeminist men have had to think about whether, or how much, to dismantle masculinity itself. This process can be a painful one, engendering guilt, resentment, and paralysis. The closest feminist equivalent to this uniquely male problem occurs when white middle-class feminist women have to confront and try to dismantle their own racism and classism. Just as some supposedly solid sisterhoods have fragmented over the resulting conflicts, profeminist groups have lost men who resented being "guilted out" or who thought they were being asked to reject everything masculine. One significant breakthrough for profeminist men is a powerful redefinition of masculinity, not as a static state but as multiple embodiments or different masculinities arising out of various social and cultural contexts.[19] Even so, the challenge of dismantling not only patriarchy but also entire concepts of what it means to be a man can be daunting and exhausting.

Another difficulty for profeminists arises out of a feminist conviction that being a man within patriarchy means that you will—whether you're aware of it or not—exercise male privilege in ways that may be oppressive to women. Among the questions profeminists have considered in forming group strategies and projects—and among the questions this book considers—are ones relating to how closely men can, or should, work with feminists and to what extent profeminists should be accountable to feminism: Can a man really say he's a feminist if he hasn't experienced life as a woman under patriarchy? Can men be true allies of feminism if masculinity has been defined as part of the problem of patriarchy? Should feminist women be worried about well-meaning men dominating feminist territory?

Despite the tensions arising at times between profeminist men's groups and feminist women, there is no doubt that profeminist groups have been inspired or at least educated by feminism. In that spirit, this book includes some feminist history and examples of activism that are most relevant to men's involvement in feminist work. Chapter 1, "Women's Struggles for Change: A Brief History," outlines major feminist campaigns and reforms undertaken during the so-called First and Second Waves of feminism. Here, I also describe some directions feminism took in Canada, Britain, the United States, and Australia in the 1960s and 1970s. Chapter 2, "There Was Liberation in the Air . . . ," focuses on men in the United States and Britain in the 1970s, who began forming consciousness-raising groups, holding conferences, and writing about what they considered the exciting question of how men might benefit from the women's movement. For a number of men, the next logical step was to form larger profeminist organizations. Chapter 3, "An Idea Whose Time Has Finally Come," tells two stories: one about the early years of the U.S.–based National Organization for Changing Men or NOCM (later the National Organization for Men against Sexism) and the other about the founding of the White Ribbon Campaign.

The two chapters that follow describe some of the organizational and political challenges profeminist groups have encountered. Chapter 4, "Trials and Errors: Being Accountable to Feminism," examines how the White

Ribbon Campaign dealt with criticisms from feminists, as well as the different strategies used by the National Organization for Changing Men and Australia's Men against Sexual Assault for keeping the lines of communication open to feminist groups. I also take a brief look at how strategies for accountability have taken theories about gender and power into consideration. An even more difficult task for profeminist organizations has been ensuring that diverse men are included and their views fairly represented. Chapter 5, "Profeminism and Inclusivity: Vexed Questions," describes how the National Organization for Changing Men dealt with conflicting views about including women, as well as whether the organization should be based on a more grassroots, regional model. An even more serious question for NOCM, though, was whether its mainly white, middle-class core was fairly representing the interests of nonwhite men, especially black men. This chapter also briefly explores, through the eyes of British and Australian profeminists, whether the antisexist men's movement can ever really be inviting to working-class men.

Some of the more successful profeminist projects have raised men's awareness of and invited men to act against men's violence to women. Chapter 6, "The Ongoing Female Holocaust," provides a context for profeminist work in this area by focusing on how feminist women activists in Canada, the United States, Britain, and Australia have tried to aid victims of domestic violence and rape and improve antiviolence legislation. In chapter 7, "Breaking the Silence to End Men's Violence," I describe the varied approaches and accomplishments of the White Ribbon Campaign, the Antipornography and Ending Men's Violence Task Groups of the NOCM, Men against Sexual Assault, and a unique men's center in Britain.

Chapter 8, "Politics and 'the' Antisexist Male," enters the bleak territory of crisis and fragmentation, focusing on conflicts and occasionally misunderstandings about what it means for men to make a commitment to feminism, particularly to its more radical principles. In this chapter, I also explore the question of male guilt and how profeminist men have dealt with it. In Britain during the 1970s and early 1980s, the men's movement never did form a significant national presence, becoming fragmented over challenges from radical and gay men about how far men should go in order to satisfy feminist goals. The U.S. national profeminist organization actively supported gay issues, and some of the executive members were gay. But after an executive member published an article in the early 1990s about his early gay experiences, describing his apparent seduction of a young boy, a number of members bitterly criticized the organization on the basis that it had lost sight of its commitment to feminism. In the wake of this crisis, the country's only national profeminist magazine stopped publishing, and the National Organization for Men against Sexism itself went into a decline from which its recovery remains uncertain.

This may seem a pessimistic note on which to end a book whose purpose is not only to inform but to suggest that profeminist men's work has a future. Appendix A ("Profeminism on the World Wide Web") lists and describes a variety of web sites and related resources and is intended to provide encouragement, through demonstration, that profeminist work itself is still alive and well and taking a variety of forms.

Through this book, I invite not only academic readers but anyone interested in gender relations, and especially in men's issues or feminism, to find out more about profeminist men's work. A great deal of research in gender relations stems from sociology, and indeed many of the feminists and profeminists whose writings I cite work within that discipline. My own background is in the humanities, and I have a longtime professional interest in exploring how written communication provides insights into people's motives, attitudes, and relationships—including conflicts. In that spirit, I have tried not to let theoretical or analytical discussions interfere too much with storytelling. Though I have interviewed a number of men, my principal method of gaining insights into profeminist men's groups has been to analyze the written documents these groups have produced. From this analysis, I have tried to piece together stories about what happened to the groups as well as provide some commentary about the importance of certain terms or arguments in the documents. For a theoretical perspective on why and how my analysis helps uncover motives and conflicts, see Appendix B ("A Method of Analyzing Profeminist Men's Motives"). Readers interested in following up on any of the other sources or theories I mention will find more information in the endnotes.

Finally, this book represents my own attempt—as a teacher of feminism and public communication—to reconcile feminist principles with my conviction that surely there is a role for men to play. Men are not the enemy, and feminism isn't just women's work. There are enough challenges to keep everyone busy; all hands are needed on deck. Admittedly, much material in this book focuses on profeminist men's failures and the fragmentation of antisexist groups or projects. But it is also important to keep in mind that there have been successes and that profeminist efforts to do feminist work and cooperate with women's groups can and do bear fruit. As this book will show, these projects vary enormously in nature and scope. Some have been short-lived, while others have spanned decades. Some take place quietly in living rooms, while others have made headlines, nationally and internationally. Many profeminists have found satisfaction in cooperating on the creative, frustrating, elusive, yet exciting prospect of dismantling sexism within their lifetimes, or the lifetimes of their children. It is my hope, and the hope of many other feminist women, that this kind of men's work will continue.

## NOTES

1. Mary Daly (1973), pp. 32–33.

2. Portland Feminist Coordinating Council Forum on the role of men in the women's movement (1974, March 19). Men's place—a separatist viewpoint. Unpublished pamphlet. From the Changing Men Collection, Michigan State University Library, 1 p.

3. Carol Tavris (1978, April), pp. 51, 78.

4. Carol Kleiman (1978, April), pp. 45–47, 77. Quote is from p. 77.

5. See, for example, Jardine (1987); Canaan and Griffin (1990); Williams (1990, April); and Porter (1992). I also discuss feminist critiques of "men 'in' feminism" in chapter 4.

6. Gloria Steinem in Kay Leigh Hagan (1992), pp. v-ix, and bell hooks (1992), pp. 111–117.

7. Lynne Segal (1997), pp. xxvi–xxvii.

8. Gloria Steinem (1970, June 7).

9. Gloria Steinem (1984, August), p. 41.

10. Some men have written specifically about their struggles to understand feminism and their relationships with feminist women. See, for example, John Rowan's (1987); various essays in Michael King (1988); Gordon Mott (1992); and Michael Kaufman (1993). Many similar stories can be found in the British men's magazine *Achilles Heel* and in Australia's *XY* magazine (though *XY* is no longer published, selected articles are available on the World Wide Web).

11. Harry Christian (1994), p. 29.

12. Quoted in ibid., p. 30.

13. Michael Flood (1993/1994, summer).

14. Harry Brod (1998), p. 207.

15. Ibid., p. 208.

16. Segal (1997), p. xxvii.

17. Steinem in Hagan (1992), p. ix.

18. Susan Faludi (1999), p. 604.

19. The concept of multiple masculinities is fully articulated by R. W. Connell (1995).

# 1

# Women's Struggles for Change: A Brief History

Much of the profeminist work undertaken by men described in this book is indebted to and inspired by feminism, and there are few (if any) profeminist men who don't acknowledge that fact. In its broadest sense, feminism means being aware of gender-based injustice and being willing to take some kind of action—direct or indirect—to redress these injustices. Feminists have generally focused on four major areas of understanding: first, that "virtually all social and institutional relations" are gendered; second, that gender relations are inseparable from a wide range of "inequities and contradictions in social life"; third, that gender relations aren't "natural" or innate but are products of history and socioculture; and fourth, that in order to change unequal or oppressive gender relations, feminists have to take political action and whenever possible, challenge "traditional race-class-sexuality-power arrangements."[1] Feminist thought and activism have a long and honorable history, and some understanding of this history is helpful for appreciating the issues and challenges faced by men who have chosen to support feminism.

I teach introductory women's studies, and occasionally students are surprised by the news that feminism did not begin in the 1960s. When asked what women were doing before that time, the response "staying at home" comes up a fair number of times. One of the great pleasures of teaching women's studies is to introduce students to Mary Wollstonecraft, John Stuart Mill, Friedrich Engels, and other early feminist thinkers. We explore nineteenth- and early twentieth-century activism in the United States, Canada, and Britain—when women and their male supporters struggled against slavery and for higher education, the vote, reproductive rights, and workplace equality. Students also find out that black women were often the sole supporters of their families and the mainstays of entire communities. They discover that women did the lion's share of men's work during the two world wars, but that middle-class women were cut out of the market during two remarkably different economic cycles: the Depression and the booming 1950s. Students realize that not all women were housewives, as illustrated by the stark contrasts between the primarily white middle-class "problem without a name" and the ongoing efforts of black, immigrant, and aboriginal women to survive and fight racism as well as sexism.

## THE ROOTS OF FEMINISM

In the late seventeenth and early eighteenth centuries, well-read upper-class women like Anne Bradstreet, Katherine Philips, Margaret Cavendish, Aphra Behn, Lady Mary Chudleigh, and Anne Finch wrote about families, work, and travel from women's perspectives. While many of their poems and other writings celebrated married love and family life, some satirized both marriage and men's attitudes—at times none too gently. Philips lamented that "A marryd state affords but little Ease/The best of husbands are so hard to please," and advised a woman friend that it was better to remain a spinster. Chudleigh warned in "To the ladies" that "Wife and servant are the same/But only differ in the name," and Finch equated marriage with a set of "unequal fetters":

> Marriage does but slightly tye Men
> Whil'st close Pris'ners we remain
> They the larger Slaves of Hymen
> Still are begging Love again
> At the full length of all their chain.

In the late eighteenth century, Mary Wollstonecraft's *A Vindication of the Rights of Woman* (1792) issued the first clear call for equality between women and men in British society. Feminist scholars also consider this work to be the first treatise on what is now called liberal feminism: very simply, the belief that women and men should be treated equally. Serious discussions of equality between the sexes were also influenced by a growing nineteenth-century concern—both in Britain and the United States—with antislavery work, which provided middle-class women reformers with some insights into the injustices they themselves suffered.[2] Slaves, like white women, could not vote or own property, had no legal rights to their own children, and could seek no redress against abuse or violence. However, middle-class white women had some access to limited employment and education, and under certain circumstances or given particular topics, they could write and speak in public forums.

Most respectable and well-published male intellectuals (for example Rousseau, whom Wollstonecraft detested) took the position that women were physically, mentally, and emotionally different from men and that these differences made women better suited to the domestic sphere. However, among the small number of men who publicly supported women's equality in the public sphere were John Stuart Mill ("The Subjection of Women," 1869/1970), and Friedrich Engels ("The Origin of the Family . . . ," 1884/1993). Mill is one of the first high-profile profeminists to be inspired by feminist women; Harriet Taylor (1807–1858), with whom he shared a long intellectual partnership before their marriage in 1851, not only read but co-authored much of Mill's writing. In some of her own essays, Taylor criticized women's economic dependence on men and argued that marriage laws needed to be radically reformed. The couple was co-authoring "The Subjection of Women" when Taylor died in 1858. Taylor's daughter from her first marriage, Helen—a women's rights activist—helped Mill complete the work.[3]

Like Wollstonecraft, Mill and Taylor had a profound effect on shaping "natural rights" or liberal feminism in Britain and North America. Grounded on Enlightenment ideals about the rights of man, the liberal feminism of Wollstonecraft, Taylor, and Mill assumed the equality of women and men and sought to entrench that equality within public institutions. Engels, who included working-class women in his analysis and drew relationships between capitalism and women's oppression, helped lay foundations for Marxist/socialist feminism. This philosophy is one of several kinds of radical feminism, all of which seek to redress gender injustice by dismantling oppressive institutions and power structures, whether economic, political, or sexual.

In the early nineteenth century, these differing stances had not yet been articulated. At that point, women in the United States and Britain were deeply interested in social reform projects that provided nurturing soil for the growth of First Wave feminism: that period from the mid-nineteenth through the early twentieth centuries when women formed mass movements to obtain basic rights, such as the right to vote. Women reformers undertook church activities, started charitable organizations, and worked in the antislavery movement. American women reformers before the Civil War pushed not only for the abolition of slavery but also, with reasonable success, for women's access to higher education. Similarly, "specific issues which engaged the attention of women at the outset of the British women's movement in 1856 were the rights of married women to own property, family welfare and better opportunities of education and employment."[4]

## GAINING THE VOTE

The philosophies of Wollstonecraft, Taylor, and Mill gave American women activists necessary tools for building equal opportunity arguments. In the latter half of the nineteenth century, American women reformers focused primarily on obtaining the vote, considering enfranchisement as "a necessary step in the process of having a say in the social and political decisions over their lives."[5] Susan B. Anthony and Elizabeth Cady Stanton are considered the main architects of this suffrage movement. Disgusted by the fact that, as women, they were not allowed to speak at an antislavery meeting in London, England, Anthony and Cady Stanton organized the world's first women's rights conference in Seneca Falls. On July 20, 1848, sixty-eight women and thirty-four men set out a "Declaration of Sentiments" whose language parallels that of the Declaration of Independence: "We hold these truths to be self-evident, that all men and women are created equal."[6] This Declaration called for women's equality in all areas of public and private life, including the right to vote.

The American feminist campaign for the vote was one among several other campaigns for women's rights gathering momentum in the mid- to late-1800s, notably property rights reforms for married women and access to all levels of education, as well as male-dominated trades and professions, such as medicine. But not all feminists in the United States agreed with this liberal agenda. Feminist historians have recorded tensions between liberal feminists and feminists demanding radical transformations in family structure or advocating free love. Though doomed to be lost causes in this puritanical era, these more radical demands anticipated the sexual revolution of the 1960s and are now associated with gains made during the Second Wave of feminism.[7]

A popular persuasive strategy used by nineteenth century women reformers was to tap into conservative views about women's maternal abilities. The witty and outspoken Canadian reformer Nellie McClung won over the prairie press with her emphasis on women's responsibilities and duties as citizens. Among other events, she staged a satirical Women's Parliament in which men were judged by their handsome appearance, and it was argued that women were naturally the guardians of the race and their vote would help to lift high the standard of morality. The notion that a woman's special role as mother "gives her the duty and the right to participate in the public sphere"[8] has been labelled maternal feminism, a set of beliefs still echoed today in some radical feminist philosophy.[9] While many First Wave women reformers passionately believed females were morally superior to males, maternal feminism can also be seen as a prudent persuasive strategy; in an era when respectable women were discouraged from even speaking in public, let alone taking a political stance, expressing reformist arguments in maternal terms made women's demands less threatening.

In the United States and worldwide, women's struggle for the vote was a long one, with many setbacks. In most English-speaking nations, women won enfranchisement piecemeal, state by state or province by province. Often this process took years, even decades. In 1894 the state of South Australia gave women the vote, but women in Victoria had to wait until 1908. In England, women undertook mass activism and encountered police violence at rallies; suffragette leaders who protested with hunger strikes were force-fed, and one protester died after being trampled by a racehorse. Yet only in 1918 were a restricted constituency of British women[10] given the vote, a grateful nation having decided they'd earned the right after demonstrating patriotism and good citizenship during World War I. Though American women began campaigning for the vote in 1848, only after 1920 did they become enfranchised. While Nellie McClung's ability to combine wit with morality helped win the vote for western Canadian women in 1916, followed rapidly by other provinces, women in Québec (who had also been organizing around suffrage since the late 19th century) were not allowed to vote until 1940. In many jurisdictions, nonwhites waited decades longer. In Canada, First Nations peoples were not enfranchised until 1960. Until 1967, Australian aboriginals were considered "flora and fauna" and not counted in the national census. That same year, they obtained citizen status and the right to vote.

## RECENT FEMINIST ERUPTIONS (OR, A BRIEF OVERVIEW OF THE SECOND WAVE)

"Ideological and social conditions were conducive to a widespread challenging of the 'status quo' and convention . . . there was a general resurgence of a radical, political ideology taking place in Europe, the USA and Australia by the mid-1960s."[11]

In the nineteenth and early twentieth centuries, topics like abolition, temperance, women's suffrage, better working conditions, and higher education for women were common rallying points for women reformers and feminists. Yet one of the reasons why the 1960s and 1970s seem so resonant for feminists, and perhaps a reason why many students think of that period as when feminism began, is that for the first time women were able to organize en masse and at all levels, from the grassroots to the highest levels of government. Popularly known as the Second Wave of feminism, this period from the late 1960s through the 1970s was galvanic. Like past moments of feminist activism and reform, feminist activism and the rich burgeoning of feminist theory in late 1960s and 1970s in many ways resembles a volcanic eruption much more than a wave. The mass activism and the public profile it helped engender gave feminists opportunities to force a wide range of women's issues onto political, legislative, and cultural agendas.

The motives energizing British, Canadian, Australian, and American feminist activism also directly and indirectly shaped profeminist men's responses and work. While these countries' distinct histories gave rise to different kinds of feminist activism, including culturally distinct concepts of profeminist activism, a number of common conditions made it inevitable that certain feminist issues would emerge. For example, according to historian David Bouchier,[12] who has compared 1970s British and American feminism, both countries experienced long campaigns for women's suffrage (which took a more militant turn in Britain); a massive involvement of women in the workforce during World War I and II; a 1930s depression and a 1950s boom which effectively excluded most middle-class women from the marketplace; and some gains in reproductive rights and sexual freedom by the 1960s.

## BRITAIN

Much British feminist thought has been influenced by a brand of socialism rooted at least partly in the philanthropy of nineteenth century women who worked for prison reform, an end to child labor, and better public health and working conditions.[13] The British suffrage movement of the late nineteenth and early twentieth centuries created stronger ties with working-class women's issues, such as higher wages and improved conditions; it was also much more militant than its United States or Canadian counterparts. The famous (or infamous) suffragettes were spearheaded by the fiery mother and daughter team of Emmaline and Christabel Pankhurst. Yet while the suffragettes presented a united front, deep divisions opened up between working-class and middle-class women. Indeed, some women resented the fact that the Pankhursts had domestic help and even "the time and money"[14] to be arrested and thrown in jail.

Working-class women in Europe and North America generally lacked the time or financial resources to organize effectively; most organizations for working-class women were created and run by middle-class women. Even so, feminist historian Marlene LeGates notes that British feminist reformists were more likely to venture into the front lines by getting themselves elected to school boards and local councils. They had a better understanding of working-class women's constraints, among them constantly struggling to balance work and childcare instead of having the choice *not* to work.[15] Socialist, and later neo-Marxist, feminists critiqued traditional family structures from several perspectives, such as recognizing that unpaid domestic work has little or no status, that the unpaid work women do supports the capitalist system, and that domestic work should be paid—or at least counted.[16]

Women's discontent with domestic subordination simmered for years, but this issue alone wasn't enough to motivate the next major eruption of

British feminist activism in the 1970s. Growing concerns about women's sexual equality and sexual freedom and the inspiration provided by Germaine Greer's *The Female Eunuch* (1970) energized much of this Second Wave activity. Greer saw a strong relationship between an artificial femininity and the development of capitalism, but she was less enthusiastic about changing the social relations of production than she was about envisioning "the lifting of sexual repression and the transformation of sexual relations." She advocated a model for "a proper, fully social form of love . . . between equals, based on the attraction of like to like."[17] Probably because Greer was more interested in sexual freedom than in other forms of sexual politics, she did not at first identify herself with the women's movement, and her work was seldom cited in British feminist writing.[18] Yet *The Female Eunuch* and Betty Friedan's *The Feminine Mystique* were among the few feminist publications to break through the mass media barrier.

By 1974, as British feminist writer and novelist Ann Oakley recalls,

> feminism was in full swing again. There was a newspaper, *Shrew*, the voice of the women's liberation workshop, and the magazine *Spare Rib* had entered the cookery section of newsagents' shops. . . . They were strident times, full of metallic demands and easy notions of utopia. . . . Women's groups listed the political requisites for their liberation: free contraception and abortion on demand, free childcare, increased family allowances, equal pay and opportunities at work, proper paid maternity leave, no more discrimination in tax and social security systems: there was a lot to be done. Meetings and conferences abounded. But, partly because the voices that were raised were not in unison, few agreements could be reached about the political strategies needed to correct the problems.[19]

Many of these meetings and conferences, as well as much of the disagreement about strategies, took place outside the political and cultural mainstream. Enormous energy infused the first major feminist gathering at Oxford in 1970, whose delegates made a significant decision to operate as an autonomous movement outside established political avenues and initiated four major demands that would shape feminist politics into the 1980s. The first two—equal pay and equal opportunity—rested firmly on a liberal platform and were not considered very contentious. However, as Oakley intimates, the political landscape of British feminism was already showing signs of a split between liberal and more radical feminist perspectives, illustrated by reactions to the latter two demands—free contraception and abortion on demand, and free childcare—which quickly became sources of conflict and controversy. This came on top of tensions created by a 1972 split between the larger women's movement and the women involved in Gay Liberation, who broke away "to form their own autonomous movement."[20] Because many feminists felt that mass public acceptance of women's demands was a high priority, lesbianism was considered a potential threat to achieving these goals.

As Bouchier notes, whenever it seemed as if an issue was being co-opted into the mainstream, significant parts of the British women's movement gravitated toward "more deeply radical positions."[21] It was rare but not unknown for men to be involved in some radical feminist work, including the National Abortion Campaign (NAC) during the 1970s. NAC maintained a strong and coherent presence throughout the 1970s, thwarting attempts by antiabortion forces to limit access. But as contraception and abortion became institutionalized in Britain, more women found the radically leftist stance taken by the NAC to be alienating. It's also interesting that men's involvement in the NAC was seen by some as an example of men dominating a women's issue[22]—a criticism that would prove to be a constant thorn in the sides of profeminists.

At the same time, separatism from men represented a significantly radical feminist position in Britain. As well as challenging profeminist men, separatist feminism was problematic for many women in the movement. Separatism is the position of some radical feminists that neither men nor women cooperating with men can be trusted. Ideally, women and men should not live or work together.[23] Adding a Marxist/socialist feminist analysis connecting patriarchy and capitalism, some separatist feminists also wondered—if capitalism exploits women, isn't that an even stronger reason for women to separate from men, who perpetuate and benefit most from capitalism?[24] Not surprisingly, an ideological gap existed between liberal feminists, who wanted equality for women within existing economic and social systems, and socialist feminists, who were committed to a working class revolution.

Yet some feminists thought it possible to take a Marxist perspective on feminism, sex roles, women's work, and even psychoanalysis, without necessarily advocating separatism.[25] Stemming from the neo-Marxism of the 1960s, this analysis focuses on how cultural and social, as well as economic, norms effectively maintain the power of ruling groups. As their political involvement shifted from the labor movement to feminism, some British feminists found neo-Marxism compatible with the goal of ending patriarchy. They began to ground their feminism on a "clearly socialist analysis which identified women's liberation with the unity of the working class and the struggle against capitalism."[26] Among the key differences between a liberal and a Marxist/socialist feminist perspective is the view of wage labor: liberals believe women need to be represented and treated equally within the existing economic system, whereas socialists "claim [women] are *exploited* as an inevitable consequence of the system itself."[27]

While Marxist/socialist feminism did not attract many street followers in the early- to mid-1970s,[28] it found a home in academe, and many of the women's studies programs that would gain toe-holds in Britain during the early 1970s were grounded on a socialist feminist analysis.[29] Events like the Women and Socialism conference in 1974 inspired the newly founded Women's Studies Group at the University of Birmingham to take up the domestic labor dispute as a research topic.[30] Adopting the revolutionary language of the left, the Women's Studies Group (which initially did include men) saw women's studies "constituted through the recognition of economic, ideological, sexual and political subordination and exploitation of a social group."[31]

Yet the Second Wave revival of Marxism—once a "starting point" for many British feminists—did not serve long as a unifying element for activists. By the end of the 1970s, front-line feminism in Britain had become less of a national movement and more a loose collection of "multifaceted action groups"[32]—each one serving different constituencies. However, feminist thought linking socialism and radical politics has continued to shape major contemporary developments in socialist feminism worldwide.[33]

## CANADA

From the 1870s on, many of the women's organizations flourishing across Canada focused on the same issues that concerned their British and American counterparts: suffrage, education, economic independence, and reproductive rights. Yet few Canadian feminists who became active in the late 1960s realized that their new movement was rooted in two traditions: a history of grassroots, and sometimes radical, women's groups drawn from workplaces, homes, or from the political left, and a legacy of established women's organizations representing a liberal feminist agenda. Among the established groups were the Young Women's Christian Association (YWCA) and the Canadian Federation of University Women, both instrumental in lobbying for the formation of the Royal Commission on the Status of Women (RCSW) in the 1960s. By the time the RCSW was formed and had issued a long-awaited report on the status of women in 1970, institutionalized women's organizations and a number of small, grassroots groups were mobilizing at the same time. Many of the former joined in 1966 to become the Committee for Equality of Women (CEW), an "old-girls" network that had the clout to call for the establishment of the RCSW. When the report—with its list of women's demands—was finally published, the CEW's chair warned that "only in joint action can we be sure that the Report will not gather dust on some Parliamentary shelf."[34] In 1971, the CEW became the National Ad Hoc Committee on the Status of Women (now the National Action Committee on the Status of Women, or NAC), a broad coalition of feminist women's groups and the most well-known representative of feminist interests in Canada. However, in trying to become a coalition "that would truly represent the variety and range of the women's movement in Canada," NAC, too, would eventually struggle with conflicts about questions of race and sexuality.[35]

By 1971, the women's movement had become established in Canadian society. As in the United States and Britain, consciousness-raising (CR) groups had formed, emerging very quickly as an effective means of grassroots organizing. Working separately from institutionalized women's organizations, grassroots feminist groups had taken hold in Canadian urban centers and had organized protests, rallies, and conferences to bring public and government attention to issues like working women's concerns, safe and legal abortions, and access to day care.

But as early as 1970, Canadian feminists began to question the notion of a unified women's movement. Could all women be brought together under a single issue? Should they be? At the first national conference on the women's movement in Saskatoon, one speaker argued that "race and class divide women too much to build a common movement," and that it would be better for women to work in separate revolutionary groups. Others wondered whether the women's movement should be confined to any one issue, possibly "narrow[ing] the scope of women's struggle for social change." Also around that period, several feminist groups experienced conflicts over ideological differences and over concerns about representation: "different politics and different strategies [had begun] to emerge, and it became clear that 'feminism' had no one meaning."[36] A major issue emerging in the 1970s was the question of sexual orientation. Paralleling similar debates within the National Organization for Women in the United States and Australia's Women's Liberation Movement around lesbianism (see below) were conflicts over heterosexual privilege and whether lesbians would be better off organizing separately. Some Canadian feminist writers have analyzed this conflict as part of the long struggle to legitimate lesbian feminism, "forcing the discussion of sexuality and insisting that feminists grapple with heterosexism." Though fraught with tensions, the debate over lesbian feminism in Canada has not, in their view, undermined women's ability to work together for change.[37]

## AUSTRALIA

Along with their British, Canadian, and American counterparts, young and newly politicized Australian women began organizing in the late 1960s against oppressive social conditions. Australian women working against sexism took inspiration from American feminist trends and activism emerging in the late 1960s, as well as from the writings of ex-patriot Germaine Greer.[38] Like their American counterparts at this time, Australian students and youth protested against involvement in the Vietnam War—their energy and anger important for motivating Australian feminist activism.

Though many Australian women working for social change in the 1960s situated themselves on the political left, they were exasperated with the fact that leftist organizations generally forefronted "the culture and priorities of the men." In their view, New Left men

> seemed capable of challenging oppressive class, cultural, and racial relationships, but found it difficult to surrender their traditional privileges concerning women. . . . it was quite apparent that the left had never considered women in a revolutionary perspective, expecting us to remain its faithful servants and supporters in the great struggle.[39]

For these reasons, many of the small Australian feminist groups forming around 1970 remained loyal to Marxist principles and adopted a politically revolutionary politics focusing on the liberation of working-class women. Yet at the same time, they rejected the New Left's hierarchical structures in favor of egalitarian, round table, consensus-based organizational models. Indeed, many of these small Australian feminist groups took a strongly oppositional stance toward not only New Left structures but New Left men. The first National Women's Liberation Conference in 1970 identified New Left men as "a major obstacle to the development of women's 'revolutionary' potential and their own liberation." For many feminists, this argument more than justified the formation of women-only groups to "develop [women's] own consciousness and sense of identity as individuals."[40]

By the early 1970s, two major strands of the Australian feminist movement had emerged. One, the Women's Liberation Movement (WLM), was powered not only by the ideals and activist history of the political left but also by a strong conviction that men should not play a significant role in women's struggle for liberation. An exemplar was the Women's Action Committee, formed in 1972. The experience of reading the United States publication *Second Year Notes from Women's Liberation* " 'exploded the minds' of the WAC members," inspiring them to believe that women the world over could be united by the common condition of being oppressed by men.[41]

But a number of Austalian women were unhappy with the women's liberationists' "anti-structure, anti-hierarchy, anti-men and anti-State attitude and style." Their belief that feminists could accomplish some change by working within existing structures characterized a second strand of Austalian feminism, exemplified by the formation of the Women's Electoral Lobby (WEL) in 1972. Representing a more mainstream approach to feminist reform, groups like WEL tended to attract an older, more middle-class, professional constituency. A number of these mainstream feminists became "femocrats," working with both government bureaucracies and feminist groups to establish various women's programs; among them publicly funded child care, equal pay, women's legal services, affirmative action, and recognition of rape and domestic violence against women. It helped that a reasonably woman-friendly Labour government was in power during the mid-1970s and 1980s, a government that in 1983 instituted a requirement that women "constitute 50 percent of ministerial short lists to boards and committees."[42]

## THE UNITED STATES

Arguably the strongest feminist eruption of the 1960s and 1970s occurred in the United States. One of the catalysts was the growing discontent of white middle-class women, many of whom had experienced some economic freedom and independence during the manpower shortages of World War II. If the swift loss of these freedoms during the 1950s and early 1960s re-established women's powerlessness, it also nourished women's discontent and inarticulated resentment, particularly within middle-class suburban homes. The first signs of these women's explosive anger were articulated by Betty Friedan in *The Feminine Mystique* and coined as the "problem that has no name"; for many women, reading this book constituted their first identification with feminism.

But this feminist eruption also occurred with other forms of social activism and rebellions. The 1960s witnessed many movements for improved human rights and freedoms, notably the Civil Rights movement, the Campaign for Nuclear Disarmament, protests against U.S. involvement in the Vietnam War, Black Power, the growing militarism of gays, and the youth counterculture movement—to name a few. A feminist consciousness that had never completely died and was now re-awakening, combined with the dramatic rise in the 1960s of social and human rights activism, helped give birth to the National Organization for Women: a self-described "fresh and more militant voice"[43] to articulate American women's demands. Formed in 1966, NOW's main goal was to bring about women's full participation in "the mainstream of American society now, exercising all the privileges and responsibilities thereof in truly equal partnership with men."[44] In this respect, NOW was staunchly liberal, following in the tradition of nineteenth century human rights feminism. NOW's main strategy was to rely on existing laws and constitutional instruments and educate the American public to adopt a different image of women, such mainstreaming considered tried and tested during the civil rights movement.

An enormous amount has been written about NOW's influence on American feminism and though I cannot do justice to it here, American feminism represented by NOW was in many ways unique in its ability to join the mainstream. Whereas many British feminist activists worked on the margins and took the radical approach of positioning themselves in opposition to established institutions, NOW adopted a more mainstream approach to feminist reform. Though NOW's actions and positions on issues have been described as "often unorthodox, uncompromising and ahead of their time,"[45] in the late 1960s the organizational structure was unexceptional (president, secretary, committees and committee chairs), and positions were filled by educated, almost exclusively middle-class leaders. These relatively nonthreatening features helped attract experienced organizers, political lobbyists, and sympathetic men.

One result of this mainstreaming was that NOW had enough clout by 1967 to pressure the federal government into prohibiting sex discrimination by the federal government and its contractors and modifying restrictive laws concerning married flight attendants (formerly known as stewardesses). At NOW's Second National Conference that same year, the leadership drew up a Bill of Rights for Women, which included demands for an Equal Rights Amendment to the Constitution, childcare centers, maternity leave rights, and—perhaps most controversial—the right of women to control their reproductive lives.[46]

While using mainstream legal and constitutional tools won some victories in the United States and inspired feminist, black, and gay activism internationally, the successes were limited enough to convince growing numbers of radical women that increased freedom did not necessarily result in equality. Indeed, conflicts and tensions were already surfacing in American feminism, particularly between women who felt that NOW's mainstream approach was appropriate and women who believed feminists needed to be more revolutionary and socially transformative. In the late 1960s, black women and other women of color criticized the women's movement—NOW and other groups—for being too "white." While a Hispanic woman was elected president of NOW in 1971, it wasn't until 1973 that NOW established a task force addressing the concerns of nonwhite women.[47] The role of lesbians represented another major area of contention within NOW, resulting in acrimonious debates throughout the late 1960s and 1970s about "lesbian policy."[48] After several years of internal agony over the extent to which NOW was prepared to move beyond a mainly white, middle-class, heterosexual worldview, NOW declared lesbian rights a "priority issue" in 1975.[49]

While the influence of liberal feminism on American women has been incalculable, a number of feminists asserted early during the Second Wave that the liberal agenda—represented by large organizations like NOW and the American Association of University Women (AAUW)—was an inadequate tool for dismantling patriarchy and sexism. Radical feminists argued, and still maintain, that women's oppression is rooted in patriarchy—social systems built on male dominance and the privileging of masculinity. Therefore, an equal rights agenda, often seen as grounded in patriarchal thought, cannot hope to end sexism and liberate women. Women's oppression will end only when the very sources of patriarchal thought are exposed, destroyed, and replaced. For American women's liberationists as well as for their Canadian, British, and Australian radical counterparts, the most effective way to start dismantling patriarchy was to reject mainstreaming and operate on the margins, often through small consciousness-raising groups.

Yet despite, or perhaps partly because of, these conflicts between liberal and radical positions, American feminism in the 1970s was full of energy; many groups were able to unite around urgent issues and raise considerable hell. One major motive for unity was a strong determination to pass the Equal Rights Amendment, first demanded by NOW in 1967. Another equally strong motive was to bring about and safeguard women's access to safe, legal abortion, a pathway opened by feminist struggles related to *Roe v. Wade* in 1973. Profeminist men—far from being cast as the enemy—played active roles in these campaigns.[50]

## REPRESENTATION, DIFFERENCE, AND FEMINIST MYTHS

Feminists worldwide, but especially in Western countries, gained voice during the 1970s. To some extent, the popular press and the public were starting to pick up on these messages about improving women's lives. But at the same time, feminist women in many Western countries throughout the 1970s were questioning the hegemony of a mainly white, middle-class, heterosexual feminist movement. For those not privy to feminist politics, groups like the Women's Electoral Lobby in Australia as well as NOW represented—for better or worse—a unified feminism, a powerful voice that demanded and lobbied for women's equal rights. In reality, the voice usually belonged to a core group of active, and some would say privileged, leaders able to network with established institutions. Given the impossibility that one group could hope to speak for all women, the dream of a unified voice articulating a universal sisterhood began destabilizing almost as soon as feminists began forming organizations. Indeed, it wasn't at all unusual in the 1970s for feminist movements worldwide to begin as united entities, emphasizing solidarity and sisterhood, and later to experience conflicts and a certain amount of fragmentation.

Like many feminists or women's liberationists during this time, Australian women hoped they could organize around one goal—ending oppression—and accomplish this goal as women together, forming one supposedly homogeneous category.[51] To some extent, this ideal held up: political differences between the more radical Women's Liberation Movement and the more conservative WEL didn't prevent these groups from fostering a number of unified campaigns.[52] But like their counterparts in North America and Britain, Australian feminists frequently found themselves at odds over issues of class, race, and sexual orientation. After a 1973 WLM conference, a group of lesbians publicly expressed their frustration at the heterosexism of the WLM, pointing out examples of how they had been silenced and belittled. As Australian feminist activist and historian Katy Reade records, women on the receiving end of this criticism reacted with shock and anger at the concept that they could be classed as oppressors. Others felt the lesbians were coming across as too self-righteous and exaggerated, and were worried about an emerging lesbian orthodoxy in which, as one straight woman put it, "the depth of my feminist conviction is questioned because I can love a man."[53]

In company with many other feminist organizations and coalitions undergoing similar political upheavals, the WLM could not neatly cover this conflict with a single organizational umbrella. Some lesbians split from the WLM and created their own women-only spaces, while others joined the WEL, which in 1974 had publicly adopted a prohomosexual agenda. To some lesbians, WEL seemed to offer a more productive environment for concrete action against discriminatory practices. Not surprisingly, though, lesbian politics co-existed uneasily with the more conservative politics of older WEL members, some of whom—according to Reade—"could not handle even talking about lesbianism."[54]

Tensions about how effectively all women could be represented by the feminist theorizing of mainly middle-class, straight, white women were also apparent in New Zealand. There, the Auckland Liberation Movement had begun as a reasonably unified and certainly active group. By the late 1970s, this movement was becoming divided over questions of race, socialism, and lesbianism. These tensions came to the forefront at a 1978 conference on the theme of socialist feminism, where, as recorded by two participants, a kind of moralizing tone made discussion of the main topic difficult. Conference organizers were criticized for a range of supposedly insensitive acts, including putting bowls of black olives on the lunch table, which presumably was seen as having racist undertones. Rather than discussing relations between Marxism or socialism and feminism, delegates accused middle-class women of oppressing working-class women, or charged that lesbians were being ripped off and oppressed by a feminist movement saturated with heterosexual privilege. This crisis resulted in a settlement within New Zealand's feminist movement: to maintain a kind of unity, women would agree with the radical feminist notion that women are universally oppressed within a dominating patriarchy. As two participants describe and criticize it, radical feminism in New Zealand became rigid and hegemonic: "the notion of women as a group invariably subordinated within a male world became a basis for our collective strength. Our solidarity was to be based in the dual certainties that women and men were clearly separate social categories, and that women were our sisters in oppression, men were the enemy."[55]

Nor were British and New Zealand feminist movements the only ones struggling with the unpleasant fallout of what began as a valid and thoughtful critique of representation. In all feminist movements in the 1970s, women of color were eloquently expressing their unhappiness at having middle-class white women reformists speak for them. These feminists believed they had the right to assert that no one who took their white privilege for granted could possibly come to grips with the experiences of nonwhite women. For their part, lesbians felt oppressed—many angry—about the fact that even after gay liberation began to make some aspects of their lives easier, a majority of feminist women "enjoyed heterosexual privilege as wives and mothers, and were reluctant to support or acknowledge lesbians for fear of provoking male disapproval."[56]

Publicly presenting a united feminist front was further complicated by the mass media's relationship with women's lib. It's fair to say mainstream media representations of feminism have not always supported the cause of women's equality. Radical feminism has been a popular media target. In the United States, a number of radical women rejected a liberal feminist approach and distrusted groups like NOW for "play[ing] into the hands of the oppressor by accepting his rules." The most radical feminists, some followers of neo-Marxism, felt that women as an oppressed group could be liberated only by setting themselves apart from their oppressors and attacking the entire capitalist/racist/sexist structure.[57] The representation of radical feminist activism has not been improved by the fact that the media has an unerring instinct for pouncing on extreme, sensational, or simply minority views and relying on these to generalize about feminism. Valerie Solanis's "The S.C.U.M. Manifesto" is one example of an extreme form of militant feminism,[58] while separatism represents the views of a small minority of radical lesbian feminists that women who truly want to overthrow patriarchy should not consort with men. Focusing on these views and blowing them out of proportion, both media and popular culture have created a monster that won't die: the hairy-legged man-hating feminist. Even in an age when it's chic to be lesbian (especially if you have a lot of income) and photos of fresh-faced, self-proclaimed lesbians adorn mainstream magazines, this hostile and homophobic imagery is alive and well.

Yet perhaps the most famous media stereotype equates feminism with bra burnings. This myth is so pervasive that people are amazed—or don't quite believe it—when presented with the historical fact that no bras ever went up in flames. In 1968 in Atlantic City, women demonstrated against a Miss America pageant by throwing beauty items like girdles, curlers, high-heeled shoes, and bras into a "freedom trash can," and voila—somehow this event "inspir[ed] the media myth of bra-burning."[59] What makes this myth especially annoying and irrelevant is that it conflates decades of activism and theory with one relatively trivial event; even decades later, this myth absolutely refuses to die.

## CONSCIOUSNESS-RAISING AND THE POWER OF WOMEN'S EXPERIENCES

The freedom trash can was only one example of a variety of radical feminist acts within and outside North America. Radical activism tended to set itself in opposition to established women's groups and mainstream institutions, preferring to operate on the margins or outside of government and corporations. But radical women didn't work in isolation from each other, nor did a few just suddenly decide to march, protest, publish a newsletter, or start a women's resources center. Many women taking part in the feminist eruption of the late 1960s and 1970s studied collective power through consciousness-raising: the tool of choice for women "who were interested in getting to the roots of problems in society."

Kathie Sarachild, who outlined the original program for "Radical Feminist Consciousness-Raising" in the United States at the First National Women's Liberation Conference in 1968, effectively defined CR as "[t]he decision to emphasize our own feelings and experiences as women and to test all generalizations and reading we did by our own experience." In a conference address in 1973, Sarachild reflected back on 1968 and how CR had not only been an exciting process, ripe with possibilities, but had nurtured some of the most well-known Second Wave feminist thought:

> There was no denying . . . that we ourselves were learning a tremendous amount from the discussions and were finding them very exciting. From our consciousness-raising meetings was coming the writing which was formulating basic theory for the women's liberation movement. Shulamith Firestone, who wrote the book *The Dialectic of Sex*, Anne Koedt, who wrote the essay "The Myth of the Vaginal Orgasm," Pat Mainardi, who wrote the essay "The Politics of Housework," Carol Hanisch, who wrote the essay, "The Personal is Political," Kate Millett, who wrote *Sexual Politics*, Cindy Cisler, who led the ground-breaking abortion law repeal fight in New York, Rosalyn Baxandall, Irene Peslikis, Ellen Willis, Robin Morgan and many others participated in these discussions. Most of us had thought we were only beginning to have a radical understanding of women—and of other issues of class, race and revolutionary change.[60]

But like mainstream women's organizations, CR groups experienced internal ideological conflicts. While the exciting dream of sisterhood helped motivate women to speak their experiences and envision strategies for change, it's reasonable to assume that no one was really prepared for what might happen when so many different perspectives ended up on the table. Explosive situations developed. As Trigiani puts it, "intense disputes over power sharing, racism, classism, and in particular, heterosexuality and lesbianism corroded the 'sisterhood.' " By 1975, most American CR groups had fallen apart.[61]

The demise of many feminist CR groups, due to the intensity of conflict over representation within and beyond the United States might suggest we should be pessimistic about the women's movement. Yet feminist work for change has never stopped, even while debates about representation have periodically convulsed Western feminist groups since the 1970s. Much of this work has increasingly taken on not only local but also global import: the 1981 women's peace camp at Greenham Common in the United Kingdom, the U.S. campaign (ending in failure in 1982) to pass the Equal Rights Amendment, the national antiviolence activism following the 1991 massacre of fourteen women in Montréal, and the United Nations Fourth World Conference on Women at Beijing in 1995—to name only a few diverse events.

Feminist women are highly aware that understanding and respecting differences is not only necessary but can be strategically powerful. For this reason, among others, feminists are unlikely to return to ideals of a sisterhood rooted in apparently universal causes of oppression. Yet women's desire to work together and change gender-based oppression is as strong as ever. For feminist women, as well as for the men who wish to support and work with women to achieve gender justice, this sense that change is possible can serve as a powerful motivator for action.

## NOTES

1. Patricia Elliot and Nancy Mandell (1995), pp. 2–25.
2. David Bouchier (1984), p. 11.
3. Kathleen Trigiani (1999).
4. Bouchier (1984), p. 14.
5. B. Ryan (1992), p. 9.
6. Trigiani (1999).
7. Bouchier (1984), p. 12.
8. Nellie McClung is quoted in Nancy Adamson, Linda Briskin, and Margaret McPhail (1988), p. 31.
9. Cited in ibid., p. 31. These authors also point out that aspects of modern radical feminism tap into maternal feminist beliefs in women's moral superiority. "Much radical-feminist writing, especially on issues of peace and violence against women, has in it the unarticulated assumption that men are inherently aggressive, violent, and self-serving. The other side of this assumption . . . is that women are inherently different from men. . . . If women ran the governments we would have peace, equality, cooperation between nations; there would be no poverty and no exploitation. To a large extent this view is based on the belief that women's special status comes from their ability to procreate" (p. 32).
10. The Representation of People Act of February 1918 allowed British women to vote if they were over 30, householders or the wives of householders, paid an annual rent of over £5, and were university graduates or held equivalent qualifications. In 1928, this act was amended to allow all women and men equal voting rights.
11. Katy Reade (1994), p. 200.
12. David Bouchier (1984).
13. Ibid., p. 14.
14. Marlene LeGates (1996), pp. 249–250.
15. Ibid., p. 253.
16. Marilyn Waring, who in 1975 was the youngest MP ever elected to the New Zealand Parliament, is one of the foremost contemporary advocates of global fem-

inist economics. Among other things, she argues that the way Gross Domestic Product (GDP) is currently calculated does not take either environmental impact or women's unpaid work into account. See her 1988 book *If Women Counted* (Macmillan) for more information.

17. Germaine Greer quoted in Terry Lovell (1990), pp. 6–7.
18. Ibid., p. 5.
19. Ann Oakley (1988). p. 3.
20. Marsha Rowe (1982), p. 15.
21. Bouchier (1984), pp. 121–22.
22. Ibid., p. 114.
23. See ibid., pp. 211–214.
24. Ibid., p. 134.
25. See chapter 8 of this volume for John Rowan's comments and description of the "Red Therapy Group"
26. Bouchier (1984), p. 135.
27. Ibid., p. 69.
28. Ibid., pp. 95, 100.
29. Women's Studies Group (1978), pp. 7–9.
30. Ibid., p. 13.
31. Ibid., p. 9.
32. Bouchier (1984), p. 123.
33. Lovell (1990), p. 4.
34. Adamson, Briskin, and McPhail (1988), pp. 51–52.
35. For a detailed analysis of the politics surrounding Canada's National Action Committee on the Status of Women, see Jill Vickers, Pauline Rankin, and Christine Appelle (1993).
36. Adamson, Briskin, and McPhail (1988), p. 49.
37. Ibid., pp. 58–60.
38. Judith Colp Rubin (1999, November).
39. Reade (1994), p. 201. The quote is from Ann Curthoys and Lyndall Ryan, two Sydney women's liberationists.
40. Ibid., p. 203.
41. Ibid., p. 205.
42. Rubin, (1999, November).
43. Bouchier (1984), p. 45.
44. Ibid.
45. See History of the National Organization for Women (1998).
46. Bouchier (1984), p. 46.
47. The History of the National Organization for Women.
48. Adamson, Briskin, and McPhail (1988), pp. 51–52.
49. The History of the National Organization for Women.
50. Michael S. Kimmel and Tom E. Mosmiller (1992) summarize profeminist initatives supporting the ERA and abortion rights. See pp. 38–40.
51. Reade (1994), p. 200.
52. Rachel Evans (2000).
53. Reade (1994), pp. 213–14. The quote about "lesbian orthodoxy" is from the December 1974 *Women's Liberation Newsletter* (cited in Reade, p. 214).

54. Ibid., pp. 214–15. The quote about how older WEL members handled lesbianism is from Reade's personal interview with a prominent WEL member.
55. Alison Jones and Camille Guy (1992), pp. 300–316.
56. Alison J. Laurie (1992), pp. 49–50.
57. Bouchier (1984), p. 50.
58. Valerie Solanis's "The S.C.U.M. Manifesto" is included in Robin Morgan (1970).
59. LeGates (1996), p. 311.
60. Kathie Sarachild (1978), pp. 144–150.
61. Trigiani (1999).

2

# "There Was Liberation in the Air . . ."[1]

## WHERE WERE THE MEN?

At the risk of stating the obvious, most men have not enthusiastically supported feminist goals: "the typical—even liberal—male responses [to the women's movement] ranged from sarcasm to peevish withdrawal."[2] When faced with women's rebellion against sexual stereotyping or activism for equal rights, Western men have generally exercised several options. Historically, the most popular choice has been withdrawing into silence or retreating into male bastions, be they boardrooms, legislative assemblies, pubs, or Monday night football. A more creative option has been to increase the variety of ways to keep women down—for example, when more women began entering nontraditional workplaces, sexual harassment was one way to remind these uppity women of their place.

A much riskier and therefore less popular male response to feminism has been to speak out or act publicly in support of feminist principles. Outwardly expressing feminist beliefs was not endemic among Western men before the 1960s. There were, of course, notable exceptions, among them John Stuart Mill, Friedrich Engels, Frederick Douglass, Ralph Waldo Emerson, Walt Whitman, and John Dewey—to name only a few.[3] As Michael Kimmel and Tom Mosmiller have documented,[4] high-profile American men have raised their voices to protest the injustices women have suffered and to support women's calls for higher education, the vote, reproductive rights, equal pay, fair treatment in workplaces, and an end to rape and domestic violence.

The middle-class liberal feminism reignited in the 1960s by Betty Friedan's *The Feminine Mystique* was part of a tradition—from Seneca Falls onward—of women and their male supporters operating within, or in cooperation with, established political frameworks. Based on the principle that women and men are equal and should have the same access to political, economic, intellectual, and social resources, liberal feminism was historically the first and often most accessible entry point for supportive men. But in the 1960s, as young people began increasingly to critique established institutions, a number of men also became attracted to the radical notion that both sexes could be freed from the emotional straitjackets of traditional gender relations. By the 1970s, it was becoming more and more difficult for thoughtful men to ignore the increasingly strong voices of women calling for gender equality and an end to sexism. Though the eruption of feminist activism in the 1960s and 1970s was destabilizing for many men, some thought the prospects for redefining masculinity were both exciting and challenging: "[w]omen were developing, and as they fought to change their roles, some men felt pressure to change too. . . . There was liberation in the air and men wanted a part of that."[5] Many men were optimistic that, by supporting women's struggles against sexism, they would eventually discover more fulfilling concepts of masculinity, just as many women were discovering much more empowering notions of femininity. By helping women to become more liberated, men might free themselves at the same time.

## MOTIVES FOR MEN'S LIBERATION

In the United States, the growing power of feminism inspired a men's liberation movement, a concept that soon became part of the cultural and social lexicon. More men were interested in changing their lives, discovering alternative concepts of masculinity, creating better relationships with women and other men, and unchaining their emotions. Profeminist sociologist Michael Messner is a little derogatory about this last goal: "a major attraction of men's liberation was the permission it gave to men to expand their definitions of manhood to include the emotional expression, 'It's okay to cry.' "[6] Yet the liberatory message promised by feminism clearly had enormous appeal to men who felt trapped by traditional masculine roles.

Much of the credit for initiating the men's liberation movement in the United States has rested with Jack Sawyer, a psychologist, civil rights activist, and author of "On Male Liberation" (1970).[7] By 1974, the message of liberation from traditional masculine roles had spread to the mass market, with the publication of *The Liberated Man* (Warren Farrell, 1974), *Men and Masculinity* (Ed. Joseph Pleck and Jack Sawyer, 1974), *The Male Machine* (Marc Feigen Fasteau, 1975), and *Men's Liberation: A New Definition of Masculinity* (Jack Nichols, 1975). Many of these publications equated men's liberation with the goal of ending sexism. For example, the New York Men's Center in 1975 printed a list of twenty-four men's liberation books available at that time, and a number of those titles explicitly linked men's liberation with feminism. Among them were Pleck and Sawyer's *Men and Masculinity*, a collectively written description of men's consciousness-raising called *Unbecoming Men* (1971), another collectively authored work called *The Forty-Nine Percent Majority: The Male Sex Role*, and an academic paper entitled "The Women's Liberation Movement and the Men."[8]

While supporting feminist principles and critiquing sexism, these writers also "stressed the equally important high costs of 'the male sex role' to men."[9] Focusing on "the experience of males who are white, middle-class, heterosexual, and live in the United States," Pleck and Sawyer argued that "power, prestige, and profit will not fulfill [the] lives" of even this privileged group. Real men were good at winning, staying cool, and repressing emotion. This last stricture, argued Pleck and Sawyer, was dangerous to men: "We suffer in many ways that may relate to the strain our emotional denial places upon our physical body."[10] A year later, Fasteau's *The Male Machine* (introduced by Gloria Steinem) pointed out that playing the masculine role harms not only men but the women with whom they live and work. The roots of misogyny lie in society's expectations of masculinity; boys learn about and adopt suitably male activities that inevitably restrict their behavior and perpetuate negative attitudes about girls and women. Describing what Nancy Chodorow would later locate within a psychological framework in her book *The Reproduction of Mothering* (1978, reprinted 1999), Fasteau argued that boys become men largely by defining themselves as "not like a girl": a strategy "practically perfect for inducing anxiety"[11] and highly conducive to engendering sexism.

## STRUGGLING AGAINST RESTRICTIVE SEX ROLES

The concept that men were restricted to particular sets of behaviors is rooted in sex role theory, first developed in the 1950s and reaching a peak of popularity in the 1970s. Sex role theory dismantled the carved-in-stone figures of the male breadwinner and the female housewife by defining them as socio-cultural constructs. According to Michael Messner, one highly influential example of popular sex role theory was Deborah David and Robert Brannon's 1976 collection, *The Forty-Nine Percent Majority: The Male Sex Role*, described as "a feminist men's movement companion . . . a collection of essays from feminists Marc Feigen Fasteau, Warren Farrell (in his feminist days) . . . Kate Millett, Joseph Pleck, Jack Sawyer and others."[12] Brannon himself—a psychologist and future co-founder of the National Organization for Men against Sexism—laid out "four main rules of the male script in this collection: 'No Sissy Stuff,' 'Be a Big Wheel,' 'Be a

Sturdy Oak,' and 'Give 'Em Hell.' "[13] For women and men interested in gender justice and personal growth, it was liberating and exciting to see female and male behaviors as changeable social constructs. But for men, it was especially important to understand how sex roles could be just as constraining and oppressive for women. Sex role theory suggested that women and men could cast off these roles and redefine gender relationships in more positive ways.[14]

However, as theorists like Messner and Robert Connell argue,[15] sex role theory has its limits—its focus on individual behaviors ignores interrelations between those behaviors and the social, economic, and institutional power structures in which we're all embedded. The fact that, after thirty years or so, many people show few signs of rejecting traditional sex roles also calls sex role theory into question. But the belief that sexual stereotypes were socially imposed behaviors that a person could adopt, reject, or change was enormously compatible with the liberatory *zeitgeist* of the late 1960s and 1970s. The possibility of changing masculinity for the better was a primary motive for many men joining the men's liberation movement.

## LIBERATIONISM VERSUS ANTI-SEXISM

Almost as soon as the men's movement took root in the United States and Britain, differences began emerging between a notion of liberation as struggling *against* sexism and *for* gender justice, and liberation as freeing men from a constricting and unhealthy masculinity. A number of men interested in men's liberation were skeptical about, even hostile toward, the women's movement. In their view, if even privileged white men were harmed by societal expectations around masculinity, then certain feminist demands—especially those concerning domestic rights, workplace equality, or child custody—were almost certainly going to be oppressive for men. By the late 1970s, more men's groups were becoming committed to fathers' and men's rights, and some of these groups indeed blamed feminists for their troubles. Connell traces this attitude to the growth of consciousness in the 1970s about men's liberation. As he sees it, "[t]he idea of 'men's issues,' created as a mirror-image of 'women's issues' in the 1970s, soon turned into a defense of men's *interests* against women's."[16]

In the early 1970s, British men interested in men's liberation shared "a strong emphasis on socialist issues like the family, the State, and work,"[17] issues inseparable from British feminist thought. But as time went on, growing numbers of liberated men became less interested in antisexist activism and socialism, and more focused on understanding masculinity, working toward self-improvement, and forging better relationships with other men. Initially, some British antisexist and liberationist men tried to work together, attempting unity through their common concern with understanding men's lives. But overall, reports of antisexist activism of that time in Britain[18] describe growing divisions among antisexist and liberationist as well as pro-gay men.

Here's a case in point: a description and critique of a 1973 Men against Sexism conference, which had about thirty attendees, indicates that British men were willing to discuss such topics as "liberation from the disadvantages of masculinity" and "liberation from sexism as a counter-revolutionary ideology"—but they were most comfortable discussing these issues mainly within the contexts of masculinity and men's lives: "Whilst the structure of the conference was based on pro-feminism, anti-sexist ideologies, the discussions rarely considered sexism. . . . The content of the conference reveals that this issue was actually low down on the men's liberationists agenda."[19]

By the 1980s, some—not all—of these liberationist perspectives had hardened into the argument that men were being victimized and guilt-tripped by women, especially feminists. A similar split between American liberationist and antisexist men developed more slowly, but by the early 1980s, men's rights adherents had moved decidedly away from groups with an antisexist orientation. In the United States, these attitudes tended to coalesce into the men's rights branch of the men's movement. As philosopher and men's movement historian Kenneth Clatterbaugh notes, men's rights adherents formed, and still form, groups to share a common awareness of the hazards of being male. Such groups build solidarity among men who are concerned about "the costs and discriminations of being masculine"[20] but are not willing to think about masculinity from a profeminist perspective.

Some of these men reason that if men are victimized in so many ways by societal expectations, why should they support feminist demands that seem likely to oppress men further? Profeminists are usually sympathetic to the notion that masculine straightjacketing harms men. Yet not surprisingly, profeminists and feminists alike have difficulty with the view that men are less powerful than women. Indeed, in the words of Bob Pease, an Australian profeminist theorist, "As we come to understand the hurts that men have suffered as men, there will be pressure to call this oppression. However, oppression is not a concept that refers only to people's feelings. It is a concept based on a political analysis of institutional power imbalances in society."[21]

On the other hand, some men felt that becoming liberated from the male sex role was, in fact, inseparable from overcoming sexism. These men saw the women's movement as a source of inspiration and ideas to improve the lives of men as well as women. The most logical response to feminism, they reasoned, was to explore how it could benefit both men and women and to incorporate feminist ideas into their own lives and relationships. The rest of this chapter focuses on what these men accomplished in the 1970s.

## FEMINISM IS GOOD FOR MEN

In thinking about relations between men's roles and women's liberation, some men publicly took the stance that feminism had much to offer men. Some years before his rejection of feminism and subsequent retreat to a men's rights stance, a leader in the U.S. men's consciousness-raising (CR) movement of the 1970s was Warren Farrell. His 1974 best-selling book, *The Liberated Man*, offered "twenty-one specific areas in which man can benefit from what is now called women's liberation."[22] Openly feminist, Farrell was on the board of the National Organization for Women and headed a NOW task force on "The Masculine Mystique." In no less a feminist forum than *Ms.* magazine, Farrell noted that the women's movement could teach men about "systematically expos[ing] the devastating feminine stereotypes," and argued that feminism's emphasis on consciousness-raising was "its most important contribution to [men]."[23] He also chided men for ignoring feminist work: "I have been struck consistently by how difficult it is for men to discuss Women's Liberation *seriously and personally* even in a consciousness-raising group. The men even seem to be afraid to read feminist literature. . . . *It is as if they are unwilling to admit they can learn from a woman.*"[24]

Farrell's view is fairly representative of those men in the 1970s who believed the women's movement offered not only a good consciousness-raising model but also a body of knowledge that men needed to understand and, when possible, apply to their own lives. Other men, though lacking Farrell's public profile, were also highly aware of and motivated by social changes wrought by women's activism and empowerment. One man's story, in a newsletter printed by a Milwaukee men's group in 1974, reveals that a primary motive for learning more about women's liberation was not to be left behind by a female partner:

> I became interested in men's and women's issues as I observed the breakup of the marriages of close friends. . . . The pattern in most of the breakups was that of the wife leaving the husband. Concerned lest that happen in my case, I got into women's liberation with a vengeance, e.g., *I* brought home my wife's first issue of Ms., and bought her subscriptions.[25]

Another prime motive for many men interested in feminism was a desire for self-understanding; they felt that women were opening up conceptual pathways that men could follow. Some informal writings from the early 1970s American men's movement are frankly (and refreshingly) rhapsodic about the possibilities for men offered by feminism. Said one anonymous writer in *Brother*, one of the first U.S. men's newsletters of the 1970s: "I don't believe I have ever felt so affected by a movement or a social development before in my life. . . . I have been digging *women* like never before, in new ways. Especially their strengths . . . women [are] so much more open, so much more plugged into the things that really count, the underlying *humane* concerns of our life, than most men!"[26] His assumptions about women's innate humaneness aside for the moment, this writer articulated a sincere male excitement and optimism about improving gender relations. At the same time, like many men exploring what feminism meant for them, he seemed a little unsure about exactly what to do in a practical sense: "What am I doing about it? At first, not much—just thinking a lot and rapping much of the time with other people. It's really fun to hang out with [women] and share in their new exuberant (although still serious) vibes . . ."[27] Apparently, his first choice of action was to listen to and learn from women. Almost thirty years later, feminist women still believe this is one of the best ways sympathetic men can determine good action strategies. But it's also possible, and I hope not too far-fetched, to read a warning in this *Brother* writer's comment that it's not good enough for men just to hang out with feminists and enjoy the vibes: "there comes a point where . . . the men have to start getting together . . . and start wading through all the incredible sexist, macho shit we're mired in. . . . We have our work cut out for us indeed."[28] Commenting about women's consciousness-raising groups, Robin Morgan has noted that a combination of talk and action was ideal for helping women realize the feminist principle of "theory correcting practice, practice correcting theory."[29] More radical profeminist men's groups followed similar practices by going beyond rapping about their feelings to taking part in demonstrations, supporting women's events, making the growing number of publications about gender available by creating resource centers or clearing houses, and publishing small newsletters.

## MEN IN GROUPS I: CONSCIOUSNESS-RAISING

For many profeminists, the first stage of their work was to analyze and apply the lessons of feminism. Interested men not only talked with women and read feminist literature, but also in the early to middle 1970s formed men-only groups to discuss what was then considered "the interesting and exciting question of the male response to women's liberation."[30] A number of these groups also encouraged discussion of men's lives and how men were being affected by forces like women's liberation. As Warren Farrell had recommended, many used a model derived from women's consciousness-raising groups, with emphasis on "sharing experiences, concerns, problems, feelings . . . rather than simply intellectualizing."[31]

Speaking one's experience and trying to make sense of it was common to both men's and women's consciousness-raising (CR) groups. The general idea of CR was to undertake self-examination with the goal of improving one's own life and the lives of others. The "bitch session cell group" model for women proposed by CR pioneer Kathie Sarachild in the late 1960s (also see chapter 1) suggested ongoing consciousness expansion techniques as the first session activity:

1. Personal recognition and testimony
2. Personal testimony—methods of group practice
   a. Going around the room with key questions on key topics
   b. Speaking out experiences at random
   c. Cross-examination
3. Relating and generalizing individual testimony.[32]

A Milwaukee men's group encouraged men to talk openly with each other by using strategies that appear loosely based on Sarachild's model. The group recorded

> concentrating on one member a night, having that member give us an autobiography of the significant things that happened to him in his life and then questioning him about them in order to clarify the emotional content of his experiences. We also use a device whereby each person in turn will talk uninterruptedly for two minutes. . . . We've also used a device whereby one person'll tell each of the others how he feels about them at the moment and the rest will reciprocate.[33]

In his article about men's consciousness-raising, Farrell describes the range of topics in his own men's group: "Violence. How we sought it. How we feared it. How we actually dealt with it. We talked about the meaning of *macho*. We talked about 'scoring.' Winning. Losing. Crying. Fucking. Fidelity. Loneliness. Sometimes we got off on eight personal trips. Sometimes there was understanding. Sometimes, none."[34]

While awareness of sexism was an important theme, these first men's gatherings also emphasized men's liberation goals of exploring positive and healthy masculinities. Effectively, men's CR groups could decide whether or not to engage politically with sexism, but for women's CR groups during the late 1960s and early 1970s, the changes sought were not only personal but political. For women, the CR process involved several stages: articulating one's experiences, recognizing and resisting oppression, developing theories and actions to eliminate oppression, and training other women to do the same. To help realize these goals, the Sarachild bitch session not only expressed and evaluated personal experience but also considered relations between practice and theory: "Classic forms of resisting consciousness, or How to avoid facing the awful truth. . . . "Starting to Stop"—overcoming repressions and delusions. . . . Understanding and developing radical feminist theory. . . . Organizing."[35] In her introduction to *Sisterhood is Powerful*, Robin Morgan notes that for some women's groups, CR gatherings constituted a first stage "before moving into direct actions," while other groups emphasized talk or study.[36] Similarly, some men's groups remained small and personal, while others expanded into men's study groups, or even entire men's conferences combining theoretical and practical topics.

## MEN IN GROUPS II: GATHERINGS AND CONFERENCES

In the early 1970s, hundreds of men's groups were forming within and outside North America. Most had modest goals: to meet regularly, discuss a range of male concerns in a supportive atmosphere, perhaps read and discuss feminist literature, perhaps start a newsletter or even a men's resource center. But some of these smaller groups had larger ambitions, among them organizing regional conferences. In certain respects, the liberationist/antisexist men's conferences of the 1970s were not unlike feminist conferences—indeed, some men's gatherings were modeled on feminist events. Common general topics included sexuality, sex roles, family and children, spirituality, power relations, and the ways in which race and class intersected with gender-based oppression. Men's conferences also usually offered sessions on such topics as violence against women, women's equality issues, and men's relations with feminism. At times, a profeminist or antisexist theme governed an entire conference.

At first, the idea was not so much to stage a conference as to gather men together—consciousness-raising writ large. The Chicago Men's Gathering of April 1973 was attended by about 100 men. According to one account, the mood was informal, encouraging men to communicate with each other.[37] In Britain, about thirty men gathered in 1973 for the first "Men against Sexism" conference, and two more national conferences were held in Birmingham in 1973 and in Leeds the following year.[38] The first men's gathering in Milwaukee in May 1974 began modestly, attended by eight random men; a second meeting in June attracted nineteen.[39] In December 1974, another Chicago Men's Gathering was billed as "a Men's Celebration." In 1975, what was likely Canada's first major men's conference was hosted by the University of Waterloo, with Joseph Pleck and Warren Farrell among the keynote speakers. It's not clear how many men came to Tennessee for the first Men & Masculinity (M & M) conference in 1975, but the fact that the program lists twenty-five sessions and more than twenty-six facilitators suggests that organizers anticipated (or hoped for) several hundred registrants:

> In 1975, a group of men who were enrolled in a women's studies course at the University of Tennessee held what they announced as "The First National Conference on Men and Masculinity," in Knoxville, TN. The following year, a second national M&M conference was held at Pennsylvania State University. Over the next five years, national M&M conferences were held in Des Moines, IA; St. Louis, MO; Los Angeles, CA; Milwaukee, WI; and Boston, MA.[40]

While the other conferences have long since folded, "Men and Masculinity" (now called "Men and Masculinities") still takes place each year and is associated with the U.S.–based National Organization for Men against Sexism.[41]

I've already mentioned some of the general topics men discussed at these gatherings. This description from the Waterloo conference not only illustrates the dominance of sex role theory at the time but also shows how organizers drew from feminism and CR methods to justify making this a men-only event:

> After much discussion with both men and women, it was decided to limit attendance at the conference to men only. Men have been talking to each other for only a short time, and the purpose of the conference, in part, is to see how far men can proceed in discussing their sex roles with each other. There is also a clear precedent for this in the women's movement. We believe that the task ahead will be one of sex role liberation for both men and women, but that men talking with men plays an important part in this.[42]

Feminist principles were also on the program for the first M & M conference in 1975, where discussions took place around forming a national men's organization whose structure would support "a feminist examination of the male role."[43] Moreover, M & M welcomed women's participation; a partial listing of panel facilitators includes six women and twenty men.[44] Various sessions at M & M throughout the 1970s emphasized the politics of antisexism. Notably, in 1977, participants issued a "Call for Ratification of the Equal Rights Amendment," describing the ERA as "a real new beginning for us in creating a just and humane society for all."[45] Out of this Call for Ratification emerged a group called Men Allied Nationally for the Equal Rights Amendment (MAN for ERA), which continued to campaign and work with feminist groups until 1982, when the Equal Rights Amendment was defeated. The theme of "Men Overcoming Sexism" governed the 1978 M & M held in Los Angeles. Among the activities was a public demonstration against rape and violence to women, and participants were invited to hear keynote speaker Barbara Wallston on the topic—"Why the men's movement must be feminist."[46]

But a number of conference activities were simply about men enjoying being with men, learning to communicate and express feelings more openly. One main goal at the Chicago "Men's Celebration" in 1974 was for men to make "an effort to emphasize the joy and fun of uniting as men in new and exciting ways."[47] The term effort is interesting, possibly implying a realization that many men might really have to work hard at having fun and being emotionally open. In a similar positive spirit, the concept of workshops was subverted at the first M & M conference, whose program instead lists twenty-five "playshops." Some of these—"Men and Dance and

Movement" and "Men's Theatre"—were obviously meant to appeal to participants' sense of fun and encourage free expression. Other playshops, of course, dealt with more explicitly political issues, like "The Black Male Experience" and "The Gay Male." In 1979, the M & M featured both workshops and playshops around the notion of love: for ourselves, between men, for society, between men and women, for children, and for our earth. Conferences routinely featured male-positive and profeminist performance artists, and some sessions poked fun at traditional notions of masculinity. At the 14th Annual M & M Conference, men were invited to participate in a "Tie Liturgy: A Ritual of Necktie Transformation." Complete with mock prayers and hymns, the ritual also had the more serious intent of asking men to think about relinquishing oppressive ties and "bind[ing] ourselves" to "those working for peace, for justice, for freedom for all."[48]

## MEN EDUCATING OTHER MEN

Outside the conference scene, some activist men relied on entertainment to educate other men about antisexism. Here, the playful was the political. In the mid-1970s, the "Isla Vista Gorilla Theater" described itself as a "men's feminist theater troupe—with woman clown and mime" and provided childcare at all performances. Likely associated with the California Bay Area–based men's group, the troupe's productions explored such topics as rape, sexism, and violence against women. The rape and murder of one troupe member prompted the others

> to reassess the politics of rape. We were soon creating and performing material based on our own experiences as men, and exploring both the obvious and the subtle roots of male sexism, the violence that leads to the oppression of women, the rape of women. . . . This production is an expression of our struggles on the path of change, a celebration of new beginnings.[49]

For other profeminists, humor was an effective strategy for getting mainstream men to understand the consequences of sexism. Done well, humor could deflect heavy-handedness. Better yet, humorous articles published in more mainstream magazines had a chance of reaching a broad audience, unlike an article published in a radical newsletter. A 1977 article with the weighty title "Overcoming Masculine Oppression in Mixed Groups" incorporated both of these strategies. It appeared not in a radical profeminist newsletter but in the left-wing magazine *WIN*. The male co-authors, members of the Philadelphia-based "Movement for a New Society," describe how men dominate mixed interactions and what they can do to change. Despite its title, the article takes a humorous approach, combining cartoons by a woman artist (one of them an enormous pig overflowing onto a conference table) with catchy headings and puns like "Hogging the Show,"

"George Custerism," and "Graduate Studentitis." As well as providing a practical, CR-based agenda for a first meeting of a men's caucus, the authors argue that positive attitudes are important for men thinking of changing themselves: "The process is a liberating one; rather than emphasizing guilt in defining ourselves as oppressor, the focus is on liberation: freeing ourselves! . . . Men need to recognize and concentrate on our qualities of love, of deep concern and caring which have been suppressed."[50]

## ANTISEXIST NEWSLETTERS: BY MEN, FOR MEN

By the mid 1970s, various antisexist, liberationist, and gay men's newsletters were being distributed. Some, like the Portland Men's Resource Center's "Principles of Unity," argued strongly that the men's movement should be linked with the women's movement: "Much of what we have learned about sexism comes from feminists and we intend to continue to learn from women. We feel the best way we can be supportive of women, and act in our self-interest, is to come together with other men in critical and supportive relationships."[51] Like their women's movement counterparts, these small publications were put together on a shoe-string budget. Reaching on average between a few dozen and perhaps a couple of hundred readers, these little newsletters often featured hand-drawn illustrations and were usually mimeographed. Any still existing now are available only in personal files or library archives.[52]

There were, at various times during the 1970s, hundreds of these newsletters and small magazines circulating locally. But some of these were especially noteworthy for various reasons: they were first, or they inspired other publications, or the writing conveys an especially resonant or poignant sense of what it meant, at that time, to be an antisexist man. While the opportunity to change their lives and improve their relationships was a prime motive for many in the 1970s men's movement, another strong motive was the desire for social justice, achieved through radical change. Not uncommonly, these motives clashed. Reading between the lines of some of the early newsletters—and often openly expressed—are signs of conflict about how closely the men's movement should be linked to the women's movement, or whether the men's movement should be more liberal or more radical.

The following brief history of what was likely one of the earliest profeminist newsletters published in the United States suggests such a clash of motives. The Berkeley-based *Brother: A Forum for Men against Sexism*, existed between 1971 and 1976. The first issue, with such articles as "We Are Men. We Are Not Beasts" and "Men's Liberation: Responding to the Women's Movement," has a strong gender-relations focus. This emphasis would soon change. As Kenneth Clatterbaugh notes, more radical antisexist men felt that the term liberationist should describe men who were comfortable with a liberal feminist stance, while antisexist should be reserved for men who were prepared to help radical women dismantle patriarchal institutions.[53] Soon, the newsletter was printing more radical critiques of sexism, militarism, and capitalism: the summer 1972 issue includes commentary on the Vietnam war and an article from a lesbian perspective entitled "Disarm Rapists; Smash Sexism." To make its radical stance clearer, the newsletter changed its name from *Brother: A Male Liberation Newspaper* to *Brother: A Forum for Men against Sexism.*[54]

By 1975, the *Brother* editors had distanced themselves considerably from liberal feminism. In an editorial, they outlined their "commitment to integrating our understandings about class oppression and exploitation with the anti-sexist position that *Brother* has taken." At the same time, they were getting worried about their increasing isolation from "contact with other men's antisexist activities."[55] The next issue on "Men and Class," published in the summer of 1976, argues that an antisexist movement must be organized on a class basis and includes numerous poems and articles around this theme.

Apart from its analysis of class and sexism (a socialist approach more common in Britain than in the United States), this issue is interesting for several reasons. First, it's the only *Brother* newsletter to list the editors' full names; many early men's group participants or writers used first names only, to promote egalitarianism and—in some cases, especially for gays—to preserve anonymity. Second, this issue looks as if it's been professionally typeset—a notable departure from previous issues, which (like most limited circulation newsletters before PCs) were manually typed and cut-and-pasted by hand. Finally, this issue would turn out to be, for all intents and purposes, *Brother*'s last. More than likely, as with many women's and men's groups, the core personnel went their separate ways because of fatigue, lack of funds, or major life changes. *Brother* may have been ahead of its time in trying to achieve diversity and inclusivity; among the variety of themes were men's liberation, antisexism, lesbianism, gay liberation, family relations, anti-militarism, and socialism. Perhaps the editors reached a political or ideological impasse and simply couldn't agree on future directions. It's also possible that *Brother*'s staff were faced with the choice of becoming bigger, more organized, and more formal, with the risk of losing their grassroots, radical edge. The full names and nice typesetting suggest a movement toward legitimation, which might in turn have provoked an unresolvable ideological conflict.

Yet *Brother* didn't die completely. In partial acknowledgement of the fact that *Brother* was a pioneering antisexist publication, the American-based National Organization for Men against Sexism (NOMAS) took the same name for its newsletter. This version of *Brother* began publishing in 1983, soon after NOMAS's earlier incarnation, the National Organization for Changing Men, was formed. The newsletter ceased publishing in 1996, when NOMAS was experiencing a great deal of internal conflict (described in chapter 8).

It's unclear whether or not conflict shortened the life of *The Chicago Men's Gathering Newsletter*, but this newsletter appears to have had different motives for operating than the 1970s version of *Brother*. Growing out of the first Men's Gathering in Chicago, the newsletter was a vehicle for continuing the movement and encouraging men to keep "working and rapping together." The inaugural 1973 issue described the newsletter as "dedicated to eliminating sexism, supporting the women's movement, and changing men's roles." Among the topics discussed were such issues as men, childcare, and the support of events like Gay Pride. Along with many others, this newsletter had a short life—less than three years. However, some small profeminist papers, like the Portland, Oregon-based *Forum for Changing Men* published by the Portland Men's Resource Center, managed to stay alive much longer. From 1974 to 1980, this newsletter focused on sexism and men's feminist activism; its editors described themselves as "changing men working to eliminate sexism in our own lives and in society at large."[56]

## PROFEMINIST MAGAZINES: SPREADING THE WORD

Not content with a small newsletter readership, some profeminists formed editorial collectives in the late 1970s with the ambitious goal of publishing a widely circulated magazine. The eldest and longest-lived of these is the British radical men's magazine *Achilles Heel*, which began publishing in 1978. In the United States, *M.: Gentle Men for Gender Justice* started life a year later, became *Changing Men: issues in gender, sex, and politics* in 1985, and ceased publication in 1994. A few other profeminist magazines existed during the 1980s and 1990s, one of the most prominent and ambitious was Australia's *XY: men, sex, politics* (1990–97).[57] But both *Achilles Heel* and *M.* began life in the late 1970s, a volatile time when the men's movements in Britain and the United States were splitting into liberationist versus antisexist camps and when antisexist men in the United States were thinking seriously about forming a national organization.

The first issue of *Achilles Heel*, which described itself then as "a magazine of men's politics,"[58] contained "a variety of articles, information and expressive art such as poetry."[59] The magazine encouraged men to re-define themselves, "a difficult and sometimes very painful" process—and also, in the editors' view, a political process. A member of the first editorial collective, who would later compile the early *Achilles Heel* articles into book form, was British antisexist activist and writer Victor Seidler. He, along with John Rowan and other British antisexist men, felt that this publication should—like their activism—reflect both a profeminist and a socialist stance.[60] Seidler's own description of the multiple goals of this magazine reflects his hopes that it would serve as a forum for dialogue among men and women. Such a dialogue, he implies, could help close the schisms among liberationist, gay, and straight antisexist men that were effectively fragmenting the British men's movement by the late 1970s (see chapter 8 for a closer look at this highly political situation).[61]

Yet *Achilles Heel* would have a rocky and irregular history. By the mid-1980s the editorial collective had collapsed, its initial optimism "replaced by a general uncertainty about the role, position and validity of anti-sexist men." Only one or two issues came out in the middle to late 1980s, by which time the magazine's self-description had been replaced by the less political for "changing men." Buoyed by the apparent health of both the men's movement and the British magazine *Men for Change*, the editorial collective recorded its hopes in April 1990: "At last we could be seeing the start of a real movement for the re-evaluation of men and their position in society. We are therefore optimistic about the future. We do realize that there is a long way to go. Men in general still have to find ways of working that are strong and assertive but not oppressive of women or each other."[62]

By 1991, *Achilles Heel* was back on course, but its self-description had changed once more to the current "radical men's magazine." This may be explained partly by the fact that, whereas earlier issues had not stated the magazine was explicitly antisexist or profeminist, the autumn 1991 issue made men's indebtedness to feminism more explicit. As well as repeating the magazine's earlier warning that it would not print anything sexist, racist, or anti-gay, the editorial collective added, "We recognize the issue of accountability to women, and welcome any contributions and comment from women."[63]

Today, the *Achilles Heel* editorial stance reflects the fact that most British men's groups have shifted from politicized antisexist activism to a broad-based concern with men's social, political or sexual lives. For example, the magazine is one of the few men's forums giving equal time to both antisexist and mythopoetic perspectives. *Achilles Heel* welcomes articles about profeminism and rejects sexist, antiwoman material, and in that sense is radical, especially compared to the usual newsstand fare. However, the magazine is nowhere near as profeminist or antisexist in tone or content as were the newsletters or magazines of earlier decades. The editors and contributors justify this decision by referring to the conflicts shattering the British men's movement in the 1970s and paralyzing it in the 1980s: keeping *Achilles Heel* open to a variety of views about men and masculinity is one way to avoid repeating history.[64]

In the United States, the profeminist magazine of note was *M.: gentle men for gender justice*, which later became *Changing Men*. Premiering in 1979, this self-described profeminist magazine, was partly intended as a male counterpart to *Ms.*—opening lines of communication and nurturing a larger men's community. The second issue (spring 1980) described the purpose and mandate of *M.* in more detail:

> *M.* is a quarterly publication for men and women who want a society free of sexism and who are discovering each other and the common need for support. As changing men we support the liberation struggles of women, third world, and gay and lesbian people. We are committed to communication, respect, and cooperation both among men, and between men and women.[65]

In the spirit of fostering dialogue between women and men, that same issue featured an interview with Marilyn French, who had recently published *The Women's Room*. French showed herself to be very open to the concept of men calling themselves feminists and doing feminist work: "If you consider yourself a feminist, you are one. . . . My idea of a feminist is a person who wants to see a synthesis of moral qualities in all people. . . . I think it's essential for the salvation of the human race, for its preservation."[66]

While only thirteen issues came out under the title *M.*, in 1985 the magazine became *Changing Men: issues in gender, sex, and politics*. For historians of the U.S. men's movement, these issues are a rich find. Articles by writers like Kenneth Clatterbaugh, Michael Kimmel, and Tom Mosmiller anticipate these writers' future projects, like Clatterbaugh's *Contemporary Perspectives on Masculinity* (1990, 1997) and Kimmel and Mosmiller's *Against the Tide* (1992). In 1992, Tom Mosmiller had described *Changing Men* as "the most significant and enduring 'publication of record' in the 20th century for men's support of feminism in the United States."[67] Fourteen issues of *Changing Men* came out between 1985 and 1994, when the magazine finally collapsed.[68] Except for academic publications like *The Journal of Men's Studies*, which occasionally publishes articles about profeminist men, there no longer exists in the United States a wide circulation vehicle for educating men about profeminism.

The kind of socialist vs. liberal split that may have hastened *Brother*'s demise was only one of several sources of conflict among antisexist men in the 1970s. Also of great concern to many men was a growing split between liberationists, many of whom tended to be comfortable with a liberal feminist framework, and antisexists, many of whom sympathized with radical feminism. Throughout the next twenty years, the unity of profeminist groups and projects would be punctuated by sharp conflicts around race, men's accountability to feminism, and differences between gay and straight perspectives.

It's impossible to say how many men's publications died out because of ideological conflicts or because the men involved felt they had to move on to other things, as did *XY*'s founding editor Michael Flood. It seems clear, however, that the larger publications tried to appeal to a wide range of men interested in changing themselves—men wanting to engage with more positive notions of masculinity and men wanting to do meaningful antisexist work. Theoretically, of course, those goals are entirely compatible.

In the afterglow of the 1970s, committed profeminist men also hoped that a new organization could set out a clear antisexist agenda without alienating undecided men, be male-positive without alienating radicals, convey a public profeminist presence without excluding or silencing diverse men, deal with different branches of the men's movement, and maintain productive relations with feminist groups. Yet fulfilling all these goals would prove enormously difficult. The next chapter tells the story of the U.S.–based National Organization for Changing Men and its early attempts to find balance.

## NOTES

1. Achilles Heel Collective (1990, autumn).
2. Barbara Ehrenreich (1983), p. 115.
3. See Michael S. Kimmel and Tom Mosmiller (1992), for speeches and documents produced by American profeminists. John Stuart Mill's *The Subjection of Women* (1869), Friedrich Engels's *The Origins of the Family, Private Property, and the State* (1884), and the work of German socialist August Bebel *Woman and Socialism* (1879) are notable for their sympathy to feminist ideas and their analyses of how social or economic conditions oppress women.
4. Kimmel and Mosmiller (1992).
5. Achilles Heel Collective (1990, autumn).
6. Michael A. Messner (1997), p. 37.
7. See Ehrenreich (1983) Messner (1997).
8. Interested readers should investigate the annotated bibliography and reviews found at "What are some good men's movement books?" linked to the Men's Issues Page (1997) of the World Wide Web Virtual Library. Online: <http://www.vix.com/men/books/reviews.html>. Retrieved 5 June 2001 from the World Wide Web.
9. Messner (1997), p. 37.
10. Joseph J. Pleck and Jack Sawyer (1974), pp. 2, 4.
11. Marc Feigen Fasteau (1975), pp. 36–39.
12. What are some good men's movement books? (1997).
13. In Messner (1997), p. 37.
14. Sex-role theory is based on the notion that being a woman or a man "means enacting a general role definitive of one's sex—the 'sex role' " (R. W. Connell [1987], p. 48). A key concept underlying sex-role theory is that sex roles are socially constructed; in other words, these behaviors are learned, not innate. Theoretically, what is learned can be unlearned; new behaviors can replace old. From this notion arises the possibility that so excited liberationist and antisexist men in the 1960s and 1970s: men could redefine the male sex role. As one 1974 writer put it, "If health, full-functioning, happiness and creativity are valued goals for mankind, then laymen and behavioral scientists alike must seek ways of redefining the male role,

to help it become less restrictive and repressive, more expressive of the 'compleat' man, and more conducive to life" (Sidney M. Jourard (1974), p. 28).

15. Messner (1997), pp. 37–38 and Connell (1987), pp. 50–53.
16. Bob Connell (1995), p. 78. Emphasis in original.
17. Mick Cooper (1991), p. 6.
18. Three sources that provide detailed descriptions of political conflicts around British men's antisexist activism in the 1970s are Rowan (1987), Cooper (1991), and Rutherford (1992).
19. Cooper (1991), p. 6.
20. Kenneth Clatterbaugh (1997), pp. 198–199.
21. Bob Pease (1997), p. 42.
22. Quoted in Ehrenreich (1983), p. 118.
23. Warren Farrell (1973, February), pp. 12–13, 15, 116–117.
24. Ibid., p. 117. Emphasis in original.
25. A Men's Group (July 1974).
26. Men's Liberation (1971), p. 8.
27. Ibid.
28. Ibid.
29. Morgan (1970), p. xxiv.
30. Men's Liberation (1971), p. 8.
31. A Men's Group (July 1974).
32. Quoted in Morgan (1970), pp. xxiii–xxiv.
33. A Men's Group (July 1974).
34. Stan Levine (1973, February), p. 14.
35. Morgan (1970), pp. xxiii–xxiv.
36. Ibid., p. xxiv.
37. *Chicago Men's Gathering Newletter* (1974), p. 2.
38. Mick Cooper (1991), p. 6.
39. About a men's gathering that was held June 2, 1974 (1974).
40. NOMAS (2000, July).
41. Information about current and past M & M conferences can be found at the NOMAS website. Retrieved 5 June 2001 from <http://www.nomas.org/conference/>.
42. Waterloo Men's Conference. (1975). Program. University of Waterloo, Ontario.
43. Ninth Annual Conference on Men & Masculinity in Washington, DC. (1984). Program.
44. First Annual Conference on Men & Masculinity. (1975). Conference program. University of Tennessee.
45. 3rd Annual Conference on Men & Masculinity. 1977. Call for Ratification. Des Moines, IO.
46. National Fifth Annual Conference on Men & Masculinity. (1978, December 29). Los Angeles, CA.
47. *Chicago Men's Gathering Newsletter* (1974), p. 2.
48. 14th Annual Men & Masculinity Conference (1989, June). Tie liturgy: A ritual of necktie transformation . . . Conference handout, Pittsburgh. 2 pp.
49. The Isla Vista Gorilla Theater. (N.d.). Brochure. In Changing Men Collection, Michigan State University Library. 2 pp.

50. Bill Moyer and Alan Tuttle (1977, November 10).

51. Portland Men's Resource Center (1980, March–April), p. 3.

52. I was able to access American antisexist newsletters and other materials from the 1970s and 1980s at the Changing Men Collections at Michigan State University Library. While this collections also has non-American documents, I found most of my materials from Canada, Britain, and Australia by visiting men who had been (or still were) active in profeminist projects and receiving permission to go through their personal files. I am profoundly grateful to these men for their time and generosity.

53. Kenneth Clatterbaugh (1997), p. 43.

54. See ibid., Messner (1997), p. 50.

55. Editorial (1975, July), p. 1.

56. *Chicago Men's Gathering Newsletter* (1973, June), p. 1.

57. In 1990, Australian profeminist Michael Flood began publishing a profeminist magazine that began life as *Wet Patch*, then later became *XY: men, sex, politics*. During *XY*'s first years, Flood played a central role in publishing the magazine. When I interviewed him in May 1999, Flood told me that for *XY*'s first few issues, he even wrote several articles himself under various pseudonyms to ensure there would be enough material. The magazine came out regularly until Flood, wishing to pass the work along, asked another group to take over in 1996. After two issues came out of Brisbane in 1997, *XY* ceased publishing, but still maintains a presence at <http://www.anu.edu.au/~a112465/XY/xyf.htm>.

58. Mick Cooper (1991), p. 8.

59. Editorial (1990, April), p. 3.

60. Lynne Segal (1997), p. 287.

61. V. J. Seidler (1991b), pp. 10–11.

62. Editorial (1990, April), p. 3.

63. From masthead *Achilles heel: the radical men's magazine* (1991, autumn) No. 12, p. 3. I should add that by 1997, the phrase "issue of accountability to women" had been replaced by "importance of dialogue with women." Chapter 4 discusses in more detail some of the tensions around men's "accountability" to feminism.

64. Amanda Goldrick-Jones (1998, summer/fall), pp. 32–34.

65. Editorial (1980, spring).

66. Duane Allen (1980, spring), pp. 6–7, 24–25.

67. Tom Mosmiller (1992).

68. While *Changing Men* was not, strictly speaking, an organ of the National Organization for Men Against Sexism, it nonetheless published many articles and much commentary by members of the NOMAS executive council. By 1994, NOMAS was undergoing upheaval (see chapter 8 of this volume), and both it and *Changing Men* were having difficulty retaining memberships and securing funding.

# 3

# "An Idea Whose Time Has Finally Come"

In the United States, the ambitious idea of forming a national antisexist men's organization was well under discussion by the late 1970s. The success of the Men & Masculinity conferences and the increasing numbers of regional men's gatherings and resource centers inspired antisexist men in the movement to bring up the question of establishing a national profeminist presence. For these men, consolidating local projects and regional gatherings into a more formal organization was highly desirable, even inevitable.[1]

The concept of a national profeminist group was not unique to the United States; in the early 1990s both Canada and Australia would initiate nationwide men's campaigns on feminist issues. But the American organization, formed in 1982, was the first to be established on a national scale and became the largest worldwide, though it was a long time in the making. This chapter describes some of the motives for creating and sustaining a viable, national profeminist organization, focusing on two groups in particular: the U.S.-based National Organization for Changing Men or NOCM (which later changed its name to the National Organization for Men against Sexism or NOMAS)[2] and the Canadian White Ribbon Campaign, formed in 1991. While these groups did not necessarily share the same motives for organizing, their founders had good reasons to believe that the time had come for diverse men to fight sexism together and on an ambitious scale.

## "SOME KIND OF ORGANIZATION WAS NEEDED . . .": THE NATIONAL ORGANIZATION FOR CHANGING MEN

Well before the first Men & Masculinity conference in 1975, men were talking about getting antisexist men organized. In a 1974 article in *Morning Due*, "Bruce" noted that if men don't organize, one of the consequences is "We will feel and be isolated." He predicted: "We will look for a community of support, but we will be forced to look for it in the women's movement because we won't be giving that support to each other. Certainly the women's movement doesn't need a lot of lonely isolated men looking for support. That is an old pattern."[3] This writer argued that men needed to rely on each other in order to do antisexist work effectively, and that forming an organization would provide the necessary support.

American profeminists appear to have made the first move toward forming a national organization at the third and fourth M & M conferences, both held in 1977. Delegates at the third conference, whose theme "Straight White Male: Wrestling with a Master Culture" suggests the enormous effort required to subvert and transform masculinity, authorized a task force to develop a proposal for a national men's organization.[4] At the fourth conference, attendees voted unanimously to form a national "Men's Alliance for Liberation and Equality" (MALE), whose membership would also be open to women. A related and very significant event at this conference, according to profeminist writer Tom Mosmiller, was the adoption of twenty-four resolutions defining the politics of the U.S. men's movement as "staunchly pro-feminist and pro-gay" and committing the movement to "racial and economic justice."[5]

### MALE and Split Ideologies

Yet after this promising start, MALE was split by conflicts at the 1978 M & M conference in Los Angeles. Much later, in 1992, Mosmiller recorded that the MALE-sponsored plenary sessions and task force meetings "were wrecked with dissension and ended in shambles." Though the force of these ideological differences tore MALE apart in 1979, the idea of a national organization was still, at the same time, "affirmed by consensus."[6] The men were determined to get back up on the horse that threw them.

A major cause of this "shambles" was the growing ideological split between antisexist men and men with other social agendas. One such agenda, men's rights, focuses on ways in which men are oppressed or discriminated against, especially in matters of family law or custody of children. Along with other theorists, Michael Messner implies that men's rights grew out of men's liberationism of the 1970s. Early liberationism "viewed feminism as a movement for human liberation," whereas men's rights groups "emphasized far more the costs of masculinity to men."[7] Messner reports that by around 1980, "men's rights discourse had all but eliminated the gender symmetry of men's liberation from their discourse, in favor of a more overt and angry antifeminist backlash. Feminism was viewed as a plot to cover up the reality that it is actually *women* who have the power and *men* who are most oppressed by current gender arrangements."[8] Many such men saw divorce and custody as the main areas of growing privilege for women and increasing oppression for men. As Connell somberly notes, "heterosexual men's activism on issues of sexual politics increasingly showed an anti-feminist face."[9]

The need to separate from perceived anti-feminist groups is highlighted by urgent discussions in the early 1980s about what a national profeminist organization should be called. In 1983, NOCM briefly clashed with a New York men's rights group also wanting to call itself "The National Organization for Men." In a letter to NOCM council members, one member recommended against competing for the old name and suggested the "National Organization for Changing Men." This letter also implies that the new name reasserts and reinforces a profeminist mandate and expresses strong disapproval of groups favoring "a reaction against [the National Organization for Women] and women's power."[10]

Then in early 1984, NOCM made its physical and symbolic separation very clear from perceived anti-woman versions of men's liberation by officially ousting Warren Farrell, who had made such a name for himself in the 1970s as a profeminist. Besides missing too many meetings, Farrell had—according to a letter written to him by NOCM's first president, Bob Brannon—"increasingly over the past three years publically [sic] and formally allied [himself] with a non-feminist 'men's rights' group which is hostile to both gay rights and feminism." Among other things, Farrell was told, "We have now reluctantly concluded that, despite your contributions to this movement of some years ago, you have now in body as well as in principle abandoned us, and betrayed our principles. . . ." By the late 1980s, NOCM (which became NOMAS by 1990) had moved far away from men's liberation,[11] especially the "men's rights" branches.

### Free Men versus Antisexist Men

The "Brief History" web page published by NOMAS describes how the Men & Masculinity conferences not only defined themselves positively as profeminist and pro-gay, but set themselves in opposition to men's rights advocates:

> During [the late 1970s], there was little formal organization, but an M&M ideology developed which was strongly pro-feminist and gay affirmative, while also emphasizing the burden of traditional male sex role restrictions, and the need to enhance men's personal and emotional lives. The M&Ms however clearly rejected the male-

self-interest philosophy of the "men's rights" movement, which appeared as an antifeminist backlash in the U.S. in the late 1970s.[12]

Providing grassroots insight into the ideological conflict between men's rights and antisexist groups is a 1982 article by Joe Interrante, an activist and writer who was heavily involved in gay/lesbian and men's movement issues. Interrante notes that as soon as the antisexist men took up issues "like freedom of choice on abortion, which conflicted with the demands of 'father's rights' groups," then—"The conflict began to surface in debates over political resolutions at the national conferences in St. Louis (1977), Los Angeles (1978), and Milwaukee (1979). And it began to emerge within local men's groups and centers, over the individual vs. social nature of men's oppression of women."[13] Forming a stable and unified national men's organization was a challenge, given the growing gap between the interests of antisexist/profeminist and those of father's and men's rights (also known as Free Men). The 1981 M & M conference was clearly sympathetic to and "reflected the diverse interests of the anti-sexist groups," with seventy-four workshops on topics such as images of masculinity, fathering, men and women, homosexuality, racism, anger, and men and violence—to name a few. But Interrante reports that in 1981, the Free Men held their own conference in Houston, Texas, the same weekend as the M & M conference at Tufts University in Boston.

The separation between profeminists and men's rights advocates was made clear as well by the perspectives each took on apparently similar topics. For example, violence—often discussed at M & M—was also a concern for Free Men. However, a workshop proposal to the Free Men conference offering "A Look at the Violence Women Do To Men" obviously took a very different tack. As it turned out, this proposal was rejected by the Free Men conference organizers. In protest, one of the proposers wrote an open letter "On Male Oppression" to the delegates at Tufts. Interrante provides excerpts from this letter in the first part of a two-part article about the state of the men's movement as of 1982. The excerpts reveal the anger smoldering in many of the Free Men and their sympathizers, especially toward feminism:

> It is oppressive to hear of universal female powerlessness while seeing the ubiquity of Women's . . . [sic] Studies, Book-store Sections, Theatre, Art Shows, Information vans, Health Centers, Radio Shows, etc. . . . It is not a little ironic, too, to hear of women's "second-class" status when they have such privilege in divorce settlements, custody hearings, draft acts, statutory rape laws, sexual harassment hearings, lifeboat seat allocations, etc.[14]

The bizarrely amusing image of feminists conspiring to fill up lifeboats and leave men floundering in the waves doesn't dilute the force of the Free

Men's anger toward feminism. This anger inevitably became one of the many insurmountable obstacles to a truly united national men's movement. In the face of such bitterness toward feminists and women, profeminists have generally found it difficult, sometimes even distasteful, to reach out and make connections with men's rights groups.[15]

The split between liberationist and antisexist men would continue to reshape the political landscape of the American men's movement. One large piece of this landscape, a descendent of men's liberation, is "mythopoetics." First coined by Shepherd Bliss in 1986, mythopoetic describes the spiritually oriented branch of the men's movement. Not unlike some branches of feminist spirituality, mythopoetics "uses myths and poetry as vehicles for accessing inner emotions, inner realities, and feelings."[16] Among the most well-known proponents of mythopoetics are writers Robert Bly (*Iron John*, 1990) and Sam Keen (*Fire in the Belly: On Being a Man*, 1991). In the early 1990s, this coverage defined mythopoetics in the popular eye—and in the jaundiced eyes of many feminists—as "men going out into the woods for male bonding and men hugging trees."[17]

But mythopoetic men do not equate their activities only with Bly's popular renderings, nor with extensive media coverage of warrior groups. One practitioner of mythopoetic healing work argues that the nature of these activities invites parallels with feminist consciousness-raising, allowing men to be liberated from patriarchal roles and expectations. This analysis suggests not only that the women's movement provided the catalyst for mythopoetic work but that this work is grounded in feminist theories about personal experience and ways of knowing.[18]

Yet for better or worse, by the mid- to late 1980s NOMAS had decidedly separated its profeminist and pro-gay mandates from the goals of these newly forming warrior groups. Only more recently have mythopoetic and profeminist men attempted to bridge this yawning gap with books like Michael Kimmel's collection *The Politics of Manhood* (1995)—a call and response between profeminist and mythopoetic men—and Edward Read Barton's *Mythopoetic Perspectives of Men's Healing Work* (2000), which includes feminist perspectives. It's also worth noting that in Britain, many men involved in antisexist work see "considerable overlap between profeminist and mythopoetic goals." While critical about romanticizing concepts like Bly's "Iron John," British men who consider themselves antisexist are much more likely to be open to the possibilities of mythopoetic work than their American profeminist counterparts.[19]

## "Unless We Act Soon . . ."

Since the 1970s, men interested in change and social transformation have long known that it's impossible to expect one large men's organization to represent men and their diversity of interests and perspectives—any more than one large organization can represent women's diversity. From 1975 on, the M & M conferences provided the closest thing to a national forum for the discussion of men's issues. But by the late 1970s, doubts had begun to arise about the long-term health of M & M, which was facing problems arising partly from emerging political schisms and partly from lack of funding. Forming a national profeminist organization became an urgent matter,[20] not only to promote antisexism but to make sure M & M would survive. However, NOMAS's description of this decision glosses over the complexities of building an organization:

> At the 1981 M & M in Boston, it became clear that some kind of organization was needed if the M & M tradition was to continue. A national membership organization was formed, and in 1982, its members elected an 18-person national council to provide the collective leadership of the anti-sexist men's movement. In 1983 the name "National Organization for Changing Men" (NOCM) was chosen.[21]

There was a sense of urgency when, in early 1980, profeminists began planning the goals and structure of this "National Men's Organization" (for the sake of simplicity, I'll use NOCM to describe the organization during the 1980s). Not only was the future of M & M possibly at stake, but profeminists were worried about what had happened with MALE at the M & M conference in Los Angeles in 1978 and Madison in 1979. This concern is conveyed in a 1981 article in *M.*—entitled "A National Anti-Sexist Men's Organization: An Idea Whose Time Has Finally Come." Of the reasons "why we think the time has come" to form a national organization, the third and last makes an unmistakable reference to groups like the Free Men and evokes a threatening image of the wrong kinds of men dominating the men's movement landscape:

> UNLESS WE ACT SOON, WE MAY LOSE OUR BEST OPPORTUNITY [authors' emphasis] . . . other "men's organizations" with different viewpoints and political perspectives have come into being and have begun to get publicity. . . . Some of these newer groups are explicitly anti-feminist and strongly homophobic. . . . Unless we become more visible on the national level soon, there is a real likelihood that large numbers of American men who are confused and looking for new perspectives will turn to these newer and narrower men's organizations.[22]

So one of the primary motives for forming a national profeminist organization was fear—or at the least, the need for damage control. If this seems ignoble, it's important to remember that many feminist women's organizations were formed with similar motives: to make sure that women's concerns would have a voice and that feminism would not be displaced by dominant ideologies. In this respect, the fledgling NOCM and more established feminist women's groups were very much in synch.

But there were also more positive reasons to organize, clearly explained in an internal letter circulated in March 1980:

> One year ago we had no sense of our identity as a group or as individuals, beyond scattered and sometimes frustrating attendance at the Nationals' task group meetings and a bone-chilling dissolution at LA. . . . Now we have our own Statement,[23] expressing our ideas and ideals. . . . A year ago we had no voice to announce in any effective public way these thoughts of ours. . . . Now we have *M.*, already planning issue #3 for summer[24] . . . alive and well and ready to foster our attempts to network anti-sexist people nationwide.[25]

The goals for this organization were ambitious: a "National Organization Agenda" circulated in the summer of 1980 lists no fewer than eighteen. Some were purely practical (dues, a telephone line, job descriptions). Others seemed practical (governing structure, organization's name, regional representation), but would also become political issues. Still other goals (a statement of principles, formation of action groups, priorities for social actions) would prove time-consuming and administratively unwieldy, but would underlie some of the organization's most notable successes and accomplishments.

The organizers were not expecting to accomplish all these goals within a year, or even two. In fact, it took about six. Here is an approximate timeline focusing on organizational groundwork, put together from various documents about NOCM:

- 1979—Statement of Principles for an antisexist men's group presented at the sixth M & M conference in Madison, WI
- 1980–81—initial planning for a national men's group
- 1981–82—striking of a Transition Committee to seek members and accept dues, followed by the election of a National Committee and formation of National Organization of Men (NOM) with about 100 members
- 1982–84—ongoing discussions and decisions about organizational structure, task (action) groups, and regional representation
- 1983—Men's Movement Forum, NOM's first public event in March
- 1984—official name-change to National Organization for Changing Men (NOCM)
- 1984—establishment of eighteen-member national council, twenty task groups, and twenty internal committees. Over 550 members claimed.
- 1985–86—drafting of new Statement of Principles.[26]

One source of inspiration for NOCM was the National Organization for Women (NOW). In a 1981 article published in *M.*, the nine men and two women most instrumental in forming the men's organization cited this well-established organization as a success story: "(N.O.W.) has more than

150,000 dues-paying members, and an annual budget of over $4,000,000; this is why they have been able to be effective in winning many battles (like the 1973 abortion decision by the Supreme Court). We too need to organize and begin to fight effectively for what we believe in."[27] Not cited were the numerous political and ideological conflicts NOW had experienced, nor the structural and organizational difficulties posed by such an enormous and diverse membership. As mentioned in chapter 1, by the mid-1970s NOW was trying to balance a mainstream, staunchly liberal philosophy with a more radical analysis. To the disgust of the radicals, the liberal agenda was still dominant. While the late 1970s/early 1980s campaign to pass the ERA provided enough of a motive to keep NOW together, the conflicts between liberal and radical feminists constantly threatened this fragile solidarity. Similarly, the profeminist NOCM would experience political and structural conflicts, though on a smaller scale. But the optimism, energy, and high levels of motivation conveyed by the earliest NOCM documents indicate that it's unlikely organizers foresaw all these formidable challenges—or chose not to submit their misgivings for public examination.

## ". . . We Want to Change Our Society . . ."

Since a number of American profeminist men had been thinking for years about forming a national organization founded on antisexist and gay-positive principles, a certain amount of infrastructure was already in place. These structures included the experience and teamwork involved in planning annual M & M conferences, the establishment of *M.: Gentle Men for Gender Justice* by late 1979, and the existence of dozens of regional men's groups and resource centers. But as with so many organizations, and usually for practical, logistical reasons, the bulk of planning and goal setting was concentrated among a core group of founders rather than distributed among regional groups. My reading of documents produced by the NOCM executive during its first two years or so suggests that this core group tried hard—sometimes to the point of burnout—to make the fledgling organization structurally diverse and open to feedback.

Early writings about NOCM[28] provide some insights into the motives of this core group. One clear area of agreement is that the new organization was prepared to welcome a wide spectrum of men (with the exception of declared anti-feminists like the Free Men). An internal letter written in August 1981 by the first core group, the Transition Committee, sets out three main reasons why men should join NOCM, and each argument seems designed to appeal to different constituents. The first addresses men with liberationist sympathies, or men who respond well to a male-positive perspective: "We [a new national organization] believe that the lives of almost all men have been limited and impoverished by the traditional male sex role. . . . We want to change our own lives to be more fulfilling and free . . ."

The second argument covertly criticizes groups like the Free Men while overtly establishing the organization's profeminist intent: "We refuse to blame women for the burdens of the male sex role. Indeed, we very strongly support women's continuing struggle for fair treatment and full equality. We take a special pride in the efforts of many men in our movement who are counseling with men who have been involved in violence against women." This passage contains a two-pronged argument. The references to fairness and equality refer to the American liberal feminist tradition favored by the NOW executive, in which activism takes place within mainstream political and institutional settings. But the references to violence against women acknowledge the goals of more radical profeminists. Consciously or not, this appeal typifies the ongoing balancing act between different profeminist groups played out in many other similar goal setting documents.

The final argument reflects an ongoing concern raised at many previous M & M conferences about fighting homophobia. It also subtly signals prospective members that gay issues will be well-represented in this organization: "We are also strongly committed to overcoming . . . the intense and irrational fear of homosexuality, which virtually terrorizes most American men and helps to hold them rigidly in the traditional male role. We strongly support equal rights for gay men and women . . ."[29] What's most interesting about this last argument, more so than the first two, is a subtle sense that the letter is preaching to the converted. Gay men are obviously the ideal readers of this section, with other prospective members/supporters as secondary readers. It's the use of language like "most American men" and the third-person "them" that indicates NOCM was not quite prepared to reach out directly to so-called "average men." In part, this may reflect the practical goal to get this organization established as quickly as possible, with reliable members who were already familiar and in agreement with profeminist and pro-gay principles—as chapter 8 discusses, the organization had clearly established itself as pro-gay.

Profeminists interested in a national group were also acutely aware of another obstacle blocking the organizational pathway: "the pitfalls of leadership issues among men."[30] As chapter 5 outlines in more detail, the core group planning NOCM felt that adhering closely to feminist consensus-based models would help mitigate the problem of competitive male leadership. In the 1981 article mentioned earlier published in *M.*, NOCM co-founder Bob Brannon and several other writers argue that enough trust and consensus has been achieved at this point to make good leadership decisions. Still, throughout the existence of NOCM and NOMAS, a strong desire for unity and consensus would be always in tension with an equally strong tendency to divide from or exclude those who don't fit an ideal profeminist profile. No group or organization, feminist or otherwise, can be exempt from that divisive experience.[31]

### A Public Portrait of Unity

The motives to achieve strength through unity and to claim a large space on the men's movement landscape are also conveyed by published descriptions of NOCM's 1983 Open Forum in New York—the organization's first major public event. The press conference statement, presented by Bob Brannon, and later printed in the organization's newsletter *Brother*, featured this sentence in large type: "there has never before been an organized national movement of men with the breadth of concern, and the determination to bring about social change, as the one we are launching today."[32] According to another press release issued after the Open Forum, "Feminist groups were well-represented, and expressed their warm support for the new men's organization. The National Organization for Women was represented . . ."[33] Topics covered at the forum included gay politics and links to antisexist groups; black men against sexism and racism; and pressures to be a "Real Man." The importance of unity comes through clearly in an article in *Brother* published after the Forum: "As each of the men and women spoke, the sense of excitement and underlying unity grew stronger and clearer, the ideological breadth and strength of the movement increasingly more apparent. . . . Seldom if ever had the growing men's movement been so unified in spirit and purpose, or its goals so clearly and eloquently described."[34] Terms like excitement, unity/unified, strength, spirit, and purpose echo the shared sense of inspiration and possibility in early 1970s profeminist writing. Obviously one major motive for this almost evangelical language—and particularly the explicit references to unity—is to promote solidarity among profeminists and de-emphasize internal divisions. But this language also evokes the optimism and energy that many men felt in the 1960s and 1970s about effecting social change and gender justice. Yet as later criticisms about NOCM's structure and ideologies would underscore, abstract motivators like "unifying" men and "disseminating ideas" would not, on their own, be able to sustain enough momentum to keep a national organization going.

## "WE CANNOT STAY SILENT ANY LONGER . . .": THE WHITE RIBBON CAMPAIGN

The NOCM was the earliest and perhaps most ambitious national profeminist organization to be formed. But antisexist men outside the United States were also engaged in projects that were national or even international in scope. The Canadian White Ribbon Campaign (WRC), founded in 1991, arose out of a unique combination of circumstances, yet it eventually became the world's largest profeminist initiative. Documents and interviews focusing on the first one or two years of this campaign[35] provide insights into why the campaign's co-founders decided the time had come to extend the feminist concept of ending men's violence against women into the consciousness of average men.

### The Montréal Massacre

One of the most horrifying events in Canadian history was catalytic in forming the White Ribbon Campaign. In the late afternoon of December 6, 1989, at the University of Montréal's École Polytechnique, fourteen young women were shot and killed. All but one was a student in the School of Engineering. The killer, twenty-five-year-old Marc Lépine, walked into the school carrying a semiautomatic rifle, shot one woman in a corridor, then entered a classroom and ordered the women to one side of the room. "You're all a bunch of feminists," he shouted, "and I hate feminists."[36] He opened fire on the women. Six died. Lépine then made his way to the cafeteria, "firing at diving, ducking students as he went,"[37] where he killed three more women. Going back upstairs to another classroom, he opened fire once more, and four more women died. Finally, the killer shot himself. His suicide letter, not published until a year after the killings, said that he wanted "to send the feminists, who had always ruined my life, to their Maker. . . . [T]he feminists have always enraged me. They want to keep the advantages of women . . . while seizing for themselves those of men."[38] The hatred in this passage, as well as the massacre itself, deeply shocked women and men alike and prompted many feminists and their supporters to take new initiatives to end violence against women.

### Identifying with Feminist Principles

Two years after the Montréal massacre, a handful of Canadian men who had been active in feminist anti-violence projects conceived the idea of organizing a national antimale–violence campaign aimed at men. In the fall of 1991, they issued a public statement—"Breaking Men's Silence To End Men's Violence"—which called on men across Canada to wear a white ribbon as a show of protest against men's violence to women. From the outset, the core founders of what became known as the White Ribbon Campaign used the term "profeminist" among themselves to describe the campaign's governing principles and goals. Using that term was intended not only to help define the campaign's main goals but convey the message to women's groups and activists that the campaign was trustworthy and ethical. In fact, identifying so strongly with feminism gave the WRC enough initial credibility with sympathetic feminists to garner a small but steady core of support through its first turbulent year. However, criticisms around the vexed question of men's accountability to feminism were leveled against the campaign in its second and third years, as described in chapter 4.

The WRC's choice to identify strongly with feminist principles wasn't simply strategic. Three of the WRC's co-founders—Michael Kaufman, Jack Layton, and Ken Fisher—had been actively involved in profeminist groups; their personal experiences with and belief in feminist activism played a significant role in shaping the WRC's choice to protest male violence and persuade mainstream men to get involved. In the WRC's earliest planning reports written in 1992, co-founders openly acknowledged their indebtedness to feminist work in the creation and goals of the campaign. In 1989, when a Québec woman's right to have an abortion against her male partner's wishes was tested in court, Kaufman created a national "Men For Women's Choice" petition, to be signed by high-profile men favoring a pro-choice stance. In 1991, Kaufman was a member of the Toronto group Metro Men Against Violence.[39] As for Layton, his support of feminist projects earned him an endorsement as a feminist candidate during his 1991 mayoralty campaign in Toronto. Liam Romalis, in his early twenties, was a WRC coordinator for two years. He told me he was brought up in a feminist household and had taken women's studies courses before he joined the WRC in 1992.

The WRC may have appeared suddenly on the Canadian media landscape, but it didn't materialize out of thin air. Like NOCM—which had a national magazine and could draw on a national network of men's centers and regional groups even before it was founded—the WRC grew out of existing men's organizations. The Ontario-based group Men's Network for Change (MNC)—of which Ken Fisher was a founding member—had been promoting men's political engagement in feminist projects, accountability to feminism, and the equality of women and men since the late 1980s. As well, the MNC had sponsored both the first National Conference on Ending Men's Violence in 1991 and the first White Ribbon Campaign.[40] As Kaufman noted in a report written shortly after the 1991 campaign, "part of our success was . . . the result of the fact we had a patiently-developed infrastructure [the Men's Network for Change] waiting to do something."[41] Other sources of inspiration for the White Ribbon Campaign were contacts the campaign's co-founders, especially Kaufman, had made with other men's groups in the United States, Britain, and later in Australia. One of these links was with NOMAS, previously the National Organization for Changing Men. Kaufman was enthusiastic about NOMAS's range of antisexist and pro-male activities and under his influence, the WRC adopted some of NOMAS's principles.[42]

All these factors—feminist experience and activism, and the examples of other national and international networks of men's groups—were significant in convincing a small number of profeminists that creating a national

Canadian campaign was appropriate and viable. But the most important motive of all was the tragedy of the Montréal massacre itself: this shooting of fourteen young women terrified and angered women, baffled and shocked men, and—at first—made profeminist men feel absolutely helpless. In interviews with me, neither Kaufman nor Layton wished to pinpoint December 6, 1989, as the sole catalyst of their initial discussions of a men's campaign against violence. But as Kaufman told me, "[After the massacre] I think more and more men became aware of the problem [of male violence]—finally! finally! finally!—you know it sunk through!"[43] Layton elaborated that the massacre was the watershed: "We all remember weeping, you know. So, it motivates you somehow. But we weren't sure what the hell to do! Except you go to the memorials, and you buy the posters, and you do what you were doing before, but somehow that didn't seem to be enough."[44]

Layton's comment captures a dilemma: the massacre was clearly a call to take action, yet concerned men felt that they didn't know exactly what action to take, or what would be appropriate. For two years after the massacre, according to Layton, all sympathetic men could do was attend memorials, donate money to women's antiviolence programs, and listen to women's experiences. Then in the summer of 1991, a series of brutal murders and assaults against women occurred in Toronto. These murders, so soon after the Montréal massacre, motivated Layton and Kaufman to take action. In early September of 1991, Kaufman received a phone call from Layton, who says that he told Kaufman—"We cannot stay silent any longer."[45]

For the WRC founders, these tragedies formed a primary motive for an action that seemed most logical at the time: creating a national profeminist campaign calling on men to end violence against women (more details about the WRC's antiviolence projects are provided in chapter 7). The WRC's decision to evoke the Montréal massacre and establish an all-male campaign—a "new angle" which attracted considerable media attention—helps explain what two or three co-founders described as the campaign's almost instant popularity. Initially, the WRC believed that this shattering of male silence was an accomplishment for men and a breakthrough for feminism.

It's interesting to consider what may have happened if NOCM had extended its membership goals from the beginning to include a broader constituency of the general public, and what arguments might have been used to motivate average men. In the long run, would a decision to appeal early on to average men have harmed or benefited this national men's organization? The White Ribbon Campaign decided from its inception that its antiviolence campaign should appeal to average men. Whether success can be measured by the fact that the WRC is visible in places like shopping malls and has expanded beyond Canada is perhaps arguable. But perhaps a strong appeal to average members of the public is worth considering as a standard profeminist strategy.

Both the NOCM and the WRC were motivated by strong convictions that they were doing the right thing at the right time by organizing on a large scale. One would think that antisexist men bolstered by such motives, and with years of grassroots activism and men's group experience, would be in an ideal position to create a nontraditional, nonhierarchical organization based on feminist principles. Yet they found themselves fighting both perceptions and realities that men's organizations are rife with territoriality and dominance and, further, that men do not listen to feminist concerns. Whether these criticisms were justified is a question the next chapter considers.

## NOTES

1. For example, Robert Brannon et al. (1981, fall), p. 7.
2. NOMAS (2000, July).
3. "Bruce," (1974).
4. I find it impossible not to wonder about uses of language like "wrestling" and "task force." Perhaps the 3rd M & M conference organizers used such terms with subversive, ironic intent. If not, then at the very least, these examples argue that part of the difficulty of subverting or transforming gendered institutions and behaviors lies in the near impossibility of transforming the metaphors that shape and are shaped by us and that inscribe notions of gender, especially masculinity.
5. Tom Mosmiller, Mike Bradley, and Michael Biernbaum (1980, fall/winter), p. 3.
6. In Tom Mosmiller (1992).
7. Michael A. Messner (1997), p. 41.
8. Ibid.
9. R. W. Connell (1995), p. 78.
10. Don Long, 1984 (9 August). Letter to NOM Council, 2 pp. Unpublished, in the Changing Men Collection. In 1989–90 NOCM became NOMAS.
11. Bob Brannon (1984, February). Letter to Warren Farrell. Unpublished, in the Changing Men Collection.
12. NOMAS (2000, July).
13. Joe Interrante (1982, summer/fall), p. 6.
14. Ibid. While Interrante harshly criticizes this antifeminist and anti-woman stance, in the second part of his two-part article he takes antisexists to task for "extreme heterosexism" resulting in "the invisibility of gay issues at workshops and conference panels" (1983, spring, p. 3). In his view—and he was scarcely alone—this was a major flaw in the men's movement antisexist branch.
15. Profeminist Michael Kimmel (1995, pp. 1–11) has recorded his uneasiness at the anger men expressed at mythopoetic retreats: "It was not necessarily a pretty sight, especially to feminist women who listened in horror as they learned what kinds of feelings were being released at these retreats. Undiluted rage against mothers, who were blamed for entering into incestuous relationships with their sons. . . .

Venomous anger at wives (mostly ex-wives, actually). . . . And seemingly incomprehensible fury at feminist women who have been agitating for transformation of institutional and interpersonal relations between women and men for over three decades." Quote is from p. 7.

16. Edward Read Barton (2000a), pp. 3–20. Quote is from p. 3.

17. Barton (2000), pp. xi–xiii. Quote is from p. xi.

18. Barton (2000a), pp. 3–20.

19. For more about British men and mythopoetics, see Amanda Goldrick-Jones (2000), pp. 246–251.

20. Brannon et al. (1981), p. 7.

21. Ibid.

22. Ibid.

23. This refers to a Statement of Principles for a national men's group presented at the 6th M & M conference in 1979. Among other things, this statement made "special note of our support for women's struggles for equality. . . . We pledge active and visible support to groups involved in the Women's Rights Movement." This section would clearly have alienated groups like the Free Men. From an unpublished letter in the Changing Men Collection.

24. The premiere issue of *M.: Gentle Men for Gender Justice*, a self-described "pro-feminist" magazine, was published in the winter of 1979 out of Madison, WI. Also see chapter 2 of this volume for more details.

25. Michael Biernbaum (1980). Dear Brothers . . . Unpublished letter (March 16). 4 pp. From the Changing Men Collection.

26. I compiled the NOCM timeline from documents in the Changing Men Collection.

27. Brannon et al. (1981), p. 7.

28. Morgan (1981, August). Dear Friend. Letter to M & M delegates. From the Changing Men Collection.

29. Ibid.

30. Brannon et al. (1981), p. 7.

31. See Appendix B of this book for a discussion of how feminist rhetorical criticism can provide some insights into conflicting motives of profeminist men's groups.

32. Bob Brannon (1983, summer), p. 5.

33. Anti-sexist Men's Forum: Success! (1983), p. 1.

34. Ibid. p. 2.

35. For example, Jack Layton (1993, August 31), personal interview.

36. Brian Bergman et al. (1991, November 11), pp. 26–30; Barry Came (1989, December 18), pp. 14–17; and Jennifer Scanlon (1994), pp. 75–79.

37. Came (1989), p. 15.

38. The text of Lépine's note is in Louise Malette and Marie Chalouh, (1991), pp. 180–181.

39. In interviews with me (1993), Michael Kaufman and Jack Layton also mentioned how their personal commitment to feminist projects had influenced their decision to co-found the WRC. Kaufman has also written articles and books on profeminism and men's lives. These include the edited collection *Beyond Patriarchy: Essays by Men on Pleasure, Power, and Change* (1987) and *Cracking the Armour* [*sic*] (1993).

40. Ken Fisher (1993), p. 43.
41. Michael Kaufman (1991, December 17).
42. Michael Kaufman (1993). His description of NOMAS is on p. 307.
43. Michael Kaufman (1993, December 3).
44. Jack Layton (1993, August 31).
45. Ibid.

# 4

# Trials and Errors: Being Accountable to Feminism

Highly aware of the rich history of sexism they've inherited, profeminist men have generally tried to replace (or displace) formal, hierarchical or exclusionary organizational structures with consensus-based, collective, feminist-inspired processes. Wanting to avoid reproducing oppressive patriarchal structures was a primary motive for profeminists to adopt a consensual, process-based approach as an integral part of their governance and decision-making. As much as possible, the ideal goal was to avoid using the "patriarchal skills, training, methodologies, perceptions" that feminist activist and poet Audre Lorde argued are "inevitably compromised and indentured by their origins." She has warned feminists: "The master's tools will never dismantle the master's house."[1]

Is Lorde right? Men organizing around feminist projects have at times been suspected of simply rebuilding patriarchy: albeit a kinder, gentler version. Often, criticisms of profeminist men's groups center on perceptions that men are not holding themselves accountable to feminist women. Instead, they charge into an issue like white knights to the rescue; blunder around like repairmen arriving too early in the morning to "fix" gender inequality; take center stage in what has been considered a feminist issue or event;[2] or simply appropriate, steal, or misrepresent feminist ideas or resources. While Australian profeminist Ben Mudge argues that "accountability is crucial for the profeminist men's movement, as well as for anti-racist white people and other similar groups," he concedes that "accountability is a process which is complicated, misunderstood and disputed by different groups."[3] No wonder, as some of the men who publish

*Achilles Heel* told me, accountability is a place where many men grappling with feminism "get stuck."

Also central to the question of accountability are tensions concerning male power and whether men can or should call themselves feminists. This chapter explores those issues, but first discusses the trial and error processes of the White Ribbon Campaign (WRC) and Australia's Men against Sexual Assault (MASA) as they tried various strategies for ensuring accountability with feminist groups. Some of these strategies represent hopeful possibilities for profeminists wanting to open up dialogue and do coalition work with feminist women.

## DEFINING THE NEED FOR ACCOUNTABILITY

The question of men's accountability to feminism is inseparable from trust. Feminist women have had enough bad experiences with men in groups that they are not prepared to trust even well-intentioned men unconditionally. Profeminists whose main goal is taking action on a feminist issue or participating in a feminist forum—any topic or set of discourses mainly shaped or controlled by feminists—have to be prepared to encounter some challenges from feminists. Men who believe in feminism must work to build trust with feminists. Such trust can be earned by creating a track record as responsible allies of feminist groups, establishing sound accountability structures, and maintaining respectful dialogue with feminists.

Yet even with all these fail-safes, profeminist groups often find it difficult to avoid criticism. Many of these criticisms revolve around a well-honed feminist fear that men, accustomed to exercising power, are more than likely to take over the forum. As Steven P. Schacht and Doris Ewing have put it,[4] profeminists can appear to be like "vegetarian foxes": seemingly benevolent and well intentioned—totally sworn off eating hens—but nonetheless dangerously likely to co-opt feminist space or even claim feminist women's hard-won power and resources, from funding to academic recognition.

Lack of clarity or agreement about how accountable men should be to feminism, and even uncertainty about what accountability means, can create all sorts of tensions between profeminist men and feminist women. For the National Organization for Changing Men in the 1980s, accountability meant creating an organization based on feminist principles: respecting process, ensuring decisions would be fair and consensual, and welcoming feminist women's participation. For the British men's magazine *Achilles Heel*, accountability has meant creating an open forum for discussion of gender issues, encouraging women to join that discussion, and refusing to print anti-feminist articles. Australia's Men Against Sexual Assault believes accountability structures should be formal, involving feminist observation of and feedback about profeminist initiatives. For the White Ribbon Campaign, accountability has involved keeping lines of communication open with local feminist activists and groups, being transparent about financial issues, and forming coalitions with feminists to accomplish short-term projects.

## THE WHITE RIBBON CAMPAIGN: INSTANT SUCCESS, GROWING CRITICISMS

Since its inception in 1991, the White Ribbon Campaign has considered itself indebted to feminist work and activism. Even so, the WRC faced criticisms from feminist women and men, particularly in its first two years, about the effectiveness of the white ribbon and the extent to which the campaign was accountable to feminist women. The WRC co-founders chose a white ribbon as the campaign's symbol because the color white means "peace, laying down arms" and in China, "mourning". During the inaugural 1991 campaign, the white ribbon was equated with a call for men to lay down their arms against women,[5] to remember the fourteen women killed in Montréal on December 6, 1989, and to support the eradication of male violence against women. The co-founders were delighted and amazed that "After only six weeks preparation, as many as one hundred thousand men across Canada wore a white ribbon. Many others were drawn into discussion and debate on the issue of men's violence."[6] After the 1991 campaign, the WRC began repeatedly stressing that it wasn't enough for men just to wear a white ribbon. That scrap of white cloth, said campaign organizers, also represented a pledge or commitment "not to condone, commit, or remain silent about violence against women." This phrase began to appear on cards attached to the ribbons during the campaign's second year.

Yet in 1992, some feminists began expressing concerns about the WRC's methods, motives, and accountability. Many of these criticisms were aired late in the year, when the WRC—by then an unincorporated non-profit society—had acquired office space in downtown Toronto, several paid part-time staff, and, during certain times of the year, one or two salaried full-time staff. At that point, publicity for "White Ribbon Week" involved a direct mail strategy as well as the production of about 1.5 million ribbons.[7] The WRC's most recent FAQ states that some women's groups criticized the campaign because "When we first started. . . . There were concerns (which we shared) about the disproportionate media attention in our first year."[8] This is certainly true, but criticisms also stemmed from worries about the accountability of this men-only group.

A case in point: a December 1992 news article described the Vancouver-based women's group WAVAW (Women against Violence against Women) as "angry the men are spending $400,000 to mail out ribbons." According to a staff worker at WAVAW, "That is comparable or exceeding [*sic*] our costs for one year of providing critical front-line services to women." In the first two paragraphs, the writer highlights the financial discrepancy between established, yet still-struggling, feminist antiviolence groups and the newly hatched WRC, casting doubts on the campaign's motives:

> For every dollar the high-profile white ribbon campaign intends to donate to women's groups across Canada this year, it is spending at least $12. And that has women's organizations asking about the real purpose of the male-controlled national campaign, if services to battered women get such a small amount compared to the $350,000 to $400,000 [the WRC] will spend this year.[9]

In this excerpt, phrases like "high-profile" and "male-controlled" imbue the WRC with much more power than their feminist counterparts, battered women who make do with a small amount of cash. The news writer equates the underfunding of women's antiviolence groups with evidence of women's oppression and victimization, while the links between men and money-terms reinforce feminist arguments that power and privilege accrue to men. Also in this article, a WAVAW spokeswoman ironically compares mailing out ribbons (implication—this is easy) with providing front-line services for women (hard work). Overall, the article portrays women's motives as well-articulated and grounded in feminist principles, whereas the men's intentions are portrayed as suspect.

Feminist suspicions about the WRC's possible misuse of power arose partly because in its first year, the campaign did not effectively communicate to feminist and women's groups the goals of its fundraising or its commitment to specific feminist political positions. It was also an unfortunate coincidence that during its first three years, the WRC faced a cash crunch. Women's groups who had been led to believe they would benefit financially from WRC fundraising found themselves disappointed. My conversations with several WRC co-founders, along with various internal documents and published articles about the WRC, confirm that the WRC set ambitious targets for financially supporting women's groups in 1992. But the campaign was unable to meet these targets in 1993 because of a budget shortfall. Unwilling to tap into the same government or other public funding sources that women's groups relied on, the WRC sought and eventually achieved charitable status, and undertook to raise funds from private sources, such as unions and businesses.

This was a risky decision, since feminist groups, many rooted politically in the left, generally consider such mainstreaming as a form of selling out.[10] And if it had been a question of taking the money and putting it into more office space, then such accusations would have merit. However, the WRC has put only a minimal amount of the money raised into facilities and staffing, relying heavily on volunteers. The bulk of funding is channeled into educational materials, such as school antiviolence curricula and videos; into organizational materials for men wishing to start their own white ribbon campaigns; and toward women's antiviolence initiatives, including women's shelters.[11] If some women's groups initially felt that the WRC's lack of transparency in the realm of funding and resources was symptomatic of a traditional exercise in male power, feminist concerns about the campaign's fundraising and finances have eased over the years.

Canadian profeminist Gordon Laird ironically suggested another reason why the campaign caught on so quickly: "[The] peculiar mix of solidarity and privilege that men bring to gender politics has suggested the secret to successful feminist promotion and fund-raising: be a guy. The White Ribbon Campaign's anti-violence action has taken a turn towards . . . mass fund-raising drives, national campaigns, media relations, corporate and governmental approval."[12] Laird deliberately laces his criticisms with terms that most of us associate with mass campaigning, publicity, and fundraising—in other words, corporate culture, only one small step from patriarchy.[13] Airing similar concerns after the inaugural campaign, the Ontario-based Kingston Men's Network for Change warned that, from its perspective, the WRC might be moving too quickly to capture media attention and funding. In a society in which "men (by and large) still control the major organs of communication," any attempts by a men's group to gain access to already scarce resources would inevitably create concerns about men taking power from women and raise question like—"Who benefitted [*sic*] from the WRC? Who was appropriated and whose power was increased?"[14]

By initially focusing on distributing thousands of ribbons, accepting and soliciting corporate donations and office space, and not clearly explaining where the money was going, the WRC left itself open to charges of exercising a particularly dangerous form of male power: creating an empire. This term, used by Judy Rebick (then chair of the National Action Committee on the Status of Women) well represents women's fears about the campaign's accumulation and control of property. Quoted in Michele Landsberg's 1992 *Ms.* magazine feature about the WRC, Rebick expressed support of the WRC in qualified terms: "If they help us fight against feminist-bashing, that's great. I just hope they won't build an empire instead of focusing on political action."[15]

Also concerning feminist critics and sparking accusations about possible empire building was whether the campaign was appropriating physical resources like funding from women, or simply compromising women's access to these resources. A number of news articles and columns written in 1991 and 1992 accused the WRC of accumulating the trappings of corporate power. In a widely publicized 1992 critique of the WRC in the *Globe and Mail*, two feminists wrote that "[w]omen are wise to question the campaign's strategy, its accountability to women, its fiscal responsibility and its basic premise."[16] Similarly, feminist groups like the National Action Committee on the Status of Women (NAC) reported they were worried about the WRC's rapid moves to secure funding, office space, and staff. According to an *Ottawa Citizen* article written a few days before the WRC's second annual White Ribbon Week, some women were wary that the WRC grew so quickly from "a few men [meeting] in living rooms" to a national campaign with "an eight-room office in downtown Toronto, hundreds of volunteers and a 1–800 number."[17]

Even Judy Rebick, otherwise a supporter of the campaign, expressed frustration with the reality of a sexist society that, among other things, gives men easier access to money and media than women. Her wording creates images of property and the trappings of corporate success, linking the WRC with men's drive to control resources. However well-intentioned they may be and however aboveboard their motives, these critics implicitly argue that even profeminists can be complicit in accepting or using forms of power that oppress women.

The most contested terms in these published articles relate to financial power, including but not limited to "fiscal," "funding," "office space," and "money." Much of the conflict around these terms is based on the notion that whoever possesses valued and necessary property items such as funding and facilities has an edge on the ability to control public discourse about an issue. Despite their good intentions, men are traditionally in a better position than women to exercise such power and take advantage of it—a concept I discuss later in this chapter. Reflecting a well-honed feminist distrust of male privilege, these criticisms of the WRC's conduct in its first two years also suggest a cause and effect relationship between any high-profile men's campaign—even one grounded in profeminism—and patriarchy, through which women are held back, controlled, or silenced.

Yet at the same time, along with the criticisms came praise for the WRC's unique mandate and overall goals. Rebick, Landsberg, and a number of front-line feminists were and are strongly in favor of men taking meaningful action to help eliminate male violence. As Rebick said in Landsberg's article, "We support the white ribbon campaign and we think it's positive that men are taking up the issue of male violence against women." In 1991, Rebick and WRC co-founder Michael Kaufman collaborated on a newspaper feature entitled "Ending violence against women is a 'men's issue' "—a piece included in WRC information packages. Well into 1994, Rebick was continuing to act as a contact and resource person for the campaign.

Despite its early mistakes, the WRC has been able to build trust with feminist women partly because campaign workers have listened to feminist criticisms and taken them seriously. In a 1992 "How to Organize a White Ribbon Campaign" package, the WRC issued an impassioned call for men to acknowledge women's experiences with male violence, to learn from and listen to women, and to take leadership from women: "Who knows better about the problem of violence against women than women? . . . [18] Interestingly, the WRC did try to implement a more formal accountability structure, a liaison committee, during its first two years. On this committee, representatives of the WRC and feminist groups could discuss WRC plans and policies. The women's role was to provide advice and, where warranted, criticism. Co-founder Michael Kaufman's vision of this committee was that it would be a formal link to the feminist community but would have no decision-making powers. According to WRC co-founder Jack Layton, this arrangement made it easier to bring issues like accountability into the open. Feminist women were able to advise that men shouldn't speak on December 6, the anniversary of the Montréal massacre, and to recommend that men—not feminist women—should be seen to take responsibility and do the work of organization and governance.[19] Indeed, Ron Sluser, another WRC co-founder, made a point of telling me that the women *chose* not to be part of official WRC policy-making: "They made it clear that our mandate was to go out and do it."[20]

WRC co-founders were also concerned that women *not* take on secretarial tasks like cutting ribbons and other leg work, as has so often happened when women joined men's revolutionary movements. For these reasons, the WRC insisted that the liaison committee be an advisory body only. Rather than diminishing women's power, the intention was to stress the importance of men being proactive and accountable to feminism. However, according to Kaufman, the liaison committee wasn't as successful as the WRC had hoped. In fact, after about two years, the committee no longer existed as such. This wasn't because feminist women weren't supportive of the WRC's work. As Kaufman explained,

> here we were, inviting women who were already completely overworked, and we said, "Here's one more responsibility we'd like you to take on." And it was a bit unfair, basically. And what happened in practice was that the women who said they were pleased to get involved either weren't all able to come, or were finding it—you know, one more thing they had to carry.[21]

Realizing that a formal liaison committee wasn't working, a group of WRC workers in London, Ontario held a one time Open Forum or community meeting in 1993, at which representatives of women's groups and the WRC expressed concerns and made suggestions about the campaign. According to the minutes of this Forum, the event was a success. Co-facilitated by a woman and a man, and governed by a nonhierarchical set of guidelines that encouraged feminist models of sharing and listening, the Forum arguably encouraged productive dialogue. Such an event was not repeated, though, possibly because it grew out of the particular context of complaints and concerns about the WRC in its first two years of operation and was motivated by a coherent, short-term, goal: getting feedback about the campaign's procedures and accountability.

The concept of women and men working together within short-term coalitions is promising and has received favorable reviews from some feminist women involved with the WRC.[22] In part, this was because the men running the campaign had had previous experiences with feminist coalition work by the time they joined or founded the WRC. In 1990, several women's and men's groups in Ontario came together to form the "December 6 Coalition"[23]—an ongoing alliance whose goals are to raise funds to help end violence against women.[24] A particularly successful coalition between the White Ribbon Campaign and the YWCA was arranged in 1994, when with the help of an advertising company, both groups worked together to create a joint national billboard campaign. The striking design featured the WRC's white ribbon logo on one half and the YWCA's red rose symbol on the other half. The text below the pictures read: "Help End Men's Violence against Women." While again, this same kind of activity was not repeated, a WRC administrator interviewed in December 1994 thought that the billboard campaign had been helpful in building trust with women's groups.

One Toronto feminist activist, Susan Van der Voght, acknowledged the logistical difficulties of building and maintaining such coalitions. Van der Voght, a former member of the WRC's Toronto liaison committee, believes these alliances should be ongoing and that they are just as important, if not more so, than temporary coalitions. But besides the workloads involved, temporary alliances between women and men may still be the best way of working together and ensuring accountability. There is a strong perception that both sexes—especially women—"still need space," as Van der Voght puts it.[25] WRC co-founder Ron Sluser echoed this comment: "there's a time when I think we need to come together, but I think there's a time when women need to continue to do their piece on their own, and men need to go off and do our piece on our own."[26] The implication is that feminist and profeminist partnerships might need to operate simultaneously in distinct spaces, together and separately, rather like the ribbon and rose billboard.

By the mid-1990s, the WRC was relying mainly on coalition work and casual, routine contacts with feminist groups to keep lines of communication open. Michael Kaufman argues that informal means have been more successful for the WRC than formal structures for maintaining accountability with feminist women. He describes their process as "informal back-and-forth . . . just the checking in and the trying things out, getting feedback, getting response." Such "back-and-forth" has been effective in helping the WRC avoid inappropriate actions. For example, Kaufman told me about one idea that the WRC had of having men go door-to-door.

When the campaign asked some women's groups what they thought, some reacted negatively, pointing out it could endanger women—what if some "guy off the street" put on a white ribbon as a way to gain entry? According to Kaufman, "we finally said, 'We'll cancel it. . . . We make mistakes, but it's a constant process of learning, trying out things, and looking towards women."[27]

The depth of concern shown by many feminist critics about the WRC as another example of male dominance might convey the idea that feminists and women's groups are reluctant to work with men. Indeed, in its first two years especially, the campaign's domination of media coverage on violence against women, along with its rapid accumulation of funding and office space, represented to some feminists a real threat of men appropriating women's already scarce resources. Essentially, this sense of a motive to power was in tension with the WRC's stated intentions and strongly implicit profeminist message. Yet it's fitting to note here that the campaign has continually made efforts to maintain productive and open relations with feminist groups and, in the process, built up a solid level of trust.

## MEN AGAINST SEXUAL ASSAULT: A MODEL FOR ACCOUNTABILITY

For Australia's Men against Sexual Assault (MASA), founded in 1989, the approach to creating good accountability structures begins with the assumption that gender differences are among the networks creating and maintaining power inequities. The usual result of these power differences is that men—particularly white middle-class men—tend to have more access than women to the kinds of resources that help enable change or accomplish concrete goals, large or small. MASA and its members have done a considerable amount of work thinking through what accountability means for men. Accountability for MASA has meant that profeminist men need to be aware of their position in relation to other groups, particularly women. With this awareness, profeminists should try "consciously restructuring [their] work in ways that ensure that it is responsible and respectful to those groups."[28]

How might this concept of accountability work in practical ways? In an article for the *Dulwich Centre Newsletter*, David Denborough, a MASA member, discusses formal accountability structures, such as having feminist women monitor men's groups. Indeed, when MASA was formed, it pledged to liaise closely with an established feminist institution—the Centre against Sexual Assault—"to ensure that [MASA's] activities would be supportive of the work of women against sexual violence."[29] Rather than setting up a formal committee, MASA simply asked feminist activists to observe some of their meetings and events. One Australian feminist activist, Marnie

Daphne, told me that her first exposure to profeminist activism was in 1992, as an invited monitor at a MASA conference. "I was cynical at first, but I was open to checking it out and giving feedback. And I was curious."

Over two days, she and another monitor, who sat just outside the circle of men, were asked to observe and give feedback at the ends of sessions. As it turned out, the monitors spent little time speaking, but rather reflected and wrote on their experience. Afterward, Daphne was still a bit skeptical about profeminist motives: "I wondered how politically committed they were to challenging sexism as opposed to getting glory or looking good." But she also became more enthusiastic, "more open" about profeminist work. If men want to be accountable to feminism, argues Daphne, they should actively engage in dialogue with and seek feedback from feminist women, but shouldn't expect women to come up with the right answers all the time. Profeminist men need to be able to challenge feminist women's perspectives when the situation warrants. As she and her fellow monitor, Adele Murdolo, wrote afterward in *XY* magazine:

> Overall our impression of the group and the weekend was quite positive and encouraging. We felt safe in what could have been a threatening environment . . . and we were impressed with the scope of the issues raised. We found the collective and consensus processes impressive, and they stimulated some new thoughts about group dynamics for us.[31]

Daphne and Murdolo raised some concerns in 1992 about the relatively formal nature of the monitoring arranged by MASA. They found the term "monitor" itself to be problematic "as it put constraints on us and other participants and took away our sense of inclusion." Also, in a well-meaning attempt to "protect" the women from "individual challenges," some of the monitors' contributions were "allowed . . . to rest unaddressed other than by nods of the head. This lead [*sic*] us to feel that at times we were unheard or ignored."[32] For Daphne, being accountable to feminism is about "establishing dialogue, seeking feedback, but not assuming women have the best answers" . . . .There should be "room for profeminist men to challenge" feminists.[33]

The formal accountability structures tried by MASA aren't usually a popular choice for profeminist groups. Indeed, critics say they can discourage men from taking responsibility for their own thinking and add to feminist women's workload. But David Denborough of MASA has doubts about the effectiveness of informal accountability structures. His story about sharing food with women makes it clear that even well-intentioned profeminist men can be oblivious to their own power in relation to women:

> One night in an Adelaide coffee shop, I was busily sharing dinner and discussing feminist politics with two colleagues—one woman, one man. When the meal was

over, the woman pointed out that I had just eaten far more than my fair share. It became clear to me during the conversation that followed that such small acts, underlined as they are by a sense of greater entitlement, are just as important as the big political picture. . . . The point I am trying to make is that simply hoping that we men will remain alert to our own sexism, and will challenge each other, seems overly optimistic.[34]

But Denborough, like Daphne and Murdolo, also has some problems with the more formal feminist monitor model used at the 1992 MASA conference: namely, that it "appears to be based on hierarchical notions of accountability in which the women are upheld as 'experts' or 'monitor' the work of men."[35]

As an alternative to either formal monitoring or informal phone calls, Denborough relates how the Sydney, Australia, branch of MASA adopted a two-tiered accountability structure. The first tier consists of formal consultation with feminist groups. Most suitable for planning major campaigns and policies, these consultations can consist of forums, meetings, or document distribution. The second tier is more intimate and ongoing, allowing profeminist men to work with women in "a space where issues can be dealt with in a more profound and trusting manner." Denborough describes a group—less formal than a committee—consisting of mainly equal numbers of women and men, experienced in activism and representing a range of backgrounds. Central to this partnership approach was the condition that the men already have some degree of trust or commitment with the women—a familiarity which could result in either contempt or trust. According to Denborough, their initial meeting took the form of a dinner party, to which the MASA men invited women who were "friends, partners and colleagues" (presumably the men ate only their fair share).[36]

Did this model work? Denborough, writing in 1994 when the model was just being established, expressed great hope that it would allow MASA to work in respectful ways. The goals of this accountability model included encouraging men to take responsibility, remembering women's diversity, reaching out to varied groups of men, and creating dialogue across both ideological and personal divides. But Denborough's analysis of these early days also highlights the fragility of this slender new structure, especially in contrast with the adamantine "master's house" it seeks to replace: "the acknowledgement of the need for accountability also brings, when I allow it, an openness and vulnerability. It is a feeling I cherish, for it brings with it the possibility of connection, but it is a feeling I run from at times. It is far safer to be guarded, self-assured, dominant, and in control."[37]

## MEN, WOMEN, AND WHO HAS "POWER OVER" WHOM

There is considerable feminist support for the idea of women and men working together, if men are prepared to help redefine or transform what "male power" means. Certain beliefs about the nature of power have informed feminist attitudes and discourses about men's power over women, and it's possible to summarize these beliefs as two general feminist approaches. The first approach is to see power as a commodity, "something that a person or group collects and has" in order to gain "influence and control" over resources and people.[38] Hilary Lips, a social pyschologist who has researched power, uses the label "power over" to describe this way of thinking about power. This framework helps explain why people might describe their relationship to an issue or set of discourses in terms like "ownership" and "territory." From a feminist standpoint, thinking of power as the ability to control others explains why many men oppress women in various ways. More positively, this framework also suggests that women can achieve "empowerment," a greater ability to shape the conditions of their daily lives.

The second major approach to power derives from postmodern theories that power is not a property that people possess, but a network of forces built into a social system, forces which work independently of individual will, intention, or agency.[39] The conditions or rules that govern power are not under our control—in other words, men don't exercise power over women so much as male-dominated institutions govern the conditions which produce knowledge, status, freedom, or the ability to make changes. Feminists argue that these conditions unquestionably have the effect of oppressing women and other marginalized groups.

Both these approaches to power—as exercised by people over others, and as exercised through a network of forces—help explain why male power or patriarchal power is so important to the question of accountability. The idea that power is something men often have over women in all sorts of day to day contexts resonates with the shared and common sense experiences of many women and feminist activists. But the second approach, whereby power is something created by and through a variety of social networks and can change shape depending on those networks, invites feminists and profeminists to look carefully at what power means for women and men under different circumstances.[40]

## GENDER, POWER, AND MEN IN FEMINISM

The early concerns about the White Ribbon Campaign's "empire building" and the MASA men's struggles with control and domination are only two possible results of men entering a feminist forum. Also rooted in unequal power relations is the question of whether men should call themselves feminists. The prospect of even well-meaning men getting too close to feminism is another source of possible tension between feminist women and male supporters. The question here is *not* whether men can believe in feminist principles or do feminist work, since the very existence of profeminist organizations, publications, and projects turns that into a "rather sterile debate," as British profeminist writer Joseph Bristow puts it.[41] But should men who believe in feminism actually *call* themselves feminists? The debate over what to call themselves is hard to separate from accountability to feminism, because like accountability, this issue touches feminist concerns about male power and men's historical tendency to dominate public forums.

On the one hand, there are perfectly good reasons for men to call themselves feminists. After all, central to many of the woman-created definitions of "feminist" from *A Feminist Dictionary* (1985) is the notion of "a person, male or female" or "someone" who recognizes women's importance and who is willing to take action against women's oppression. A magazine called *The Wise Woman* has defined a "feminist" as "A person, female or male, whose worldview places the female in the center of life and society. . . . Also, anyone in a male-dominated or patriarchal society who works toward the political, economic, spiritual, sexual, and social equality of women."[42] Andrea Dworkin also leaves open the possibility that men can call themselves feminists by using a neutral pronoun in her definition: "To be a feminist means recognizing that one is associated with all women not as an act of choice but as a matter of fact."[43] That men can legitimately call themselves feminists is also implied by feminist critics who do not believe that it's valid to equate feminism with the state of being female. British feminist Rosalind Delmar takes some feminist theorists to task for this conflation and argues that feminism's adoption as a "blanket term to cover all women's activities urgently needs to be questioned."[44]

Some profeminist men are also quite comfortable with the "F-word." In the 1998 collection *Men Doing Feminism*, Patrick D. Hopkins tells his story of "How Feminism Made a Man out of Me" and concludes:

> Feminism should be about gender and the structures of sexism and oppression that arise from hierarchical evaluations of gender, not about the problematic ahistorical category of woman per se. . . . Further, feminism should be characterized by adherence to a basic set of beliefs and political positions. . . . [T]he core of feminism would be *feminist* positions, not *women's* experiences. As a result of this characterization, men can be feminists.[45]

On the other hand, many feminists—female and male—prefer to reserve the term feminist specifically for *women* who are doing work by and about women, placing women in the center of analysis, and drawing motivation from their own experiences within patriarchy. The concept of experience is key to equating feminist with female. Michael Kaufman, among others, feels that the term profeminist expresses the fact that men can engage in feminist analysis toward social change. But as Kaufman said, "The other half of feminism is a theory emerging from women's experience. . . .

[U]ltimately, it doesn't emerge from my experience."[46] Similarly, Michael Kimmel, a national spokesperson for NOMAS, has focused on the centrality of women's experience to explain why profeminist is a better term for supportive men:

> to *be* a feminist, I believe, requires another ingredient: the felt experience of oppression. And this men cannot feel because men are not oppressed but privileged by sexism. . . . To be sure, some men do feel oppression, but we are not oppressed *as men*. . . . And to *be* a feminist, one needs to share the feminist analysis and vision as well as to experience that oppression. Men who support the struggle for gender equality may be called "anti-sexist" or "pro-feminist." I have used 'pro-feminist' because it better states their positive support for women's struggles.[47]

On a more personal level, men (particularly straight men) often experience unpleasant social effects when they identify themselves with anything associated with femininity. I know men who willingly support women's equality but laugh nervously when I ask them if they'd be willing to call themselves feminists. Tom Digby, editor of *Men Doing Feminism* (1998), says that when he describes himself as a feminist, "Most men and some women respond to my self-characterization with acute embarrassment. . . . [W]omen's embarrassment seems to center on how my being a feminist diminishes my manliness, while men seem to think I'm crazy."[48] In her "Foreword" to that collection, Sandra Bartky acknowledges that:

> Few men benefit professionally, not just in academia but in most work environments, from too close an alliance with feminism; such alliances tend more to discredit a man than to advance his career. Coming out for feminism regularly earns a man not only the distrust of many feminist women, but the scorn of "manly" men, who charge him with having been "pussywhipped."[49]

The label "feminist men" received mixed reactions at two public lectures I gave, both entitled "Can Men Be Feminists?" Younger men and older women were open to the concept, though most of the women were amusedly convinced that older men would rather die than call themselves feminists. Of the three older men who attended the lectures, two listened politely and one glared ferociously. It perhaps didn't help that I referred to feminism jokingly a few times as "the F-word."

But even supportive men tend to avoid the term "feminist" for a wholly different, political reason: their awareness of men's traditional, historical role as women's oppressors. Supportive men understand that the term "feminist" can signal a deep commitment and a willingness, as White Ribbon Campaign co-founder Jack Layton has put it, to "take leadership" from the women's movement. But they also understand that adopting the term "feminist" could be interpreted as a power play, a bid to appropriate women's hard won, burgeoning influence on public thinking about gender issues. In other words, men do not come with guarantees that calling themselves feminists means a sincere commitment to questioning and changing oppressive power structures (for that matter, neither do feminist women). In the words of a British feminist academic:

> So how are we to read a man who says that he is a feminist? Is this an example of patriarchy appropriating the strengths of feminism in order to defuse its radical implications, in order to contain it or make it answer to a masculine framework? . . . Confessional writing by men tries to convince the reader that they have laid down their arms. . . . The whole debate is written through a jungle of anxiety. Can men be inside feminism? On what terms can we allow ourselves to ask, are men already here?
>
> What is surely more interesting than the *legitimacy* of men's claims to entry is their *motives*. . . . How do male "pheminists" . . . fantasise [*sic*] about what it's like "in here"? . . . Evidently this new form of male desire demands a strong—and suspicious—feminist diagnosis.[50]

Casting doubt on the motives of would-be male "pheminist" colleagues, this critic suggests that men who would be feminists are expressing a deep-seated desire to be included. And indeed, considering what some antisexist men wrote in the early 1970s about wanting to be part of the excitement, there are likely some grounds for this suspicion. Still, it seems a bit sad and ironic to criticize men for wanting to be included in feminism when so many other men refuse to be associated with anything containing the prefix "fem."

An especially scathing criticism of men calling themselves feminists, also in *A Feminist Dictionary*, claims that a man calling himself a feminist represents a "male appropriation of language no less stupidly defensive than a white man imagining himself a 'black radical.' " The writer (a man, incidentally) suggested that "pro-feminist" is the appropriate word to describe "the male who works towards feminist goals"[51] (see the introduction for views about what profeminist means). Less harshly but just as firmly, scholars like Peggy Kamuf, Alice Jardine[52] and Tania Modleski[53] interrogate the "men in feminism" question explicitly as a problem in gender and power relations. Sounding warning notes about feminist men appropriating women's power, Modleski believes that men—especially men in groups—have a tendency "to . . . deal with the threat of female power by incorporating it," creating a "male feminization" that is "empowering to men and disempowering to women."[54]

Since the early 1970s, some feminists have held the position that there is little or no place for men in feminism—that indeed, "separatism"[55] is politically necessary for women to be free of oppression. An extreme position is that women should not "have to have anything to do with men. . . . Until all women are lesbians there will be no true political revolution."[56] Other separatists believe men should be excluded from women's politics, though not necessarily from women's personal lives. In a one-page statement prepared in 1974 for the Portland Feminist Coordinating Council Forum on the Role of Men in the Women's Movement, the anonymous author noted that men "are beginning to express an interest in Feminist politics." But because men are inextricably part of the "existing social order" responsible for restricting women, men should not, indeed could not, be part of the women's movement. Rather, "Separate consciousness-raising is necessary in order that each sex can establish their own identities in an atmosphere void of social pressure." The writer was careful to make a distinction between political and social/sexual separatism, suggesting that the question of whether women should have relationships with men is "a personal question each woman must answer for herself."[57]

For their part, profeminist men are often sensitive to the possibility that at the very least, feminist women need their own separate spaces. But the question of how closely men should work with women to accomplish feminist goals is vexed. In *Men in Feminism* (1987) an academic collection arguing that men's relations with feminism are contested, Richard Ohmann implies that men must be prepared to answer to women but not leave the struggle entirely up to women. In his view, men are "on extended probation, still learning. . . . But I don't see drawing back from the knowledge that feminism is our fight, too."[58] Stephen Heath, another contributor to this book, does not feel it is appropriate for men to claim space in a feminist forum: "the most any man can do today [is] to learn and so to try to write or talk or act in response to feminism, and so to try not in any way to be anti-feminist, supportive of the old oppressive structures."[59] For other feminist men, the problem of calling themselves feminists lies in perceptions about men's political and social power, especially men's historical tendency to dominate public discourse. During an online discussion in the early 1990s about the men "in" feminism debate, one scholar offered the view that men who call themselves feminist might be accused of "invading feminist mental and political space . . . regardless of our own political alignment with feminism and desire to participate."[60]

Even for men comfortable calling themselves feminists, the question of how to be accountable to feminism continues to pose a challenge for men as well as for the feminist women they work with. Still, the experiences of the WRC and MASA raise hopes that profeminists and feminists can engage in clear and open communication, share information and ideas, and work on some projects together. Maintaining accountability doesn't mean men have to seek permission for every move they make, nor does it mean waiting passively for feminist women to give them the OK. But in a world in which men have historically had more access to public spaces and resources than women, a world in which men gathering in groups has often meant bad news for women, feminists have a right to know what profeminist men are planning. At the same time, feminists have an obligation to be open-minded to profeminist men and their proposed projects and to listen respectfully when men who believe in feminism have ideas to share.

## NOTES

1. Audre Lorde (1981), p. 99.
2. The White Ribbon Campaign was accused several times in its first two years of "taking centre [*sic*] stage" in choosing December 6, the anniversary of the Montréal massacre, as the focal point for its White Ribbon Week. Many feminists considered this a day for women to mourn and remember.
3. Ben Mudge (1997).
4. Steven P. Schacht and Doris Ewing (1997, summer/autumn), pp. 34–36.
5. White Ribbon Campaign (1991, December 1–6). This one-page "inaugural statement" publicly announced the campaign in November.
6. White Ribbon Campaign (2000, March 23).
7. Sherri Davis-Barron (1992, November 24), p. B1.
8. White Ribbon Campaign (2000). About us. Available online from: <http://www.whiteribbon.ca/aboutus/>. Retrieved May 24, 2001.
9. Kim Bolan (1992, December 2), p. A1.
10. For some feminist activists, relying on corporate funds—or "mainstreaming" as Canada's National Action Committee on the Status of Women calls this tactic—is a form of selling out (from a study for NAC by Lee Lakeman (1992).
11. For information about the White Ribbon Campaign's "money matters" as of late 2000, see <http://www.whiteribbon.ca/aboutus/>.
12. Gordon Laird (1993), pp. 16–18.
13. I read through several of the White Ribbon Campaign's marketing and fundraising proposals and found that the campaign seemed to appropriate the language and some of the methods of corporate culture for its fundraising efforts. Given that the WRC had decided not to approach governments for money (to avoid competing with feminist organizations), their appeal to corporations was a logical but misunderstood decision. It's hard to say which offended critics most: the fact that a supporter donated an eight-room office in the prestigious Toronto Eaton's Centre or that the WRC did not hesitate to use "corporate language" as a persuasive strategy.
14. Craig Jones (1992, winter), p. 7.
15. Michele Landsberg (1992, November-December), pp. 16–17.
16. Cathy Crowe and Carolyn Montgomery (1992, November 27), p. A25.
17. Davis-Barron (1992, November 24).
18. White Ribbon Campaign (1992).
19. Jack Layton (1993, August 31).
20. Ron Sluser (1992, December 2).
21. Michael Kaufman (1993, December 4).
22. Susan Van der Voght, a Toronto feminist activist who did some work with the WRC, believes more permanent arrangements allowing women and men to work together are preferable to one-time coalitions.
23. Now called the "December 6 Fund of Toronto," this coalition is still highly

active as a volunteer organization raising money "to help women build lives free of violence." For more information, go to <http://www.dec6fund.ca/index.htm>. Retrieved 6 June 2001 from the World Wide Web.

24. One of the concerns about the WRC appropriating women's work centered around the fact that workers in the December 6th Coalition and the WRC were both trying to distribute buttons and ribbons at the same time in 1991. As Susan Van der Voght recalls, the media's attention was diverted to the WRC. This prompted the coalition to contact the WRC in 1992, so the coalition played a large role in the WRC's decision to "step away" from December 6.

25. Susan Van Der Voght (1995, January 5).

26. Sluser (1993, December 2).

27. Kaufman (1993, December 4).

28. David Denborough (1994), p. 45.

29. Bob Pease (1997), p. 69.

30. Marnie Daphne (1999, May 9).

31. Marnie Daphne and Adele Murdolo (1992, spring), p. 28.

32. Ibid.

33. Daphne (1999, May 9).

34. Denborough (1994), p. 45.

35. Ibid., p. 47.

36. Ibid., p. 50.

37. Ibid., pp. 53–54.

38. Hilary Lips (1991), p. 4.

39. Ibid., p. 5. This way of thinking about power as a network of forces exercised by any given social system is indebted to Michel Foucault's definition of power as ubiquitous and systemic, a complex set of relations "exercised from a variety of points in the social body" (in Smart [1985], p. 122).In describing power as matrices, webs, or networks of discourses that shape the production of "truths," Foucault problematizes the concept of power as something individuals can exercise or change, let alone "own," despite all efforts of individual agents to do so (also see Foucault [1990], pp. 97–98; Smart [1985], p. 77; Foucault [1984], p. 56).

40. See Simon Pratt and Robin Tuddenham (1997, summer/autumn), pp. 23–25. Pratt and Tuddenham argue that Foucault's interrogation of how and where power is exercised and its "invisibility" in certain contexts has important implications for understanding situations when men feel powerless. "Perhaps Foucault offers us insights into our sense of uncertainty as whole and troubled men. The roles given always elude and escape us" (p. 25).

41. Joseph Bristow (1992), pp. 57–79. Quote is from p. 72.

42. In Cheris Kramarae and Paula A. Treichler (1985), p. 161.

43. Ibid.

44. Rosalind Delmar (1986), p. 11.

45. Patrick D. Hopkins (1998), pp. 51–52.

46. Kaufman (1993, December 4).

47. In Michael S. Kimmel and Thomas E. Mosmiller (1992), pp. 2–3.

48. Tom Digby (1998), p. 1.

49. Sandra Bartky (1998), p. xiii.

50. Linda Williams (1990, April), pp. 63–65.

51. In Kramarae and Treichler (1985), p. 161.

52. Peggy Kamuf (1987), pp. 78–84; Alice Jardine (1987), pp. 54–61.
53. Tania Modleski (1991).
54. Ibid., p. 7.
55. "Separatism" has often meant a political stance largely grounded in lesbian feminism. According to some feminist theorists, there is also an association between "separatism" and woman-centeredness (see Edwalds and Stocker [1995]).
56. In Kramarae and Treichler (1985), p. 158.
57. Men's place—A separatist viewpoint (1974). Portland Feminist Coordinating Council Forum on the Role of Men in the Women's Movement. Unpublished handout in the Changing Men Collection.
58. Richard Ohmann (1987), 182–188. Quote is from p. 187.
59. Stephen Heath (1987), pp. 41–46. Quote is from p. 9.
60. Allan Hunter (1993).

# 5

# Profeminism and Inclusivity: Vexed Questions

Building trust with feminist women has not been the only major challenge facing profeminist men trying to create and maintain a large, viable organization. Another problem is inclusivity—an ongoing concern that the mainly white and middle-class core of profeminist men's groups doesn't fully or fairly represent the wide range of diversities and differences among men. Feminist groups have also, of course, been subject to intense scrutiny from nonwhite and working-class women, among others, about how inclusive the sisterhood really is—or isn't. At times, the debate following episodes of scrutiny and criticism has been bitter enough to create severe fragmenting (see chapter 1). For profeminist men, earning the trust and cooperation of men outside this core has been an important and daunting task, especially for group organizers and founders. The challenges facing these men have been considerable.

This chapter focuses on how, in its organization building efforts, the National Organization for Changing Men (later the National Organization for Men against Sexism) dealt with three major questions of inclusivity: involving women in the organization, decentralizing decision-making structures, and—also of vital importance to profeminists in Australia and Britain—trying to work respectfully through differences centering on race and class (chapter 8 looks closely at the politics of gay representation).Though NOCM's main goal was to ensure that the widest possible spectrum of men would be equitably represented and would feel welcome in the organization, a question coming up early in the organization's history was whether feminist women should be involved in the organization's decision-making.

## MEN ONLY? PROS AND CONS OF EXCLUDING WOMEN

Should a profeminist organization invite only men to join? This seemingly separatist question is fairly benevolent within a profeminist context. The founders are usually trying to emphasize that (1) this work is men's responsibility and (2) feminist women already have enough on their plate without having to oversee a bunch of men. But the associated goals of wanting to avoid overburdening busy women while making sure men do their share have to be balanced against the appearance of creating yet another old boys' club.

One of the first issues addressed by founders of the brand new National Organization for Changing Men[1] was whether women should be encouraged to join or take part in governance. Initially, NOCM was open to women's involvement at the planning level; two of the eleven members of the 1981 Transition Committee issuing a call for "A National Anti-Sexist Men's Organization" were women.[2] That same year, a set of resolutions presented at the 7th National M & M conference by the "Task Force on Men's Movement" stated clearly that a national men's antisexist organization should not be separatist and should maintain various alliances with women. One way to do this, suggested the task force, was to keep membership open to women "with the understanding that we are a men's organization primarily devoted to men's issues and, whenever appropriate, to preserve men's space."[3]

In 1982, a bulletin announcing the new organization's structure included a brief section entitled "Is This Organization Open to Women?" The first response to this question is succinct: "Certainly it is. Anyone who agrees with our Statement of Principles and pays their dues is entirely welcome to join." But about half-way through the section, the writers echo the 1981 task force's argument about keeping the organization centered on men: "Our focus is and will remain on men's issues and on men's growing role in opposing sexism and sex role conditioning. We would not want to lose our special identity as the unique voice of anti-sexist American men."[4] Clearly organizers were trying to balance between maintaining ties to feminist women and preserving what the 1981 task force called men's space. It's tempting, from a feminist women's perspective, to read the phrase "lose our special identity" in a way that suggests a fear (or at least mild concern) that women will try to take over the agenda. But concerns about gender-based territoriality are barely hinted at here. Indeed, the final paragraph of this section reinforces a positive image of women's relations with NOCM, noting that women comprised about 7 percent of the total membership and had had some influence in shaping the new organization: "Women have been present at all of our national meetings and have contributed in many ways to the vitality of the movement to date. We recognize and value their contributions."[5]

Yet it seems the "woman question" remained open for discussion within NOCM, for in 1984–1985 a document listing the pros and cons of excluding women was circulated amongst the organizers.[6] This document, awkwardly entitled "Against excluding women/Reasons for excluding women," begins with the statement—"As a basic principle, no group which is open to the public is justified in excluding people solely on the basis of their sex." This seems to be a strong argument, considering the group's aim was "to eliminate the habit of sex discrimination." However, the document also mentions an "automatic exception" to the nonexclusion principle in the case of "beginning C-R [consciousness-raising] groups" or workshops on sensitive issues, though exclusions would have to be carefully considered to avoid reproducing traditional patterns of sex discrimination.

The document mentions the fact that feminist groups have set a precedent for excluding men. In the name of equal play, could a profeminist men's group justify excluding women? From a feminist perspective, the document answers "no":

> Because of their long history of tangible and psychological oppression, it is currently justifiable for women to exclude men from events when they so choose. The same right should not exist for men. Anti-sexist men—however good their reasons and/or intentions—are still men, and do not have the right to exclude women from their meetings or organizations.

Implied within the phrase "are still men" is an assumption about men's drive for power. The unspoken argument is that men, given half a chance, will use gatherings with other men to reinforce the old boys' network and consolidate their power over women. How would it look if an antisexist organization took on the trappings of a male conspiracy? Similarly, the "Against/Reasons for" document also argues that enforcing a men-only rule could tarnish the image of NOCM: "Even if anti-sexist men did have valid and compelling reasons for limiting their meetings to men, they should still be sensitive to the impact this action would have on the public. . . . It would make the concept of anti-sexist men appear ridiculous. . . ."

Even worse, a men-only policy might encourage the public to lump NOCM in with *all* men's organizations, including anti-feminist groups. As the document wryly puts it, "It would give great amusement and comfort to conservatives, who have their own reasons for wanting to exclude women." The document also noted that including women would also allow men a chance to learn from feminism, creating "a valuable and vital forum of feedback and insight." There was every hope that both sexes in dialogue would generate new and unexpectedly powerful ideas.

But to provide a balanced view and material for discussion, the "Against/Reasons for" document presents arguments in favor of excluding women.

The first argument in favor returns to the feminist precedent of excluding men and suggests there may be compelling reasons for the organization to "support the broader principle that exclusion-on-the-basis-of-sex is not in itself always wrong."[7] Indeed, NOCM received some feminist support for this argument in an article published in the newsletter *M.* by a feminist woman delegate at the 1984 Men & Masculinity conference. Paula Brookmire felt welcome and was positive about attending the event, yet at the same time, she had mixed feelings about whether women should be allowed unrestricted access:

> I have had mixed feelings about being a woman at these conferences. My strongest feeling—and the one that keeps bringing me back to the conferences—is the sense of support and sensitivity and understanding I get from the men and women here. It is similar to the early [National Organization for Women—NOW] conferences, where a strong sense of sisterhood and support brought everyone to a psychological and physical closeness. But at times I have felt like an intruder, and perhaps rightly so.
>
> I remember many of the women's conferences I have attended, and I recall few men there, if any. There was often a hostility to men or, at least, a need for distance from them. . . . I occasionally wondered if that same need was perhaps going unfulfilled at the national men's conferences, which were trying so hard to declare their support of women and the feminist movement. I thoroughly understood why some workshops were closed to women, and I wondered whether that was enough. . . . There was a cohesion to the group, a brotherhood, that I wasn't really a part of, and I was glad to see it.
>
> I was also pleased to see an attempt to develop a dialog between the men's movement and the women's movement, or, to be more specific, between this branch of the men's movement and members of NOW. . . . [8]

Brookmire's comments can be read as justification for some men-only events, which is not the same thing as excluding women from main events or operations, or failing to keep lines of communication open.

But some men were concerned about the fact that women were gaining considerable power to shape and even dominate discussion of feminist issues. It was possible that women might try to control a men's profeminist agenda. This fear is mentioned in the "Against/Reasons For" document, with a reference to a national men's conference in Los Angeles where "one very forceful and assertive woman dominated an important meeting for several hours." From a feminist standpoint, a woman dominating a men's gathering is much more the exception than the rule. But if a man, even an antisexist man, equates a dominant feminist with inordinately high expectations for men, or even "guilting men out," then the risk of paralysis or feelings of powerlessness is high, as theorists like John Rowan and Victor Seidler have made clear. Without discounting the very real effects of being "guilted out," the fact that many men find it difficult to listen to a feminist is—as profeminist Michael Kaufman has also implied—a sad fact.[9] As many women have found, even a moderate feminist stance is often interpreted as strident. Profeminist activists have found time and again that men more readily accept feminist arguments from other men.

However, the "Against/Reasons for" document also gives a more benevolent justification for NOCM to exclude women: their absence would force men to work harder at communicating among themselves: building "warm, caring, trusting, and emotional" relationships with other men while avoiding traditional "male bonding." Similarly, the process of "unlearning sexism," entailing emotional pain and reawakened memories of "what it has meant to be a man under patriarchy," is "often" more difficult with women around. The document finally suggests that formal liaisons and joint events with feminist groups, along the lines of those discussed in chapter 4, would be more productive than the two extremes of allowing women free access to all parts of the organization, or cutting them out entirely.[10]

## NOCM: INSPIRED BY FEMINIST PROCESS

Profeminist men have done a considerable amount of soul-searching around the question: how feminist should we be? The depth or type of commitment to feminism can affect organizational structure or decision-making, determine whether a group should publicly support feminism in their literature, guide whether women can or should be part of the group or contribute to governance, and—in some ways most significant of all—help determine how a profeminist group or project is accountable to feminist women.

The National Organization for Changing Men tried to avoid traditional patriarchal structures, a choice acknowledging some preliminary concerns about forming a U.S. antisexist men's organization. In the early- to mid-1970s, profeminists were already worried about the dangers of reproducing the oppressive structures of traditional male institutions. Late in 1974, men attending a sex roles workshop were inspired enough by their experience to talk about forming a larger organization. But an article about this workshop, written the following year in a Madison, Wisconsin, men's newsletter, expressed concern that men might have "difficulty realizing and stopping the process of being defensive . . . a main form of this defensiveness is to explain, theorize, and write statements about liberation instead of dealing directly with feelings and issues."[11]

That same year in an issue of the newsletter *Morning Due*, "Bruce" wrote that the fear is very real that men would get organized, only to fall back into "[t]he old 'Competition' pattern." He argued that good relations and dialogue with feminist groups would help prevent profeminists from recreating oppressive leadership structures. "I feel that we are safe in organizing if we remain close to other movements, and very close to the women's movement, accepting and seeking advice, criticism and guidance from women. . . ."[12] Respecting grassroots concerns about maintaining close ties to the women's movement, NOCM maintained that its primary focus on improving men's lives and fighting against sexism should not exclude—and should even invite—feminist women's involvement and input.

Feminism and feminist process laid significant groundwork for men wanting to create a shared, participatory, nonhierarchical form of governance. At one point, there were even suggestions that the Men & Masculinities conferences, already closely tied to the national organization, should adopt a structure more conducive to feminist political activism, as in this excerpt from a memo to the National Council:

> Up til [*sic*] now, the M & M conferences have emphasized the personal over the political and organizational. . . . [W]hat I am proposing is a transitional phase to bridge between a conference with a personal growth orientation emphasis to one with a more political emphasis. This . . . would better balance the personal growth orientation with political activities than is now the case and, in essence, create an institutionalized environment to develop the novice into a feminist political leader.[13]

While the National Organization for Changing Men never became a seedbed for feminist political leadership, from the beginning the founders adopted a major goal of supporting feminism and encouraging men to do anti-rape and antiviolence work. A 1983 bulletin announcing the formation of what was then the "National Men's Organization" spelled out men's support for "the continuing struggle of women for full equality" as a second top priority, after improving men's lives and before overcoming homophobia. The bulletin noted that issues of rape and violence were a "particular concern." The writers also envisioned women and men united by overarching goals: "Feminist women and men can work together to change the unjust patriarchal system, and to escape from the sex roles and power imbalances that have so often made women and men view each other as enemies."[14]

This ideal notion of unity and an end to the gender wars was somewhat supported by existing practices since, as already noted, women were welcome to join NOCM, and some women were actively involved in organizational planning. A letter sent to members in January 1983 reporting on the progress of the new organization listed two women on the national council, and mandated a committee to establish and maintain liaisons with feminist groups. The goal to deepen ties with feminism becomes apparent in the second issue of the organization's fledgling newsletter *Brother*, which featured reviews of several feminist publications. Some of the articles—"Dowry Deaths," "Black Men against Sexism and Racism"—argued that feminism can inform and enrich men's lives in various ways. The 1983

Open Forum announcing the establishment of NOCM, described in chapter 3, strongly conveyed the impression that this men's organization enjoyed the support and trust of feminists.

## "The Other Side of the Coin"

Perhaps inevitably, concerns arose about whether NOCM was becoming "anti-male," or leaning too far toward radical profeminism. In 1983, a critique of the new national men's organization was circulated at the Men & Masculinity conference in August. The writer, Roy Schenk, argued that feminism is anti-male. The handout he supplied also promoted his book, *The Other Side of the Coin: Causes and Consequences of Men's Oppression*, which was on sale in the registration area unless banned by M & M conference organizers. In accordance with many men's rights adherents, Schenk believed NOCM was guilty of submitting to women's unreasonable demands and, by buying into a feminist agenda, was encouraging reverse sexism. To quote an especially pungent section of his critique—

> Is [NOCM's] behavior anti-male? Of course not, though current and past actions do make one wonder sometimes (e.g. censorship and tearing down leaflets and posters). In general, though, I believe the behavior is just due to an abysmally low level of consciousness of the intense oppression men experience *as men* [author's emphasis]. . . . This is coupled with their INTENSE NEED FOR APPROVAL FROM THE WOMEN IN THEIR LIVES [author's emphasis]. And these tend to be women who expect their men to uncritically kiss ass to the feminist movement regardless of how sexist feminists may act. . . . But that is pathetic you say? Of course it is pathetic! These men need our pity not our rage.[15]

Schenk also echoed the call of more moderate critics that NOCM should adopt a more overtly male-positive stance and include a phrase like "pro-male" in its statement of purpose. Of course, his hostile rhetoric would clearly have alienated men interested in striking a balance between the apparent polar opposites of profeminist and pro-male. Yet the idea that a profeminist organization should also be pro-male (but in a feminist supportive way) was taken very seriously by NOCM organizers, and would also become foundational to the White Ribbon Campaign.

## Pro-Male Rhetoric

In no small part because of profeminism's uncomfortable relations with more conservative men's groups, being pro-male was an idea which committed antisexist men handled with kid gloves in the mid-1980s. Some members felt the national organization was already focusing too much on male-positive aspects and should become more politically aware. In a 1985 article in *Brother*, Ken Fremont-Smith analyzed men's varying reactions to profeminism and concluded

> I want to see the men's network encourage personal growth within a political or social-change context. Too often personal growth is the be-all and end-all, with the unsettling result that we gather to nurture each other but don't know quite what to do once the hugging is over. The lack of political context is one of the reasons for the vagueness of the men's network.[16]

Comparing a 1983 informational brochure with a version likely distributed in late 1985 and 1986 shows that NOCM consistently attempted to balance being profeminist with being male-positive. The 1983 version[17] first explains in general terms how this men's organization will help men "unlearn much of the old-fashioned Male Role, and . . . live freer, happier, and much more fulfilling lives." A lengthy paragraph "acknowledge[s] that much of what we have learned about the problems of the Male Role has come from the insights of the women's movement. . . . We, as men, strongly support the continuing struggle of women for full equality." There is mention of women and men working together to change patriarchy, particularly gender and power imbalances.

Whether NOCM's attempt to balance profeminism and pro-male "ism" had any effect on the disappointing membership numbers in 1984 and 1985 probably can't be determined. It's not unusual for organizations to find they gain new members but lose some former ones. By 1984 it was clear that NOCM was not expanding nearly as quickly as hoped, if at all. In an article in *Brother*, Tom Mosmiller lamented that "less than 200 people voting on the name change and then again in the spring '84 election was disappointing and frightening . . . we are attracting new members but not keeping old ones."[18]

Coincidentally or not, the 1985–86 NOCM brochure "Join Us for Change," projects a stronger pro-male stance.[19] Gone are the hallmark terms of antisexist rhetoric—"patriarchy," "power," and "feminist." The organization's purpose is described as providing "a network of support and resources for men and women committed to positive changes in men's roles and relationships." NOCM is rooted in "community and regional-based efforts of men and women working for change in male roles" rather than overtly indebted to the women's movement. This brochure also discusses in more detail than the 1983 version some of the negative consequences of "traditional masculinity." These include crime, imprisonment, violence against women, and homophobia, underscoring the message at the end of the brochure—"It's time for a change!"—and the closing invitation to join NOCM. While a commitment to feminist causes is still apparent, the more pro-male language in the 1985 brochure creates some distance from what could be perceived as a radical and possibly threatening feminist agenda.

In the late 1980s, NOCM's closeness to feminism was still creating mixed feelings. The pendulum seemed to swing even further away from taking a feminist stance—but not for antifeminist reasons. In the description of a workshop held at the 1989 Men & Masculinity conference entitled "What Should the Relationship Be between Pro-Feminist Men and Feminism?" the proposed goal was to "explore the idea that for pro-feminist men to call ourselves feminists may not be an act of liberation. Instead it may be a way of perpetuating men's traditional theft of women's energy."[20] This concern with men's theft of feminism occurred at a time when a fierce debate about men's place "in" or "with" feminism was gathering steam in the late 1980s and early 1990s—almost two decades after antisexist men in Britain and the United States first became inspired by the possibilities of feminism. Perhaps it's no coincidence that within academe, concerns about men's relations with feminism only began to arise as men's studies started gaining footholds at some universities.[21] But whether within or outside academe, men who supported feminist goals were becoming hypersensitive to the possibility that not only their actions but their very use of the term feminism might encourage men to exercise traditional male patterns of domination. In other words, men could—even inadvertently—move into the feminist arena and take over women's painstaking work, ideas, and resources (for more details about this debate and the associated question of male power, see chapter 4). By the 1990s, profeminist organizations were reserving the term feminist mainly to describe the nature of the principles and projects they supported.

## HOW REPRESENTATIVE SHOULD THIS ORGANIZATION BE?

For other NOCM members, the issue wasn't so much whether the organization was feminist enough, but whether it was prepared to include men from the grassroots. A significant number of members appear to have believed that an enlightened men's organization inspired by feminist process should have invited representation from small and regional men's groups. But NOCM's executive group was concentrating on "solidifying management," "rules of procedure," "organizational growth," and "principles"—the language of organizational growth displacing that of the grassroots. NOCM also tried to encourage a wide range of action-projects by setting up specific task groups for diverse men to join. Various minutes and reports, as well as some material published in the newsletter *Brother*, suggest that the very structures intended to make NOCM a diverse and representative organization involved tremendous amounts of planning, complex organizational mechanics, and no small degree of frustration.

In 1982, the newly elected NOCM council met and adopted a jointly proposed "innovative structure"[22] intended to make it easier for every member to contribute to the organization. In Barry Shapiro's words, "We didn't just copy other organizations; we designed a structure that uniquely reflects the philosophy and values of the men's movement."[23] At the heart of this structure was the concept of seventeen National Task Groups, each focusing on a particular topic or issue such as men's violence, fathering, homophobia, or rape. The Council also created thirty Action Positions, envisioned as leadership roles for any members interested in helping to build the organization. Members volunteering for an action position could choose among a range of responsibilities: recruitment, process leader, national conference planner, men's movement organizer, liaison to feminist women's groups, publications editor, or leader of one of the seventeen task groups—to name only a few. Essentially, the idea (or ideal) was to move away from a "top down" approach in which elected executives performed all major duties, and instead encourage and enable as many members as possible to participate in governing the organization.

The fact that NOCM's governance was centered around a core group of executive member-activists is hardly unusual in volunteer run organizations, where the dedicated few take on an often inordinate number of tasks. In theory, NOCM had a variety of goals and recognized many different constituencies, which fell under the auspices of the task groups and action positions. Each task group was headed by its own coordinator, who in turn reported to the executive. Though task groups were designed to attract diverse men—such as black, gay, disabled, or Chicano—as well as invite all members to participate in the work of the organization, throughout the 1980s various commentators criticized NOCM for being too elitist as well as failing to represent more men.

This impression of elitism was also supported by a lack of regional representation, which many members considered a major shortcoming. According to one former executive member,

> I am firm in the belief that the structure of our organization (as detailed in the by-laws) is seriously flawed by . . . the omission of any provisions for the creation of local chapters. . . . [T]he failure to have local chapters . . . doesn't give us much in the way of a mass, democratic organization. All we have is a highly-concentrated elite of 18 National Council members without a representative constituency talking to ourselves, and claiming to be leaders of a few hundred non-based members.[24]

### Growing Pains

Tensions about representation likely were not eased by the fact that the National Organization for Changing Men (NOCM) had a fairly complex set of by-laws and resolutions first drawn up in 1982, then revised and expanded in 1984.[25] Like most by-laws, those of NOCM focused mainly on process issues and procedures, and what turned out to be a long-drawn-out development of a Statement of Principles. As NOCM gained members and recognition, its governing structures also grew in size and complexity. By April 1984, when NOCM claimed over 550 members, the original council of nine had expanded to eighteen and the seventeen task groups to twenty, and there were twenty internal committees.[26]

A positive interpretation of this expansion indicates a thriving organization whose many and diverse members were keeping busy on a variety of projects. But a quarterly report dated October 1984 gave a total membership of 350, noting there had been no renewal solicitation over a three-year period.[27] If so, and only 350 members were being represented by so many council members and committees, then it wasn't surprising that eyebrows were being raised. Indeed, the author of this quarterly report, Ron Smith, had mentioned some concerns earlier in the year about the expansion of NOCM governance and its impact on membership. Smith was confused by "the splitting up of membership related functions into several different action positions without a formal mechanism to guide them," and made several recommendations for changes in the organizational structure concerning membership committees.[28] Tom Mosmiller, NOCM's co-chair, publicly expressed his concerns about irregular communication among council members.[29]

The NOCM National Council's apparent lack of communication—along with a perception that the organization's structure was unclear, unwieldy, and nonrepresentative—created concerns for members throughout the mid-1980s. In 1985, NOCM was also trying to recruit Hispanic, Oriental, and handicapped members to sit on the council, none of whom had yet been represented. Yet in 1986, it appears the NOCM executives had bitten off more than they could chew. The council passed a resolution to terminate seven Task Groups, including Reproductive Rights, Men and Health, and Racism and Sex Roles, and asked task group leaders to agree that their groups would accomplish a minimum number of goals each year. The intent was not "to punish or chastise but to stop what [the council] believes is the deceit of advertising the existence of Task Groups which effectively do not function."[30] Essentially, the NOCM council began downsizing, and it's perhaps an unfortunate irony that the first casualties were task groups (albeit inactive ones), initiatives that had been expected to attract diverse men and encourage a wide range of participation.

## NOM/NOCM—Centralized or Regional?

NOCM's decision in 1981, against the wishes of a number of members, to adopt a centralized, at-large Executive Council instead of a regional structure is worth examining, since it has implications for diversity and inclusivity. A tendency to distrust centralized structures and celebrate local governance was already well in place long before NOCM. Jack Nichols, writing to the New York Men's Center in 1976, insisted that free men could govern themselves:

> An elected regime, after proving a few times that it is 'liberal' becomes—day by day—exceptional and exclusive. It assumes privileges covertly. . . . Men are wise enough and good enough to gather in local groups—sharing affinities with other groups—and creating ad hoc committees to handle immediate situations without resorting to political infighting. . . . Almost every spirited movement becomes—too early—encrusted with the bickering of bureaucratic do-gooders who are, in fact, a kind of managerial priesthood. . . .[31]

This profound distrust of big government is an extreme view not shared by the majority of men's groups, but Nichols wasn't alone in arguing strongly for a regionally based men's organization. In 1977, a report written by a "Task Force on the Possibilities of a National Men's Organization" (probably presented at that year's M & M conference) strongly recommended not only both "a national organization and regional grouping of local men's organizations" but that "the national should grow from the regional." For added protection against a consolidation of power, the task force cautioned that the organization "should avoid placing a single person in a spokesperson role."[32]

Four years later, at the 7th National Men & Masculinity Conference, yet another task force rejected a centralized structure. A series of resolutions proposed by a "Task Force on Men's Movements: National, Regional and Local Organizations" called for an organization "whose leadership is collective and non-competitive and whose members are a federation of regional groupings."[33] This task force specifically proposed eight "autonomous regional structures initially centered around existing men's groups throughout the country."[34]

It must have been a shock to many M & M attendees and prospective members of the new organization to discover that, instead of regional representation, the Steering Committee had chosen a more centralized structure and an at-large election process. In the fall of 1981, an editorial in *M.: Gentle Men for Gender Justice* supported the new organization-to-be but expressed "dismay" at "the absence of any mention of 'regional' representation." The magazine *M.* unequivocally criticized this decision for the following reasons:

> This [structure] not only eliminates the movement's stated preference—and ours—for regional representation, but also raises some difficult questions: (1) Doesn't a national at-large election give an unwarranted and unhealthy advantage to nationally known authors and spokespersons and those with high media exposure . . . ? (4) Isn't a regionally elected Council a more balanced and non-hierarchical—and ultimately a more trustable [sic]—basis for decisions and actions?[35]

## A Close Look at the Debate about Regional Representation

In late 1982, the steering committee, which had become the newly elected NOCM Executive Council, decided to reserve one council seat for "the current regional movement on the west coast" and a second seat for "the next regional group to become active."[36] It seems clear that this decision was made after some exchanges in 1982 between the highly active California Antisexist Men's Political Caucus (CAMP Caucus) and the NOCM steering committee. The regional movement on the west coast was most strongly represented by the CAMP Caucus, which had written to the steering committee in July expressing concern that the fledgling national organization was apparently not considering regional representation. The letter stresses CAMP's support for the national organization but not for the current structure, and asks NOCM to replace at-large with regional representation:

> we are frustrated that regional leaders like us who have been actively organizing, promoting and supporting men's movement activism at the grassroots level are excluded from the national steering committee by an election procedure which favors those with national reputations. . . . We share . . . a strong concern that the new national organization be regionally oriented and committed to decentralized and democratic process. We are afraid that a national steering committee whose members lack involvement and daily contact with active anti-sexist men's movement groups might develop in an hierarchical fashion . . . [37]

Resonant terms like "share" and "democratic process," as well as the letter's opening congratulatory remarks, convey a sense that the CAMP Caucus was aiming for constructive criticism of a concept it otherwise supported. However, it is possible to anticipate that some readers would react defensively to terms with negative connotation like "frustrated," "excluded," "lack involvement" and "hierarchical." Such terms would easily tap into profeminist men's fears of rebuilding old patterns of patriarchy and hierarchy.

In his response to the CAMP Caucus challenge, Bob Brannon (on behalf of the Executive Council) began on a positive note, making it clear that organizations like the CAMP Caucus were outstanding and would be excellent models of regional branches. "I am personally an advocate in the direction of regionalism," Brannon wrote. "Local men's friendship and action networks . . . are the best possible support for men who are trying to change." But he also pointed out "certain realities" mitigating against a regionally based structure for NOM: "Foremost among these is the simple fact that, with one possible exception, *there is currently not one single active REGIONAL men's movement anywhere in the United States*. That is a sad fact, but a fact nonetheless."[38] Under those circumstances, regional representation would entitle parts of the country with no existing men's organizations to a seat on the council. "Isn't this," writes Brannon, "a violation of the fundamental democratic principle of equal representation?"

In the middle of this letter to the CAMP Caucus (the middle being the classic location for secondary arguments or bad news), it becomes clear that Brannon is troubled by some of the arguments used by the CAMP Caucus. Using language as challenging as CAMP's, he refutes their claim that "a single resolution passed many years ago at the 4th annual [M & M] conference" commits the national organization to a regional structure. "To be blunt, that was a long time ago and many things have changed." Brannon also points out that since that time, efforts to create regional organizations had largely been unsuccessful.

Throughout the 1980s, members and critics of NOCM and NOMAS would continue to cite the organization's centralized structure as a deterrent to grassroots activism. By choosing "an exclusive, nonrepresentational style of decision-making," wrote one disgruntled member in 1987, and by not providing for chapters or for other kinds of decentralization, NOCM had "simply cut off our own lifeblood."[39] It's understandable that NOCM's choice of a centralized rather than regional structure could be seen as a barrier against inclusivity.

## WORKING-CLASS MEN AND PROFEMINISM

"The anti-sexist men's movement has, on the whole, baulked [*sic*] somewhat at addressing issues of work and class . . . as a result of class divisions inherent within capitalist society, [the middle-class men's movement] does not share much cultural ground with working-class men."[40]

In feminist and profeminist organizations, differences around race, class, and sexual orientation have been especially contested, prompting a range of reactions from passionate debate to out-and-out fragmentation. For American profeminists, issues of race (see below) and sexual orientation (see chapter 8) have taken up more discourse space than discussions of how class differences affect men's lives. But for profeminists in Britain and, to some extent, Australia, looking at how class contributes to gender oppression has played a large role in men's antisexist work. Whether working-class and middle-class men can work together to end sexism has been of some concern for British and Australian profeminists.

In Britain, Andrew Tolson's *The Limits of Masculinity* (1977) raised awareness about the possibility that class shapes concepts of manly behavior.[41] When Tolson observed British men in the 1970s, he noted that "working class masculinity is characterized . . . by an immediate, aggressive style of behavior"[42] as compared with that of middle-class men. Tolson saw a cause and effect relationship between a patriarchal working-class man's demand for absolute power in the home and the fact that the same working-class man is "individually powerless, a mere calculation of the capitalist economy."[43] This form of male aggression, he argued, shapes relationships with other men as well as with women, and is often at odds with feminist goals of gender equity.

Twenty years later, an issue of *Achilles Heel* devoted to the theme of "Men and Work" revisited the complex issue of how men's work shapes their conceptions of gender and family relations. Written by two women, the article "Flexible Work Patterns for Men" explores how professional and managerial men are starting to take advantage of job sharing and flexible hours in order, among other things, to "meet some domestic responsibilities."[44] But the authors point out that "[m]anual workers are still underrepresented" in job-sharing schemes, "perhaps because of lower salary levels." In other words, a large schism still exists between the ways working-class men and their middle-class/professional counterparts conceive of "work." Could this mean that middle-class men are more likely than working-class men to think of helping women with child-raising and household chores as legitimate "work"—especially if the structures governing professional or managerial workplaces make it easier for middle-class men to be profeminist in their daily lives?

British profeminist theorist Victor Seidler argues that we cannot understand masculinity, family relations, or male power without also understanding the conditions controlling work and production:

> When people say that "men are not oppressed," especially heterosexual men, since they have power in a patriarchal capitalist society, not only do they forget the nature of class relations, but they also fail to explore the power capitalist production routines and disciplines have over the lives of both working-class and middle-class families. A man is not even free to develop a closer relationship with his children, if he is forced into the routines of shift-work.

But Seidler also points out that men on shift work are not the only powerless men, making the case that "the constraints of the office, school and hospital" also control men's lives. Following Tolson and employing a feminist socialist analysis, Seidler suggests a strong relationship between "the ways scientific management has brought tighter control and regulation" into workplaces and men's experiences as relatively powerless.[45]

Examining relations between class and male power also helps us understand situations when class and masculinity become fluid or changing constructs, disrupting traditional notions of masculinity. As Australian gender theorist Bob Connell suggests,

> new information technology became a vehicle for redefining middle-class masculinities at a time when the meaning of labour for working-class men was in contention. This is not a question of a fixed middle-class masculinity confronting a fixed

working-class masculinity. Both are being reshaped by a social dynamic in which class and gender relations are simultaneously in play.[46]

Since the early 1990s, a number of Australian profeminist activists have tried to articulate or query what it means for profeminism to consider class as well as race. According to one writer, Adam Hughes, white middle-class men generally "have time and space and safety to reflect on issues that black men, migrant men and working-class men do not always have."[47] But possibly in tension with Connell's notion that middle- and working-class masculinities aren't necessarily static is Hughes's description of how class is conveyed through different language-performances:

> It can be maintained that an important part of working-class masculinity is an almost deliberate self conscious inarticulateness: a reliance on glib one-liners about the world, personal matters, and one's own feelings. How is a self-consciously articulate middle-class man to find common ground with these men long enough to convince them that he is not a wanker, that he is worth listening to?

In 1993, the Australian profeminist magazine *XY* published an issue on men and class. Among the topics explored were the lives of men under capitalism, the stigma of unemployment, and the views of an English group called "Men against Sexist Shit" about working-class men and the anti-sexist men's movement. This latter article stated quite baldly that "middle-class anti-sexism, like pacifism, is the politics of the privileged." A major problem, the anonymous writer argues, is that middle-class "lefties" have monopolized antisexism and rendered it unattractive, and to some extent inaccessible, to working-class men. The writer describes middle-class anti-sexism in terms—"limp-wristed, dungaree-wearing"—that no doubt many middle-class readers would consider highly stereotyped and even offensive. He is equally blunt about what his concept of antisexism does and doesn't include:

> It's about sharing my experience, getting rid of guilt, being positive, overcoming my fears and any hang-ups. For me it's not about . . . acting effeminate and it's not about role reversal. It's about doing my share of the work with kids, learning to listen. It's about responsibility for my actions . . . and getting myself sorted out. I think the insecurities fetched about by living in a fucked-up, alienated capitalist society are what creates "sexist" behavior.[48]

The Australian profeminists contributing to this issue of *XY* are generally pessimistic that men's antisexist work will ever be anything but primarily middle-class–identified. One writer, Mike Leach, maintains that the men's movement as a whole is "unlikely to attract many working-class men." As he puts it, "[m]ost working-class men do not have the energy, leisure time, or personal freedom necessary for such involvement." However, Leach believes it's possible for the men's movement to start fighting sexism in workplace culture. This is "probably best achieved through joint projects with trade unions,"[49] an arrangement not unlike certain kinds of coalition work between feminist groups and profeminist men.

## A HETEROGENEOUS MOVEMENT?

American profeminist groups from the 1970s onward have also been troubled by the fact that profeminist men are mainly middle-class and white. In the early days, many men's movement enthusiasts were also predominantly straight. For example, one of the first American men's groups, formed out of Milwaukee in 1973, was successful at encouraging discussion and activism through 1979. A probable reason why this group survived as long as it did was that it encouraged (or didn't discourage) a kind of controlled heterogeneity.

The group's membership was limited to about eighteen, and there were times when the group was closed to new members in order to build existing relationships and trust. Ages ranged from early twenties to early forties; there is no mention of race; and the implication is that the core group was mainly or perhaps entirely heterosexual, as evidenced by the phrase "encompassing varying degrees of openness to gay experiences" used in a 1974 description of the group's recent gatherings. The variation in ages, marital/parental experience, and openness to homosexuality constitute the heterogeneity in this group. The description notes that "there's perhaps more homogeneity in politics and life style, though the former isn't a central part of our discussions."[50] I had access to several documents produced by this group from 1974 to 1979, and none mentions racial or sexual diversity in the context of group discussions or make-up (though to be fair, these issues did come up at conferences that the Milwaukee group helped organize).

The principle that most profeminists were members of a privileged group of oppressors created some dissonance and guilt that, in some cases, loomed larger than the original goals of ending sexism and patriarchy. In 1973, the radical men's newsletter *Brother: A Forum for Men against Sexism* alerted readers about these dissonances and their possible consequences for a unified men's movement: "It seems to us that the so-called men's movement has not been able to sustain very much organized activity or energy because of the knotty contradictions in its base (mostly white, middle class straight men) and its process (how critically or supportively these men relate to each other)."[51] The following year, *Brother* published a survey of American men's groups. The goal was to summarize and share the current state of antisexist activity. While the *Brother* editors were "encouraged by the beginnings of an analysis and practice linking social and economic class with issues of sexism and political power," they also issued this warning:

The people currently engaged in gay male and men's movement activities are predominantly white and identify as "middle class." If those movements are only a defense of the privileges associated with that social position, an attempt to reform and preserve male power by straights or to gain a share for gays, then they will be self-defeating movements.[52]

Like *Brother*, a newsletter called *Morning Due: Voices of Changing Men*, published out of Seattle between 1974 and 1977, began life as "a way for men to reach out to other men, opening discussion and dialogue."[53] By 1977, the newsletter had changed its name to *Morning Due: A Decent Men's Journal*. In what appears to have been the final issue (there is mention that the journal was broke) the editors note that "Our politics and our collective have changed a lot in the past year, evolving in the direction of class politics, and seeing dialectical materialism as tools for our struggle. . . ."[54] The relationship between antisexism and economic or class reform—so fundamental to British feminism—was given priority by only a small number of American men's groups and collectives.[55] Groups that did take a more radical political stance experienced conflicts that, as in the case of *Brother*, contributed to if not directly caused the group's demise (also, lack of funding was a constant problem for newsletters). The wording of these editorials suggests a mixed sense of excitement and frustration about the different political directions being taken by different individuals in the collective. At this fairly early stage in American profeminist activism, well-intentioned men were finding it difficult to bridge the gap between the theory of male solidarity and the realities of difference and diversity—let alone the demands of radical politics. Time and again, the struggle not to exclude has been subtly undercut by language that seeks to be inclusive, as in this brochure describing upcoming sessions for the 1984 M & M Conference: "The social analysis presented by such diverse social movements as gay rights, worker's rights, single parenting, civil rights, and so on, are also examined as they interface with the men's movement."[56] The implication here—one I believe to be entirely unintentional at the time—is that the norm is white, middle-class, and heterosexual. Describing diverse social movements as forces that interface with the men's movement defines them as outside the norm. This sense of uneasiness about where diversity belongs would continue to trouble antisexist or profeminist organizations throughout the 1980s and 1990s.

## "WHY IS THIS MEN'S MOVEMENT SO WHITE?"

American profeminists since the 1970s have publicly and often voiced their awareness of and sensitivity about racial issues. The structure and goals of the National Organization for Changing Men [NOCM], as well as the National Organization for Men against Sexism [NOMAS], were inclusive: the organization intended to acknowledge, respect, and include multiple perspectives and areas of difference, including race. For example, the concept of black men against sexism and racism was introduced during NOCM's inaugural 1983 Open Forum. By 1984, the organization's seventeen task groups included one on "Racism and Sex Role Issues of Minority Men." Commenting on these attempts at racial inclusivity, profeminist sociologist Michael Messner maintains that by the mid-1990s, the organization had integrated antiracist work to the point where it became part of the political discourse of NOMAS and more men of color were taking leadership roles in the organization, representing altogether a "rare example" of diverse men working together "toward common goals."[57] But critics noted that "[NOCM] remained an organization that was made up of predominantly white, professional-class men (and some women). Although the organization "welcomed and sought Black men's participation . . . over the year, few blacks participated."[58]

There are conflicting accounts about how successful NOMAS has been as an inclusive profeminist organization. But without question, debates over racial representation occurred, and some were bitter. In 1991, NOMAS decided to go ahead and hold the annual Men & Masculinity conference in Arizona after the Reverend Jesse Jackson and civil rights groups had called for a tourism boycott of Arizona. That state had rescinded the new national holiday in memory of Martin Luther King. In response to NOMAS's decision, noted radical profeminist John Stoltenberg (author of *Refusing to Be a Man*; also see chapter 7) resigned his longstanding position as chair of the Ending Men's Violence task group.[59] Another former NOMAS member saw this decision as a sign of the organization's "internal racism" as well as its "lack of commitment . . . to combatting racism."[60] NOMAS's decision to ignore the Arizona boycott was interpreted by many as confirmation that this mainly white organization wasn't truly prepared to represent or respect the views of black men.

In 1992, black feminist writer and theorist bell hooks expressed concern that the white middle-class profeminist movement wasn't doing enough to invite black men's views and participation. Outspokenly supportive of men's participation in feminist work, hooks described attending, with a gay black male colleague, "one of the major conferences focusing on men who are concerned with confronting sexism and challenging patriarchy and heterosexism." As hooks reported,

> We were both disturbed by the complete lack of any emphasis on race. We were disturbed by the discussions of masculine identity that were based on the assumption that all men share equally the rewards of patriarchal privilege in this society. . . . There were few black men present. And there was no real emphasis on outreach. It was definitely (as some all female feminist gatherings and conferences have been) an exclusive meeting for the "in" crowd.[61]

One black member of NOMAS posed the question of race and inclusivity very bluntly in a 1993 article published in *Changing Men* (formerly *M.*). In "Why Is This Men's Movement So White?," Michael-David Gordon pleaded with white profeminists to recognize their own unspoken racism:

> If we have any intention of truly changing the power institutions and relationships that we live in, and liberating ourselves in the process, then we've got to confront the demons that haunt us and keep us away from the truth. *We have got to name our racism. We have got to confront white supremacy*. . . . I am a Black man, feminist and bisexual, who feels a solidarity and a kinship with you white men. . . . But along with fear around confronting male power, I also feel your fear of me. *Are you afraid of me?* Are you afraid of who and what I represent? Are you afraid of my blackness? . . . Why do we spend so little time talking about race and racism in our men's groups? . . . In our organizations and meetings I want to see white men give up the "power seat" as a matter of principle and purpose. . . . I challenge you to make us people of color a part of your daily lives and work. I challenge you white men to not behave as if you were the center of the universe. . . . I challenge our movement to reach men who don't see what's in it for them. . . . I challenge you to make the men's movement truly accessible—i.e. affordable . . . to all.[62]

The challenge of not only making the men's movement more accessible to black men, let alone eliminating sexism against black women, is complicated by what Manning Marable calls the distortions of racial stereotyping. The sexual and racial stereotyping of black men cannot be separated from the reality that black men undergo kinds of systemic socioeconomic and political discrimination that white men simply do not experience. Marable believes that black women's and men's common struggle against racism is more urgent than eliminating sexism. Racial equality "transcends the barrier of gender, as Black women have tried to tell their men for generations."[63] However, Robert Staples warns that public schisms between blacks over sexual relations, notably the 1991 Anita Hill–Clarence Thomas hearings, have the "potential for increasing tension and conflict between Black men and Black women. . . . Only time will tell."[64]

Writing from a white profeminist standpoint, Michael Messner notes that it's quite rare for men of color to argue that patriarchy is more oppressive than racism. Rather, "the discourse of racialized masculinity politics in the United States has tended primarily to be concerned with the need to strongly assert men of color's rightful claims to "manhood" as a means of resisting white men's racial (and often also, simultaneously, social class) domination . . ."[65] So perhaps it was not surprising that in 1995, Nation of Islam leader Louis Farrakhan led thousands of black men in what became known as the Million Man March, a rally and prayer session at Washington, D.C. and that supportive black women were asked to "stay home" that day,[66] Yet this one march attracted far more black men concerned about social injustice than a hundred profeminist rallies. In combination with the criticisms of black profeminist men about organizations like NOMAS, the fact that this march took place raises a vital question: can a profeminist organization created mainly out of the experiences of white middle-class men address respectfully and without fear the ways in which sexism is complicated by the multiple obstacles facing black men, let alone black women? As the next chapter will briefly outline, even an apparently universal feminist concept like ending violence against women becomes highly complex and contested when viewed through the lenses of race, class, and historical differences.

## NOTES

1. During its first year, the National Organization for Changing Men was called "The National Organization for Men."
2. Robert Brannon et al. (1981), pp. 6–7.
3. Task Force on Men's Movement: National, Regional and Local Organization (1981).
4. Barry Shapiro (1982b, October).
5. Ibid.
6. Against excluding women/Reasons for excluding women, 1984–85, National Organization for Changing Men. Unpublished document, 4 pp. From Changing Men Collection.
7. Ibid.
8. Paula Brookmire (1984 winter), pp. 3–6.
9. Michael Kaufman (1993, December 4).
10. Against excluding women.
11. S. LaVake (1975), *Turning Point: A Men's Newsletter* (Madison, Wisconsin), p. 2. From Changing Men Collection.
12. "Bruce" (1974).
13. Ron Smith (1984, January 27), p. 2.
14. Announcing . . . a national anti-sexist *men's* organization, 1983. Pamphlet. 2 pp. From Changing Men Collection.
15. Roy Schenk (1983).
16. Ken Fremont-Smith (1985, June), pp. 1, 8–9. Quoted from p. 9.
17. A National Anti-Sexist *Men's* Organization (1983). National Men's Organization brochure. 2 pp. From the Changing Men Collection.
18. Tom Mosmiller (1984b, fall), pp. 1, 8–9.
19. Join us for change: NOCM (1985–86). The National Organization for Changing Men brochure. 2 pp. From the Changing Men Collection.
20. What should the relationship be between pro-feminist men and feminism?, 1989, *Menergy: celebrating the profeminist men's movement: 14th Annual M & M Conference* (1–4 June). Conference handout. From the Changing Men Collection.
21. Profeminist groups against sexism and violence, as well as men's discussion and support groups, have existed since the 1970s. But academic theorizing around the politics of men's relations with feminism followed more slowly. In 1984, the Modern Languages Association presented two sessions of papers on "Men in Fem-

inism." After that and well into the 1990s, the temperature of the debate heated up, fueled by books like *Men in Feminism* (Jardine and Smith, 1987), *Women Respond to the Men's Movement* (Hagan, 1992), *Between Men and Feminism*, (Porter, 1992); and conferences like the "Men and Feminism Colloquium" at Cambridge University in 1990.

22. The proposers were Joseph Pleck, Robert Brannon, Barry Shapiro, and Bob Morgan.

23. Barry Shapiro (1982b, October).

24. Sam Julty (1983). Unpublished memo. From the Changing Men Collection.

25. One NOCM document (undated) proposes a "consensus decision making process" represented by a four-level flowchart. The document, which appears not to have been created by the organization, has detailed descriptions of levels of concerns that could arise in decision-making: "minor concerns," "reservations," "non-support," and "blocking concerns." While consensus is the guiding principle, this process seems somewhat hierarchical and convoluted, and I suspect some found it intimidating.

26. This information was printed on a brochure for the Ninth Annual Men & Masculinities Conference.

27. Ron Smith (1984, October 8).

28. Ron Smith (1984, July 24).

29. Mosmiller (1984a, fall), pp. 1, 8.

30. Task Group Coordinator (1986). Unpublished memo to task group leaders, National Organization for Changing Men, pp. 2–3. From the Changing Men Collection.

31. Jack Nichols (1976, February 10).

32. Task Force (1977). The Possibilities of a National Men's Organization. Unpublished report. From the Changing Men Collection.

33. Task Force on Men's Movement: National, Regional and Local Organizations (1981).

34. "The country" also included parts of Canada, namely Vancouver, B.C., as well as Toronto and Windsor in Ontario—all probably unaware that they'd been annexed.

35. Editorial (1981, fall), p. 1. Since NOM/NOCM had a council rather than a president and vice-president, etc., in theory there was no one single spokesperson. However, as the organization took shape between 1981 and 1983, Robert (Bob) Brannon played a significant role. Elected chairperson of the new council in 1982, Brannon wrote, among other things, a number of the planning documents and calls for membership, the press statement for NOM at the March 1983 Open Forum in New York City, and various articles for the organization's newsletter *Brother*. Other council members at various times included Tom Mosmiller (who also served as an NOCM co-chair), Barry Shapiro, Harry Brod, and Joseph Pleck who also had high profiles; some, like Pleck, were already well published and others soon would be. At the same time none, including Brannon, seems to have been exempted from less glamorous duties like recording and compiling minutes.

36. Shapiro (1982).

37. CAMP Caucus (1982, July 13).

38. Bob Brannon (1982, July 21), p. 1. The underlining and capitals are the author's.

39. Norberg-Bohm (1987, June), p. 4.
40. Mike Leach (1993, spring), pp. 14–17.
41. Andrew Tolson (1977).
42. Ibid., p. 28.
43. Ibid., p. 30.
44. Linda Collins and Pam Walton (1996, spring/summer), pp. 28–30. Quote is from p. 28.
45. Victor J. Seidler (1991a), pp. 42–43.
46. Connell (1995), p. 80.
47. Adam Hughes (1992, autumn), pp. 12–13. Quote is from p. 13.
48. Men Against Sexist Shit. (1993, spring). pp. 19.
49. Leach (1993, spring), p. 17.
50. "A Men's Group" (1974). Unpublished memo. Milwaukee: Men's Resources Center (July), p. 1. From the Changing Men Collection.
51. Berkeley Brother (1973).
52. The Brother Collective (1974, fall), pp. 1–2.
53. "Collective Statement" (1974).
54. "Collective Statement" (1977), p. 3.
55. As Messner (1997) notes—"In the United States, despite some efforts by socialist feminists to organize women workers . . . and despite a highly influential presence in organizations such as the Democratic Socialists of America (DSA), socialist feminism never developed a significant activist base outside of academia" (p. 55). Messner adds that despite this low profile, socialist feminism has played an important role in "much of the U.S. profeminist movement" (p. 55). This is evidenced by the efforts and principles of groups and collectives like *Brother*, who focused on the economic inequalities underpinning sexism.
56. Ninth Annual Conference on Men & Masculinity, 1984, Washington, DC. Brochure.
57. Messner (1997), p. 101.
58. Quoted by Messner (1997), p. 101.
59. John Stoltenberg (1997).
60. Geov Parrish (1992).
61. bell hooks (1992), pp. 115–116.
62. Michael-David Gordon (1993, summer/fall), pp. 15–17.
63. Manning Marable (1997), p. 447.
64. Robert Staples (1997), pp. 191–192.
65. Messner (1997), p. 71.
66. The October 16, 1995, "Million Man March" was described by Louis Farrakhan as "a day of atonement and reconciliation," an opportunity for black men "to take responsibility for their own lives and families, and to dedicate themselves to fighting the scourges of drugs, violence and unemployment." For the source of these quotes, go to <http://www.usatoday.com/news/index/nman010.htm>. An academic article, "Myth of the Million Man March," published in the magazine *Bad Subjects: Political Education for Everyday Life*, provides an interesting analysis of the March in relation to feminism and various branches of the American men's movement. See <http://eserver.org/bs/23/newitz.html>. Black women's feelings about being told to "stay home" and not participate in the march were mixed. See <http://www.cnn.com/US/9510/megamarch/10–16/women/index.html>.

# 6

# "The Ongoing Female Holocaust"

Worldwide, feminist activism against male violence toward women has not only involved creating safe spaces for victims but trying to dismantle rigid sets of public attitudes and stereotypes: particularly the often unspoken idea that only a few stray women on the fringes of society are really at risk. Slowly, the ongoing problems of men's violence against women and children—as well as, to a lesser extent, men's violence against other men—are becoming areas for serious public discussion and for broader civic work beyond the struggles of feminist groups. Yet these activist groups are owed much credit for this gradual transformation in public attitudes, and profeminists wanting to lend their support are usually quick to acknowledge that much of what they have done, and are still doing, to end violence against women is built on a solid foundation of feminist women's activism. Indeed, most profeminists insist that men doing work against violence to women should take leadership from feminism.

In that spirit, this chapter highlights feminist activism against male violence in Canada, the United States, Britain, and Australia from the 1970s through the 1990s. This overview is necessarily brief and cannot do justice to the extent of feminist thought and activism involved in trying to end violence against women. Still, I hope to provide some insights into the kinds of feminist leadership that profeminists consider important, as well as create a context for chapter 7—a close look at some anti-male violence projects undertaken by profeminist men entering this highly political area.

## CANADA: RAISING THE STAKES OF THE DEBATE

In both Canada[1] and the United States, early combined efforts in front-line anti-violence work and feminist analyses of sexual violence "heralded the coming of age of the contemporary women's movement."[2] For many feminists within and outside North America, violence against women is not only a central topic of analysis and protest but has been a primary motive for organizing. Indeed, the "springing up of community-based rape crisis centers and battered women's shelters out of the first consciousness-raising groups in the United States and Canada"[3] prompted greater recognition of violence to women as an important topic for feminism and a key issue in struggles for equality.

One of the most influential radical groups in Canada was the Toronto-based Women against Violence against Women (WAVAW), formed in 1977. This group argued, among other things, that men should be excluded from International Women's Day celebrations.[4] That same year saw a national day of protest against violence to women on November 5. In 1978, Canada's first "Take Back the Night" march was held in Toronto.[5] But not much of this late 1970s radical feminist activism against violence to women was filtering into the realm of institutionalized policy making. In the early 1980s, those in power still considered issues like "family violence" or "wife battering" to be private concerns—or worse, the butt of bad jokes. When a Canadian parliamentary committee introduced a report on family violence into the House of Commons in 1982, male Members of Parliament laughed outright.[6] This time, the joke backfired: the MPs' laughter actually served to focus public attention and outrage on the issue. By June 1983, a federal/provincial committee had been formed to propose ways to deal with wife-battering. But radical organizations like WAVAW continued to protest that, as long as patriarchy and masculinism existed, violence against women—"the ongoing Female Holocaust"—would rage unabated.[7] Quite obviously, a large gap still separated feminist positions on violence to women from public attitudes.

In the early 1980s, popular attitudes about violence to women were still, for the most part, entrenched in the Stone Age. One case in point: within a six-month period in 1982, one young woman in Toronto was raped and left in serious condition, and a number of other women were raped or assaulted in that same city. It was "as if, suddenly, somebody had declared violent, anonymous war on the women of the city. . . ."[8] According to two researchers at the University of Toronto's Centre of Criminology, one characteristic of the ensuing "moral panic" was to explain away the attacks using women as "the locus of the problem,"[9] essentially blaming the victim. The women were wearing provocative clothing; they were walking alone at night; in other words, they basically "asked for it." Legislation has since changed; no longer can a woman's sexual history, mental state, or attire be offered as defense evidence in a rape case.

The tragedy of December 6, 1989, when fourteen young women were fatally shot at Montréal's École Polytechnique by a man whose suicide note claimed he hated feminists, had one positive outcome: more people began publicly discussing the problem of violence against women and taking feminist work in the area more seriously. The days when Members of Parliament joked publicly about wife-beating were now over. These gradual shifts in attitude have also been encouraged by feminist efforts to educate decision makers and push for policy reform. At least on paper, governments within the last ten years have shown more willingness to examine the problem of violence against women. In 1987, the Canadian federal government announced major funding initiatives in response to a new report on wife abuse, *Battered But Not Beaten.*[10] In 1989, a subcommittee on the Status of Women was formed, which compiled a report on violence to women entitled *The War against Women/La Guerre Contre les Femmes* (1991). Two years later, the federally appointed Canadian Panel on Violence against Women published the less contentiously titled *Changing the Landscape: Ending the Violence, Achieving Equality.*

Yet feminist work against violence has been hard to detect—and feminist voices hard to hear—against the cacophony of casual violence in the media, portrayals of women as sex objects, and images of macho masculinity permeating North American and, increasingly, global cultures and media. The most extreme manifestation of violence against anyone, mass murder, is unfortunately more common in the United States than in the other countries mentioned in this book: Canada, Britain, or Australia. This is not to imply for a moment that mass murders haven't occurred in these countries, or that mass murder fails to shock and sadden Americans. But there is no doubt that the December 6, 1989, shootings, which some Canadians called "U.S.–style killings," had a profound impact on public discussion within Canada about violence against women, turning it almost overnight into a subject of often contentious debate. Later, activists used the massacre to rationalize certain legal reforms, particularly more restrictive gun control laws. The aftereffects of the massacre also made it possible for Canadian profeminists, particularly the White Ribbon Campaign and the Halifax-based group Men for Change, to raise awareness about a feminist issue among men who would never otherwise considered themselves involved in these issues.

Indeed, it's fair to say that public awareness in Canada about the role of violence to women in perpetuating gender inequalities has been growing since the 1990s. But while public reports are all to the good, one of the greatest frustrations for activist feminists—and not only in Canada—is knowing that large gaps still exist between government initiatives and practical action, particularly in the form of funding. In Canada, sustained lack of funding for supporting the elimination of violence to women has been a major problem, although interestingly, the government found $10 million to research and compile *Changing the Landscape*.[11] As former National Action Committee on the Status of Women chair Judy Rebick argued, "the government can find pots of money to wage war but cries deficit when money is required to improve services to victims of male violence."[12] Indeed, by the late 1980s, feminist groups were maintaining that "despite the increase in opportunities and the changes in legislation, attitudes, and social consciousness," women in North America were still faced with an array of gender-based inequities, not the least of them "escalating violence."[13]

The problem of violence has been particularly acute for First Nations or aboriginal women in Canada. As a First Nations law professor, Patricia Monture-Angus (formerly Monture-Okanee) pointed out that for aboriginal women the idea of violence in a sense of physical or sexual abuse is inseparable from the violence of racism.[14] Aboriginal oral traditions speak of times when women's independence and dignity were valued; when a man abused a woman, the community intervened—not merely to punish but often to provide spiritual guidance and healing. A 1990 study indicated that First Nations women dealing with abuse from men today are forced to do so within a westernized, patriarchal framework "deeply imbued with sexism, racism, and classism. . . . In urban areas, these women lack support from extended families and groups."[15] In 1992, the Aboriginal Circle of the Canadian Panel on Violence against Women underscored the dire effects of violence and racism on aboriginal women: "it is recognized that the women of First Nations communities have special needs as demonstrated by rates of suicide for females at a rate of 7.5 time the national average, the highest for any group in Canada; and by raises [*sic*] of abuse estimated as high as 80% in some published reports."[16]

Monture-Angus, a professor of law, does not "believe for a minute" that aboriginal men are inherently more violent than non-aboriginal men. Rather, she locates much of the "violence" within a criminal justice system that was

> never consented to by First Nations. Yet you put the weight of that whole system on our backs. Because of the over-representation of First Nations people in prisons, if the rape laws are made harsher, or if capital punishment is legalized, disproportionately more First Nations men will be serving the sentences for those rape convictions. I also suspect that First Nations women will disproportionately be the victims of rape, not necessarily by First Nations male perpetrators.[17]

Indeed, the critique of Monture-Angus represents the fact that more aboriginal women in Canada are speaking out. Increasingly, non–First Nations feminists working to end violence against women are being reminded that aboriginal women's perspectives and experiences arounc ferent, and that aboriginal women "must be provided roo. the power to define."[18]

## THE UNITED STATES: FEMINISTS AGAINST RAPE, VIOLENCE, AND PORNOGRAPHY

Seeking funding and legislative solutions to the problem of sexual violence has long been a priority for American feminists as well as women worldwide. In the United States, "in 1970, there was no such thing as a shelter for battered women." In 1978, the National Coalition against Domestic Violence (NCADV) was formed out of a gathering of "over 100 battered women's advocates from all parts of the nation [who] attended the U.S. Commission on Civil Rights hearing on battered women in Washington, DC." Serving as a clearing house for information as well as a referral center, NCADV has also undertaken to change public policy and legislation affecting battered women and their children. Notably, NCADV worked with federal legislators to develop priorities for Victims of Crime Act (VOCA) funds for battered women's programs, supported the Domestic Violence Offender Gun Ban in 1996.[19]

The NCADV, along with other advocates working against violence to women, also lobbied for the development and passage of the 1993 Violence against Women Act. This significant piece of legislation came about not only through feminist lobbying but the facilitation of a high-profile profeminist, Senator Joseph Biden. In 1990, the U.S. Majority Staff of the Senate Judiciary Committee had compiled a series of frightening statistics showing that American women were increasingly likely to be sexually assaulted or raped:

- The most serious crimes against women are rising at a significantly faster rate than total crimes: during the past 10 years, rape rates have risen nearly four times as fast as the total crime rate.
- Every hour, 16 women confront rapists; a woman is raped every 6 minutes.
- Every 18 seconds, a woman is beaten; 3–4 million women are battered each year.
- Since 1974, the rate of assaults against young women (20–24) has jumped almost 50%. For young men, it has decreased.
- Three out of four women will be victims of at least one violent crime during their lifetimes.
- A woman is 10 times more likely to be raped than to die in a car crash.[20]

The 1993 Violence against Women Act (VAWA) was shaped by the same hands as a 1992 report entitled *Violence against Women: A Week in the Life of America*, compiled by the Senate Judiciary Committee under the signature of Senator Biden. In the "Introduction" to *A Week in the Life of America*, Biden notes somberly: "the nation does not fully comprehend the magnitude and severity of the problem of violence against women. . . . I have come to believe more firmly than ever that this nation will be powerless to change the course of violence against women, unless and until its citizens fully realize the devastation this violence yields."[21] This clearly profeminist report was the result of two years of hearings overseen by Biden on rape, domestic violence, and legal protections. The hearings and the report were followed in 1993 by the Violence against Women Act, a piece of "comprehensive legislation" with $300 million in funding attached to help rape and assault victims, promote education, and protect accusers' rights.[22]

Along with securing the right to an abortion and equality in workplaces, ending rape and preventing male violence were consistently at the forefront of feminist concerns during the 1980s and 1990s. American feminist writers have been leaders in bringing the darkest manifestations of male violence into the light of public discussion. Classics like Susan Brownmiller's *Against Our Will: Men, Women, and Rape* (1975) took the sex out of rape and redefined it as an act of power and domination. A reconceptualized notion of rape, along with the work of later American theorists like Andrea Dworkin and Catharine MacKinnon, has inspired various attempts to create rape laws and penalties that treat the problem more seriously.

Very broadly, MacKinnon criticizes the practice in the United States and Canada of defining rape as "sexual assault" and making sexual violence "part of the law of assault" rather than recognizing it as "a special law of sex" unto itself. Depending on one's perspective, this more gender neutral treatment of rape can be seen as a move toward recognizing that both women and men can be victims of sexual assault, or an attempt (inadvertent or not) to obscure the fact that rape is an act of power perpetrated mainly by men against women.[23] MacKinnon herself confronts the gender-neutral redefinition, for among other things, the neutral term can obscure the fact that rape is much more likely to be a crime committed by men against women.[24]

What many feminists considered to be further groundbreaking research on rape and sexual violence was conducted on college campuses in the mid-1980s. The researcher, Mary Koss, a professor of family and public health, published her results in the October 1985 issue of *Ms*. For antiviolence feminists, Koss's findings were a loud wake-up call. According to the Project on the Status and Education of Women of the Association of American Colleges (1987):

> Mary Koss . . . surveyed approximately 7,000 students on thirty-two campuses on behalf of *Ms.* magazine and found that one in eight women were the victims of rape. One in every twelve men admitted to having forced a woman to have inter-

course or tried to force a woman to have intercourse through physical force or coercion; that is, admitted to raping or attempting to rape a woman. Virtually none of these men, however, identified themselves as rapists. Similarly, only 57% of the women who had been raped labeled their experience as rape; the other 43% had not even acknowledged to themselves that they had been raped.[25]

By 1990, Koss had published her results in several academic journals and had co-authored a further study for the U.S. Department of Justice. Complementing the statistics compiled for Senator Biden's report, the work of Koss and her co-authors illustrated that younger women were at high risk of being raped, particularly by men they knew (so-called "date rape"). The authors noted that "The definition of rape employed in these statistics is the one formulated by the FBI for its Uniform Crime Report, which is the narrowest official definition." Among the alarming statistics they compiled on date rape and that became widely publicized are the following:

- 1 in 5 adult women will be raped at some point in their lives.
- 1 in 3.5 adult women will be attacked by a rapist.
- 1 in 7 of the women now in college have been raped.
- 1 in 4 of the women now in college have been attacked by a rapist.
- More than half of college rape victims are attacked by dates.
- More than 4 out of 5 rape victims know their attackers.
- 1 in 15 rape victims contracts a sexually transmitted disease as a result of being raped.
- 1 in 15 rape victims becomes pregnant as a result of being raped.
- Only 7% of all rapes are reported to police. By comparison, the reporting rate for robbery is 53%; assault, 46%; and burglary, 52%.
- Less than 5% of college women report incidences of rape to the police.
- More than half of raped college women tell *no one* of their victimization [authors' emphasis].
- The number of women raped in 1986 is fifteen times higher than officially reported in the National Crime Survey.
- The number of college women raped in 1986 is fourteen times higher than officially reported in the National Crime Survey.[26]

Throughout the late 1980s and into the 1990s, Koss's studies generated considerable controversy and sometimes bitter argument among various women who considered themselves feminists of one sort or another. Activists who felt Koss's figures accurately represented the "chilly climate" on campuses for women were demanding proactive measures to control date rape. And indeed, on many college campuses in the United States and Canada during the 1990s, administrators were quickly formulating sexual harassment and date-rape policies and openly discussing strategies for preventing date rape and sexual assault in orientation presentations. In the United States, the justification for such action was provided by the array of statistics gathered by researchers like Koss and institutions like the U.S. Department of Justice, and the increasing publicity being given to issues like date rape.[27] In Canada, it's fair to say that one aftereffect of the 1989 Montréal massacre was to raise awareness of what many feminist academics had earlier defined as a chilly climate in colleges and universities.[28]

On the other side of the Koss controversy are those who feel the 1985 study results were inaccurate, skewed, or politically motivated. Christina Hoff Sommers has been among the most vocal critics of one particular statistic generated by Koss's 1985 study—that one in four college women have been attacked by a rapist. According to Sommers,

> "One in four" has since become the official figure on women's rape victimization cited in women's studies departments, rape crisis centers, women's magazines, and on protest buttons and posters. . . . Koss and her colleagues counted as victims of rape any respondent who answered "yes" to the question "Have you had sexual intercourse when you didn't want to because a man gave you alcohol or drugs?" That opened the door wide to regarding as a rape victim anyone who regretted her liaison of the previous night.[29]

Sommers is considered by many antiviolence feminists and activists as a conservative whose views undermine feminist struggles against male violence.[30] But there are other reasons why antiviolence feminists react negatively when women who think of themselves as feminists appear to betray the cause. For one thing, any criticism of antiviolence research can be seen as a weapon for antifeminist men. And indeed, various men—some of them stridently antifeminist—have suggested that studies like Koss's encourage anti-male–violence feminists to go over the top in attacking men and to justify putting male victims of violence at a lower priority level. The sad fact is that, worldwide, general lack of funding for and public interest in anti-male–violence projects renders the search for solutions into a zero-sum game. This situation does nothing to discourage divisions arising among those who, in other circumstances, could conceivably be allies in social transformation.

No less controversial for many feminists has been the debate around pornography. For many radical antiviolence activists, pornography—"violence against women through sexual and violent images"—is the main motivator of male violence. Radical American feminists had earlier asserted the harmful effects of porn, expressed in Robin Morgan's famous statement "Pornography is the theory, rape is the practice." Large-scale American anti-porn activism began around 1979, when the influential New York–

based Women against Pornography (WAP) was formed. In 1980, WAP "mobilized 7,000 women for a march in New York."[31]

Andrea Dworkin's groundbreaking book *Pornography: Men Possessing Women* (1979) had also just been published. Dworkin saw pornography as inseparable from men's systemic abuse of women. Her arguments soon after became closely associated with the work of a theorist in feminism and the law, Catharine MacKinnon, whose main interest was in delegitimizing porn by redefining it as a kind of sex discrimination. Together, they created the often-termed "MacKinnon-Dworkin ordinance" passed by the City of Minneapolis in late 1983. This ordinance "authorized any woman to sue the producer or distributor of a pornographic work for 'trafficking in pornography' on the grounds that 'pornography' is a form of sex discrimination." The MacKinnon-Dworkin ordinance also set out a complex definition of pornography as "the sexually explicit subordination of women, graphically depicted, whether in pictures or words":

> Pornography . . . also included one or more of nine elements . . . women . . . presented dehumanized as sexual objects, things, or commodities; . . . presented as sexual objects who enjoy pain or humiliation; . . . presented as sexual objects who experience sexual pleasure in being raped; . . . presented as sexual objects tied up or cut up or mutilated or bruised or physically hurt; . . . women's body parts are exhibited . . . such that women are reduced to those parts; women . . . presented as whores by nature; . . . presented being penetrated by objects or animals . . . presented in scenarios of degradation, injury, abasement, torture, shown as filthy or inferior, bleeding bruised or hurt in a context that makes these conditions sexual.[32]

This definition went beyond generalizations, presenting a broad and detailed classification of porn's harmful effects and receiving high praise from many feminist activists as well as from radical profeminists.

But defining porn so broadly has raised concerns about freedom of expression.[33] The division between so-called anti-porn and anticensorship feminists has been deep and bitter, and views are still sharply divided about whether censorship is an appropriate or an extreme solution. While the porn versus censorship debates are far too complex and broad to discuss in detail here, the basic positions can be sketched. Feminists and profeminists against pornography argue that since porn is "at the root of violence against women,"[34] censoring porn—like not yelling "fire!" in a crowded theater—is a justifiable restriction to freedom of expression. On the other hand, feminists against censorship argue that anti-porn movements "espouse a Victorian view of women and their physical, emotional and sexual abilities that is out of sync with the reality of many women's lives."[35] Other feminists take the view that it's possible and indeed necessary to differentiate between porn and erotica—restricting the first while celebrating the second.[36] Still others find it ironic that the feminist movement that fought so long for women's right to sexual expression is divided in the 1980s and 1990s over whether to censor certain forms of it.

Feminist debates around issues like campus date rape or pornography ironically underscore the extent to which antiviolence activism has focused mainly on the concerns and experiences of white middle-class women. In the words of one professor of Afro-American studies:

> White women's experience is often substituted for all women's experience, although it is only a part of the whole category of women . . . Black women and other women of color are not viewed in universal terms. Yet black women deal with the interlocking oppression of race, sex and class, unlike white women, most of whom view their oppression almost exclusively in terms of gender.[37]

In some ways not unlike Canadian and Australian aboriginal women, black American women can't easily separate violence from layers of racism, but in this case the racism has been troweled on by a history of slavery and its aftermath. As black feminist theorist Patricia Hill Collins has illustrated, slavery defined black women as "sexualized," and rape became a "fundamental tool of sexual violence" to control black women. So central an experience was rape that it became "a prominent theme" in black women's fiction. Black women also run a considerable risk of losing their lives in a domestic dispute; as of 1995, 47 percent of black women murdered were killed by acquaintances and 43 percent by family members. Black women at all socioeconomic levels can be victims of violence; moreover, a black woman without a job or means of financial support "begins to believe that she can live with the violence."[38]

Yet within societies in which racism has been and still is institutionalized, not only black women but black men are caught up in "interlocking race, gender, and class oppression."[39] For this reason, black women have been more reluctant than white women to treat men as the opposition. Collins acknowledges that black women reporting rape or sexual violence have been victimized by family members and their communities: effectively seen as traitors to their race.[40] Black women have been slower than white women to participate in anti-rape movements, partly for this same reason. But for a long time, the white feminist movement in the United States defined sexual violence in terms of male against female, not considering that for blacks, sexual violence is also an effect of racism and internalized hatreds that poison gender relations. As black feminist writer and theorist bell hooks has expressed it, "feminism is often seen as one of the 'weapons' women have used to belittle men."[41] Black women against violence are certainly not prepared to excuse rape and violence perpetrated by black men, any more than by white men. But a number of black American feminists—among them hooks and Collins—do not separate sexual violence and sexism from institutionalized or culturally sanctioned racism. They believe it is more productive for black women, whenever possible, to work with rather than against black men to end racism, sexual violence, and other forms of sexism.[42]

## BRITAIN: WOMEN NEVER "ASKED FOR IT"

Divisive politics has made it challenging to sustain a national feminist antiviolence effort in Britain. In the early 1970s, when the British Women's Liberation Movement (WLM) was gaining momentum, the problem of domestic violence was an especially high priority. According to scholars who have researched British feminist work against violence in the 1970s and 1980s, "The sheer scale of domestic assault shocked the women who became interested in the issue." In 1975, members of the WLM agreed to establish a national coordinating body to fight domestic violence: the National Women's Aid Federation. These efforts, along with sustained feminist publicity, caught the attention of politicians. That same year, a parliamentary select committee on violence in marriage established that domestic violence was a "social rather than an individual problem."[43] In 1976 the Domestic Violence and Matrimonial Proceedings Act was passed,[44] allowing courts to attach a power of arrest to injunctions restraining abusive men.[45] By 1977, nearly 200 refuges (women's shelters) had been established in the United Kingdom.

Yet stereotypical attitudes about men's violence to women—that women are the problem, that they ask for it—have been difficult to dismantle. British feminist Yvonne Roberts notes that in 1975, the British House of Commons Select Committee on violence in marriage "advised against a series of national conferences on the issue, as this 'might well create new and greater demands for resources than could be met.' " Especially compromised by both lack of resources and lack of power were black and immigrant women. Like black women in the United States, many were discriminated against both sexually and racially, by restrictive immigration laws and by police violence. But black women in Britain who sought help in refuges were often misunderstood by the white women who operated them, operators often unable to understand that black women were often considered traitors if they called the police. "Racism poisoned relations in many refuges, promoting guilt and irritation amongst white women and righteous anger on the part of black women."[46]

Political schisms within feminism did handicap antiviolence work to some extent. But it was also difficult for politicians and the public to take domestic violence and rape seriously when the police themselves generally did not. In 1983, the *London Times* quoted an assistant commissioner of London's Metropolitan Police as saying that domestic disputes should be categorized "along with 'stranded people, lost property and stray animals' so that the police could get on with 'real crime work.' "[47] In the mid-1980s,

Elizabeth Stanko called these elaborate rationalizations "the rhetoric of protection," and noted the prevalence of this rhetoric in the trials of men accused of sexual assault:

> There are special ingredients available to assist attorneys, judges and jurors with their task of assessing credibility and truthfulness for women. . . . One such ingredient, being "nice," is a value for women. . . . "Nice" girls, for example, don't accept rides from strangers, don't go into pubs alone, don't walk the streets at night, are "chaste," in essence, are passive, compliant, sexually controlled within respectable boundaries.[48]

Dismantling the myths that trivialized rape was one priority for British antiviolence feminists in the 1970s and 1980s; providing support systems for victims of rape was another. A group of women who began meeting in the early 1970s gave birth to the London Rape Crisis Centre [*sic*], which opened in March 1976. Other centers soon appeared throughout England. These were not actual places but telephone lines, and calls were taken by trained rape counselors—still the main form of rape crisis work today. By the 1980s, the view that "all sexual coercion is a form of rape" gradually gained ground in Britain,[49] a view upheld by American studies such as the one conducted by Mary Koss in 1985.

Addressing domestic violence, mainly through the women's refuge movement, and campaigning against rape have been the main areas of feminist work against violence in Britain. Yet as of the early 1990s, only one anti-domestic violence group—Women's Aid—has been able to maintain a national presence since 1975, when the Women's Liberation Movement began to split over the question of how to deal with men's violence to women.[50] This split is illustrated best in a debate about the relationship between maleness and violence: a debate still ongoing, but more vociferous and less subtle in 1975 than now. Some feminists have held the position that, simply put, all men are violent or inherently violent, so feminists should separate from or interact as little as possible with male power structures. Other feminists, particularly socialists, have generally believed violence is inextricably part of capitalist society. In Britain, men treating violent men are much more likely to accept social and psychological explanations than theories that sanction separatism. This kind of profeminist work, though not necessarily grounded in socialism, acknowledges how systems and institutional power structures perpetuate or encourage male violence.

## "DISTINCTIVELY AUSTRALIAN" ISSUES ON VIOLENCE AGAINST WOMEN

"Although early feminist interventions against violence drew both their framework and their focus from the women's movement in the UK and the USA, in many ways their origins are also distinctively Australian."[51]

According to Gail Mason, a "distinctively Australian" publication, Anne Summers' *Damned Whores and God's Police*, showed links between violence against women and the "physically and sexually violent history of the early Australian colonies."[52] Not only the women convicts transported from Britain to Australia between 1788 and 1852, but women in general were often the objects of sexual stereotyping and abuses ranging from rape to essentially forced prostitution. Among other indignities, a convict woman had no rights even if she found a man. According to Robert Hughes (*The Fatal Shore*, 1986), "a settler could simply throw a convict woman out when he was tired of her." If convicted of disorderly conduct, a convict woman could be punished in a variety of ways short of flogging, including being led through the streets with a rope around her neck.[53]

This often violent early history has informed Australian feminist work on rape awareness and prevention as well as the elimination of domestic violence. Australian feminists started campaigning for rape law reform as early as 1972, well before the publication of books like *Against Our Will* (Susan Brownmiller, 1975) and *The Politics of Rape* (Diana Russell, 1977). According to Mason, in the late 1970s, the radical ideology inspired by Brownmiller defined rape as "an act of intimidation, through which all men kept all women in a state of fear" and dominated Australian feminist activism against rape. The Melbourne collective of the group Women against Rape issued an anti-rape Manifesto in 1975, defining rape as a " 'paradigmatic instance' of women's oppression."[54]

The analysis that all men could commit rape and sexual violence was also connected to the idea, developing in the 1970s and 80s, that antiviolence activism could unite the Australian women's movement. In the 1980s, Australian feminists began to redefine rape and sexual abuse as part of a larger continuum of violence. Their concept of violence as pervasive and systemic was influenced partly by the theories of Catharine MacKinnon and Andrea Dworkin (discussed above).[55] However, the concept that all men are considered possible offenders and oppressors indirectly created some tensions when, at one point, Australian profeminist men wanted to support the most well-known anti-rape event: "Reclaim the Night." Beginning in the late 1970s, this yearly event was adapted from the American and Canadian "Take Back the Night" marches and has, over the years, featured not only marching and songs but even, in the mid-1980s, the burning of a male effigy in the Melbourne city center. During the 1990s in Melbourne, profeminist men volunteered to play a supporting role during "Reclaim the Night" marches. During the years in which feminists who knew and trusted these men were organizing the march, this plan worked well. But when other women later challenged this decision on the basis that "Reclaim the Night" should be strictly for women, the Melbourne profeminists reluctantly backed away.[56]

The continuing efforts of Australian feminists to intervene in legal and public debates have expanded the definition of male violence against women even further. A 1992 Position Paper of the National Committee on Violence against Women considers male violence as "behavior by the man, adopted to control his victim, which results in physical, sexual and/or psychological damage, forced social isolation, or economic deprivation, or behavior which leaves a woman living in fear."[57] Defining violence not only as deed but as intent has opened up possibilities for feminists in Australia and elsewhere to theorize how cultural norms, and even the language of sex and gender relations, reinforce oppressive attitudes about rape. Recently, a researcher has argued that a useful feminist anti-rape strategy would be to disrupt and dismantle what she calls rape scripts. In Australian as well as in other Western cultures, a rape script places women in the role of endangered and fearful, whereas men become predators, "legitimately violent and entitled to women's sexual services."[58] This suggestion is grounded on the theory that the language we use not only constructs the ways we think of rape but gives rape a particular cultural meaning. Thus, we should focus at least partly on language as a preventative measure, displacing the rape scripts victimizing women and demonizing men with alternative discourses emphasizing women's "will, agency, and capacity for violence." Then the possibility exists not only for preventing rape but "transforming the destructive experience of rape for women."[59]

Going hand in hand with rape prevention in Australia have been efforts to expose and address domestic violence. As late as the mid-1990s, not much information had been collected about the extent of domestic abuse in Australia, though one researcher estimated in 1993 that about 3 percent of women living in the Australian Capital Territory had requested space in a women's refuge.[60] But like their British and North American counterparts, white Australian feminists began national campaigns in the 1970s to expose, address, and eliminate domestic violence. Along with establishing a national women's refuge movement, by the 1980s a significant number of Australian feminist activists and thinkers were critiquing the family as "a screen behind which there was abuse of women and children."[61] This critique was taken up mainly by white middle-class women, some of whom chose to separate themselves from men and live in collective women-only houses or communes. These women had concluded that living with men not only exposed them to personal risk but gave "tacit support to a patriarchal system which enslaved women and privileged men."[62]

But white women's critique of and rebellion against the nuclear family failed to account for the experiences of aboriginal women. Not unlike black women and immigrant women of color in the United States and Britain, aboriginal women in Australia were torn between the reality of domestic violence and the need to stay united with aboriginal men. Both sexes faced (and still face) racism and discrimination, but aboriginal women remained disenfranchised long after white women won the vote. They were devalued by the white women who used them as domestic servants as well as sexually stereotyped and denigrated by white men, many of whom treated aboriginal women violently, perpetuating "patterns of behavior which outlasted the 'final frontiers' of white colonisation [*sic*]."[63]

Most tragically, aboriginal women watched their children being forcibly removed in the thousands by an Australian government intent on assimilating them more easily into white culture. Despite the testimonies of aboriginal women and men and concerted protests by enlightened white women in Britain and Australia during the late 1920s and early 1930s, these removals continued for decades.[64] Faced with this struggle to keep their families together, aboriginal women have, not surprisingly, felt excluded by the anti-family and at times anti-male emphasis of white Australian feminism.

Aboriginal and non-English speaking immigrant women also had to wait longer than white women to be served by Australia's powerful women's refuge [shelter] movement, the chief weapon in this country's fight against domestic violence. Starting in the 1970s as a grassroots organization that was part of the feminist movement, the refuge movement represented an important linking of health and housing issues, later institutionalized when a single Ministry of Health and Housing was established. The refuges offered some options beyond a welfare system that sought "to preserve the family—even if it was violent." However, while the Australian government began supporting women's refuges in 1975, funding "waxed and waned" until 1985, when both state and federal governments put "consistent, long-term funding" into place.[65]

In 1993, the Women's Emergency Service Network (WESNET) was formed. Not unlike Women's Aid in Britain, WESNET provides a coordinated approach to addressing domestic violence on a national scale. WESNET's purpose and vision is "to ensure that all women and children can live free of domestic and family violence. We do this by lobbying, research and debate, networking and resourcing and community education."[66] Tied in with WESNET, all Australian refuges are run autonomously so they can best answer to the women and communities they serve.[67] However, as of 1997, only five women's refuges had been established for non-English-speaking women, even though a national survey conducted overnight in 1994 indicated that 29 percent of the women using refuges were non-English-speaking.[68] The activism of aboriginal women helped establish, among other projects, the Cawarra Aboriginal Women's Refuge and the Moree Wirraway Women's Housing Cooperative, which also provides emergency shelter.[69] By 1997, there were approximately seven full-fledged refuges throughout Australia for aboriginal women as well as a scattering of safe houses and outreach services, according to researcher Deborah Saltman.

This total, says Saltman, is not nearly enough.[70] Making this problem particularly grave is the fact that aboriginal women are ten times as likely to be homicide victims as nonaboriginal women.[71] As well, though there is a high rate of nonreporting among aboriginal women, a 1994 study estimated that "one-third of the Northern Territory's Aboriginal women were assaulted each year."[72] Overall, mainly white women and women within mainstream Australian society have begun to benefit from linking the refuge movement to health issues and recognizing that domestic violence is a widespread, societal problem. Saltman is pessimistic about the possibility that women's needs will be met anytime soon as long as "white views of health, housing and welfare" continue to prevail.

## NOTES

1. Nancy Adamson, Linda Briskin, and Margaret McPhail (1988), pp. 291–292.
2. Constance Backhouse and David H. Flaherty (1992a), p. 185.
3. Ibid.
4. Adamson, Briskin, and McPhail (1988), p. 72.
5. Ibid., p. 301.
6. Linda MacLeod (1987), p. 1.
7. Adamson, Briskin, and McPhail (1988), pp. 291–292.
8. Sophia E. Voumvakis and Richard V. Ericson (1984), pp. 4–5.
9. Ibid., p. 73.
10. Adamson, Briskin, and McPhail (1988), p. 4.
11. Vivian Smith (1993, July 30), pp. A1, A3.
12. Ibid.
13. Adamson, Briskin, and McPhail (1988), p. 5.
14. Patricia Monture-Okanee (1992), p. 193. This writer, now known as Patricia Monture-Angus, is a citizen of the Mohawk nation and a professor of law in the Native Studies Department at the University of Saskatchewan.
15. Barbara Cassidy, Robina Lord, and Nancy Mandell (1995), p. 29.
16. Assembly of First Nations (1992, June 24).
17. Monture-Okanee (1992), pp. 198–199.
18. Ibid., p. 199.
19. About NCADV (2000).
20. Majority Staff of the Senate Judiciary Committee (1990).
21. Senator Joseph R. Biden (1992).
22. Major goals of the proposed Violence against Women Act are mentioned in Biden (1992). Slated to expire after seven years, VAWA was reauthorized by the U.S. Senate in October 2000, passing by a vote of 95–0 and promising $3.3 million "to address violence against women over the next five years." According to the National Coalition against Domestic Violence, much credit for this success is due to the intense and organized lobbying of domestic violence and sexual assault advocates. The NCADV's report on the reauthorization can be found at <http://www.ncadv.org/>.
23. Catharine A. MacKinnon (1992), 186–192. Quote is from p. 188.

24. Backhouse and Flaherty (1992b), p. 10.
25. As cited in Ellen Sweet (1995), pp. 10–20.
26. From Mary P. Koss, W. J. Woodruff, and P. G. Koss (1991).
27. The range of differing positions on dealing with date rape and other forms of sexual violence in the United States during the 1990s is well articulated in Adele M. Stan (1995).
28. For perspectives on the "chilly climate" for women in Canadian, American, and European universities, see Paula J. Caplan (1994).
29. From Christine Hoff Sommers (1999).
30. Some of the argument over Koss's results has been fairly nasty. Many feminists, including writers like Susan Faludi and some *Ms.* editors and regular contributors, see Koss's work as a solid confirmation of their own experiences and the messages they had been trying to convey for years about violence against women. Among Koss's detractors have been so-called "conservative" women who consider themselves feminists, like Katie Roiphe and Christina Hoff Sommers. These women have suggested that antiviolence feminists overreacted to dubious results (particularly the 1985 ones) and helped create a culture of victimization. Koss herself responded sarcastically to Roiphe's question that if one in four college women had been raped, "Wouldn't I know it?" and took issue with Roiphe's reading of the study results in a letter to the *New York Times* (Koss and Fitzgerald, 1993, June 14). In her article "The Real Issue" (see n. 29), Sommers has questioned the reliability not only of Koss's methods but of other sources, like the FBI and the U.S. Bureau of Justice Statistics. Camille Paglia has frequently criticized feminists for promoting date-rape hysteria and for demanding a top-down rules and policies solution rather than "female awareness and self-control" (Adele M. Stan [1995], pp. 21–25). Faludi, on her part, has dismissed Sommers, Roiphe, and Paglia, among others, as "pod feminists" who are more interested in media exposure than in ending sexism (see Faludi [1995] March/April], pp. 31–39).
31. David Bouchier (1884), p. 206.
32. Quoted in Christopher M. Finan and Anne F. Castro (1996). MacKinnon (1987, p. 176), closely paraphrases this definition. The text of the ordinance can be found in Andrea Dworkin and Catharine MacKinnon (1988).
33. Finan, cited above, is highly critical of what he considers MacKinnon's successful attempts to censor free speech. Engaging the spectrum of opinions on whether North American—especially U.S.—society is taking reasonable steps to end sexual violence or is entering a new era of puritanism is Stan (1995), a collection of articles by authors ranging from Dworkin and MacKinnon to Camille Paglia.
34. Barbara Ryan (1992), p. 114.
35. In Pat Califia (1994). The website <http://www.wacc.org.uk/womedia/porn.htm> represents one of the most interesting side-effects of the anti-porn/anti-censorship debate: some radical feminists have found themselves sharing views—though for very different reasons—long held by right-wing or Christian thinkers about restricting porn. In this context, it's not surprising to find a well-written, carefully referenced article on a Christian website that presents anti-porn and anti-censorship views, but that ultimately comes down on the anti-porn side. Ellen Willis's 1979 essay, "Feminism, Moralism, and Pornography" presents a more typical feminist argument against "antipornography": its proponents not only risk allying

themselves with the religious right but set themselves in opposition to entire constituencies of women, like sex industry workers (see pp. 41–49).

36. Margaret Atwood (2000) tries to distinguish porn from "joyful and life enhancing" sexuality (see pp. 347–353). Ambivalent views about the value of censoring porn—specifically using the Dworkin-MacKinnon ordinance—are apparent in a sampling of feminist opinions published by *Ms.* magazine in 1994. A performance artist notes that "many women . . . choose to use and participate in porn, and that's not an act of self-abuse. It can become a tool to discover your own sexual power" (see Pornography [1994, January/February], pp. 42–45).

37. Audrey Thomas McCluskey, quoted in Susan Williams (2000, February 25).

38. Show Your Respect for African American Women: Councilwoman Fields' Statement at the Candlelight Vigil for Black Women Who Have Been Victims of Violence (June 19, 1995).

39. Patricia Hill Collins (1990), pp. 176–177.

40. Ibid., p. 179.

41. bell hooks (1992), pp. 111–117. Quote is from p. 116.

42. Also see Marable (1997), cited in chapter 5.

43. Joni Lovenduski and Vicky Randall (1993), pp. 305–307.

44. Liberty Ross (1998–99).

45. Lovenduski and Randall, p. 313.

46. Ibid., pp. 309–310.

47. Yvonne Roberts (1992), pp. 162, 167.

48. Elizabeth A. Stanko (1985), p. 91.

49. Lovenduski and Randall, pp. 322–324.

50. The Women's Aid Federation of England (WAFE) is the umbrella organization for a variety of local Women's Aid chapters. As "the key national charity in England for women and children experiencing physical, sexual or emotional abuse in their homes," WAFE provides resources and information about services, and operates the National Domestic Violence Helpline. Go to <http://www.womensaid.org.uk/>. Retrieved May 6, 2001.

51. Gail Mason (1998), p. 337.

52. Ibid.

53. Robert Hughes (1987), pp. 253–254. Hughes's chapter "Bunters, Mollies and Sable Brethren" (pp. 244–281) details the treatment of women, homosexuals, and Aboriginals between 1788 and 1852.

54. Mason (1998), p. 337.

55. Ibid., 339–340. Many Canadian feminists also evoked the concept of "a continuum of violence" to help explain the 1989 Montréal massacre (see esp. Malette and Chalouh [1991]).

56. From personal interviews with Bob Pease (1999, May 6) and Marnie Daphne (1999, May 9).

57. Mason (1998), pp. 342–43.

58. Sharon Marcus (1992). Fighting bodies, fighting words: a theory and politics of rape prevention. In J. Butler and J. W. Scott (Eds.), *Feminists theorize the political.* New York: Routledge. Quoted in Barbara Sullivan (1995), pp. 184–197. Quote is from p. 196.

59. Marcus (1992), in Sullivan (1995), p. 196.

60. Kate Pritchard Hughes (1997), pp. 1–29. Quote is from p. 15. The Austra-

lian Domestic and Family Violence Clearinghouse has since compiled a number of recent studies conducted in Australia and elsewhere on women's fear of crime, "femicide," child abuse, and domestic violence, among other topics. Abstracts of these studies and information on availability can be found by clicking on the "Databases" link at <http://www.austdvclearinghouse.unsw.edu.au/>. Retrieved May 27, 2001.

61. Ibid., pp. 14–15.

62. Ibid., p. 16.

63. Sevgi Kilic (1997), pp. 30–51. Quote is from pp. 44–45.

64. Fiona Paisley (1998), pp. 168–173. Quote is from pp. 172–73.

65. Deborah Saltman (1997), pp. 232–233.

66. Source: the Women's Services Network home page <http://www.wesnet.org.au/>. Retrieved May 27, 2001.

67. Saltman (1997), pp. 233–234.

68. Ibid., p. 234.

69. Jan Larbalestier (1998), p. 390.

70. Saltman (1997), pp. 235–236.

71. Mason (1998), p. 343.

72. Saltman (1997), p. 235.

# 7

# "Breaking the Silence to End Men's Violence"

For many profeminists, one of the most important things men can do is join women in their struggle to end male violence against women and initiate their own antiviolence efforts aimed at men. Feminist women have not always uncritically supported men's antiviolence work, and profeminist men have at times felt uncomfortable about entering this particular feminist territory. But antiviolence work has been one of the most high-profile forms of profeminist activism. The surprise value of men speaking out on a feminist issue has even, at times, succeeded in capturing public attention at national and international levels. While profeminist groups have encountered their share of obstacles and experienced failures, it's important to keep in mind their successes. With that aim, this chapter describes the varying forms of antiviolence work done by groups like the White Ribbon Campaign, the U.S.-based Ending Men's Violence Task Group, and Men against Sexual Assault in Australia, which mounted its own white ribbon campaign. This chapter also looks at a unique partnership between feminists and men working against men's violence at a British antiviolence treatment center.

## CANADA'S WHITE RIBBON CAMPAIGN: REACHING OUT TO "AVERAGE MEN"

In 1991, during the week of December 1 to 6 (the second anniversary of the Montréal massacre), passers-by in cities like Toronto, Kingston, and Ottawa were intrigued to see men distributing white ribbons at subway stations and street corners in exchange for donations to battered women's shelters and programs for violence against women. The media, piqued by the unusual sight of men doing feminist activism, peppered the organizers and supporters of this "White Ribbon Campaign" with questions like—"Why are men doing this?" and "Why wear a white ribbon?"

As far as the WRC was concerned, the answer to the first question could be summed up in two general convictions. First, men should not just passively support, but take action to end violence against women. Second, *all* men—or as many as possible—should get involved, not just those on the political left or the small minority interested in social reform. To include mainstream men in its commitment to end male violence, the campaign had to define itself from the beginning as an inclusive, grassroots effort "by men, for men."[1] The White Ribbon Campaign's inaugural publicity statement of November 1991 asserted that violence against women is a form of warfare. If male attitudes toward women, violence—and indeed masculinity—are "the problem," then a change of male attitudes can be, and should be, "part of the solution."[2] The campaign's emphasis on naming the problem reveals the extent to which these men relied on feminist beliefs to shape their own convictions about violence against women—particularly the principle of naming men as the agents of violence and admitting that men have been at war against women. But the focus on men as part of the solution also shows how, from the beginning, the WRC tried to balance the potentially negative, off-putting notion of naming or even blaming men with a more positive message that not all men are violent and that men can do something about violence.

The answer to the question—"Why wear a white ribbon?"—is summed up in this excerpt from a 1998 article about the WRC in the newsletter *Education Wife/Assault*:

> If we are ever going to see an end to systemic violence against women—men are going to have to shoulder their responsibility and get involved. That was the premise when, in 1991, a handful of men, reflecting on the commemorative events held for 14 women killed in Montreal on December 6/89, decided to start the White Ribbon Campaign.
>
> The white ribbon appeared as an ideal symbol that could be worn by men as a means to express a personal pledge not to commit, condone, or remain silent about violence against women. And because we knew that others would ask: "What's that ribbon for?" the ribbon seemed a likely way to provoke discussion and debate.[3]

The 1991 White Ribbon Campaign was arguably the first time a group of men had ever begun and sustained a national protest about a feminist issue.[4] A major goal of the first White Ribbon Week was embodied in the slogan-like phrase "Breaking Men's Silence To End Men's Violence" in the WRC's inaugural publicity statement. Early WRC planning reports reinforce the impression that in December 1991 a dramatic shattering of male silence on violence against women occurred, and that for the first time men talked openly and publicly about the problem. It's true that the campaign received considerable media attention in Toronto as well as some national news coverage. Men were talking, but not the hundreds of thousands enthusiastically described in co-founders' reports written just after the first campaign.

The white ribbon did have considerable value as a symbol, especially in the early 1990s, before there were ribbons for every cause. As the campaign's main symbol, the white ribbon was designed to be instantly recognizable, cheap, and easily accessible to men everywhere. For the organizers of the first campaign, decorating public spaces with ribbons and wearing ribbons in public areas were seen as absolutely necessary to create public attention and curiosity. According to reports written after this first campaign, these strategies of accessibility and visibility were so successful that, according to early campaign literature, "men and boys in their millions were talking to each other" about the WRC and male violence.[5] Indeed, for the WRC, the visibility of the ribbon prompted curiosity and encouraged discussion about male responsibility and commitment among men.

But within the first two years of the WRC's existence, the campaign co-founders were insisting that wearing a white ribbon signified not only men's willingness but a concrete commitment to do something to help end violence against women: linking this conspicuous symbol with the promise of action. Indeed, the WRC's slogan for the 1992 campaign, "Get Involved," reinforces the connection between the white ribbon and men's involvement in responsible action. Again and again, the WRC's co-founders have stressed taking responsibility as both goal and motive.

But what specific responsibilities have men who wear white ribbons been asked to take on? Feminists felt it was essential that men participating in the WRC were prepared to do something concrete and meaningful; otherwise, wearing a white ribbon was just an empty gesture. This issue came to a head in 1991, the very first year of the campaign. Canadian feminists and profeminists were furious when former Conservative Prime Minister Brian Mulroney and many Members of Parliament wore white ribbons during the 1991 White Ribbon Campaign. For many feminists, Mulroney embodied drastic funding cuts to women's and feminist initiatives and had failed to act responsibly against male violence.[6] Critics suggested that wearing a white ribbon was a safe way for men to express liberal sentiments without having to follow through with, say, increased spending on women's programs. Even more disturbing was the prospect—raised by some feminists and profeminists—that a small minority of men might wear a white ribbon to show women they were a "safe date." That sent shudders down more than a few spines.

Very aware of criticisms that the white ribbon could be seen as an empty gesture, the WRC began, from 1992 on, explicitly defining the white ribbon not only as a symbol of male responsibility but as a commitment to take action. Each ribbon came attached to a card defining what the ribbon means and asking men to make a pledge or commitment "not to condone, commit, or remain silent about violence against women." The WRC's informational and publicity materials encouraged men to be more personally aware of violence and openly support women's antiviolence work, help fund women's work and projects, or publicly protest against male violence.

The idea that support should also be financial was heavily stressed in the first two years of the campaign. Co-founder Michael Kaufman, in a December 1992 letter to the editor of a Toronto entertainment weekly, *NOW*, argued that financial support of women's groups, programs, and shelters is fundamental to men taking responsibility and committing themselves to ending violence: "The goal of the campaign is not simply for men to wear a ribbon for a week. . . . We strongly support increased funding to women's programs and we urge elected officials to make a public commitment to support all efforts to end violence against women and to promote equality in a way that is consistent with the wearing of a white ribbon."[7]

From the beginning, the WRC had also an educational mandate. To help fulfill this, the campaign began sponsoring various events during the year to raise money to create antiviolence educational materials for men and boys. Donations from business and industry were solicited and noted on a "corporate honour [*sic*] roll." But along with a thank-you letter, the WRC encouraged donors to be involved in some way: raising or discussing the issue of male violence in the workplace, starting an in-house white ribbon campaign, or doing something public as a company. In other words, the WRC believes donors have a responsibility to take other forms of practical, and perhaps riskier, action than handing over a check.

The WRC's current website makes it clear that "White Ribbon Week" is one of the most visible and important events for the campaign, whether in Canada or in other countries. "Each year, we urge men and boys to wear a ribbon for one or two weeks, starting on November 25, the International Day for the Eradication of Violence against Women. (In Canada we wear ribbons until December 6, Canada's National Day of Remembrance and Action on Violence against Women.)"[8] This week of fundraising raises money to meet two major goals: supporting feminist antiviolence initiatives and educating men about ending violence against women. Toward the first goal, the WRC has supported local women's groups, and portions of the money raised from selling ribbons go to women's shelters. The second goal also involves helping "to help create an atmosphere and consciousness where violence against women is unacceptable in our society."[9] Thus, while financially supporting women's groups year-round is one way to help satisfy feminist demands for practical action against male violence, promoting men's awareness of male violence is an important, complementary form of action that, in the long run, plays an essential role in supporting women's antiviolence work.[10] Both kinds of action are congruent with the WRC's profeminist mandate: it's time for men to take responsibility for ending male violence.

## MEN ENDING MEN'S VIOLENCE IN THE UNITED STATES

Today, men from California are joined in a public demonstration by anti-sexist men from many states and from countries as far away as Sweden and France. Our demonstration will focus on male violence to women and to other men. Here in Los Angeles, we men have earned the title of "Rape Capital of the World" for our city. . . . Yet our action today, and the men's movement itself, demonstrate that some men are beginning to examine and reject the kinds of roles that result in such violence and isolation. (Statement at 5th National Conference on Men and Masculinity, Los Angeles, Dec. 30, 1978)

American men were not motivated by a large-scale national tragedy like the Montréal massacre to take responsibility for ending violence against women. But American profeminists have been keenly aware of the day-to-day violence permeating American society, and have long drawn relationships between this culture of violence and traditional masculine behaviors and roles. Since the 1970s, the extent—and often the passion—of American feminist antiviolence and anti-porn activism has inspired profeminists to make antiviolence activism a top priority. A key principle underlying North American profeminist antiviolence activism is that education and raising public awareness are effective means to end male violence.[11] According to the sociopolitical models on which many profeminists base their approaches, violence isn't necessarily hard-wired into men; violence can be unlearned.

### The Late 1970s: Reading, Writing, Acting against Violence

As documented in Kimmel and Mosmiller's book *Against the Tide*, American profeminists have a history of speaking out against many sources of women's oppression, including domestic violence and rape. But in the 1970s, men began initiating projects explicitly aimed at raising men's awareness of violence or helping abusive men. In 1976, a group in Champaign, Illinois, may have been one of the earliest American men's groups to form around an anti-rape theme. The "Men's Task Force against Rape and Sexism" outlined basic goals and objectives for a men's group against rape. Undertaking an intense thirty-two–hour training session, the task force issued a twenty-five–page training packet in March 1977. In 1977, the Men and Maculinity conference in St. Louis inspired one group of six men to form a study group. Members read feminist literature on rape and violence (among them, Susan Brownmiller's *Against Our Will*) and received training in crisis intervention from a local women's center. This small study group grew fairly quickly[12] into a counselling and resource service for violent and abusive men. Known as RAVEN (Rape and Violence End Now), this organization achieved a national profile and was active well into the 1980s as a counselling and educational center and resource clearinghouse.

One notable success story is the Oakland Men's Project of California, which in 1979 started community education and counselling programs to help stop male violence. Co-founded by Paul Kivel,[13] a well-published antiviolence activist and counselor, the Oakland Men's Project is still active. Also in 1979, a statewide alliance of men called the California Anti-Sexist Men's Political (CAMP) Caucus formed around profeminist and antisexist goals. While not specifically focused on violence education or prevention, the CAMP Caucus placed a high priority on men taking individual and collective actions that might help mitigate violence. The extensive list includes "tell men that you don't think rape jokes are funny"; "when approaching a woman in a deserted area, keep your hands visible, walk so that women have a clear path, and be aware that to every woman, any man is a potential rapist"; and "find out how to start a counseling program for men who batter."[14] The CAMP Caucus also composed a men's pledge to stop rape, which since the early 1980s has been adopted and acknowledged by several other men's antiviolence and anti-rape groups.[15]

### Antiviolence and the Men & Masculinity Conferences

An antiviolence or anti-rape theme has also informed a number of annual Men and Masculinity gatherings. Demonstrating against rape, assault, and other forms of violence such as back alley abortions, men took to the streets on December 30, 1978, at the 5th Annual M & M conference in Los Angeles. The following year, conference delegates were presented with a resolution against rape and violence to women. In the 1980s, M & M conferences continued to feature antiviolence issues in the program, including a 1983 workshop entitled "Why Men at a 'Take Back the Night' March?" and a keynote address in 1989 by a feminist involved with battered women's issues. In 1990, the entire conference was thematically devoted to "Ending Men's Violence: Pathways to a Gender-Just World." The keynote speakers included bell hooks—an outspoken supporter of men's involvement in feminist activism—and John Stoltenberg, the radical anti-pornography author of *Refusing to Be a Man* and, a chief organizer of the Ending Men's Violence Task Group. In the wake of the 1989 Montréal massacre, which was discussed extensively in the American profeminist press, the M & M conference in 1992 sponsored a workshop on "The White Ribbon Campaign: Mobilizing Men to Take Action," facilitated by WRC co-founders Michael Kaufman and Ron Sluser.

A fair question to ask here is whether some conference attendees were uncomfortable with the topic of male violence—inseparable as it often is from the powerfully persuasive and threatening argument that as a man, you must be part of the problem. An article by Tom Mosmiller, a keynote speaker at the 1991 Men & Masculinities conference, gives the strong impression that the 1990 conference on "Ending Men's Violence" was somewhat contentious in tone. Mosmiller writes that the 1991 conference conveyed "a remarkable atmosphere of mutual support and affirmation which had been sorely lacking at the previous [conference]."[16] While not wanting to read too much into this comment, it would not have been surprising if a conference around a topic so fraught with emotion and often subject to polarization had *not* been fractious at times. Issues like male guilt and men's accountability to feminism—not to mention the vexed question of pornography—would almost certainly have engendered some debate, unease, or anger.

Some might say that discussing male violence at conferences isn't as effective as getting the message out on the street. But as long as agreement does not break down completely, debate and discussion are valuable symbolic acts that can lay essential groundwork for more practical or concrete action. In that respect, the 1978 demonstration in Los Angeles is an apt example of profeminists combining symbolic with street-level activism. The fact that men's involvement in "Take Back the Night" was on the M & M conference agenda also shows the reverse: street activism was shaping the discussion, allowing profeminists a chance to reflect on their practices and plan more effective strategies.

## The Antipornography and Ending Men's Violence Task Groups

Some of the most dramatic profeminist antiviolence initiatives in the United States originated with two task groups under the auspices of the National Organization for Changing Men. The Ending Men's Violence (EMV) and Antipornography task groups quickly became associated with a radical antiviolence and anti-porn stance, in large part because one of NOCM's most high profile activists, John Stoltenberg, strongly sympathized with the radical feminist work against male violence represented by Andrea Dworkin and Catharine MacKinnon.

Both task forces were created in the mid-1980s, shortly after NOCM was formed. The main inspiration for the antipornography group appears to have been a 1983 workshop conducted by Stoltenberg and Bob Brannon at the M & M conference. As Stoltenberg reported to the NOCM's co-chair in May 1984, "The great interest expressed in that workshop I took to be a measure of potential interest . . . around the issue of pornography and antisexist men's relation to it (see n. 17)." Stoltenberg worked with Brannon and Michael Kimmel to chart the future of the group, which quickly achieved Stoltenberg's initial objectives of forming a New York–based men's group for anti-pornography activism as well as starting a newsletter. The group, Men against Pornography, came together after taking a "tour" of Times Square conducted by Women against Pornography.

In December 1983, Stoltenberg was invited to write in support of the MacKinnon-Dworkin ordinance against pornography being considered at that point by the Minneapolis City Council; his letter was subsequently included in the record of testimony at the hearings. Stoltenberg also reported he had almost a dozen speaking or media engagements in 1983 and early 1984 around the issue of pornography, and in all cases he identified himself as chair of the Antipornography Task Group of NOCM.[17] Clearly, Stoltenberg not only identified closely with this issue but was in many respects the driving force behind NOCM's antipornography efforts. In the first newsletter of the Antipornography Task Group, Stoltenberg wrote: "I feel very heartened about the existence of this task group. I can envision it becoming a form [sic] in which men's voices on the issue of pornography can be raised, voices that are grief-stricken, voices that feel called to speak out against pornographers' manipulation and corruption of sexual feelings. . . ."[18]

Not surprisingly, given his strong adherence to the radical anti-porn feminism represented by the MacKinnon-Dworkin ordinance, Stoltenberg is easily located on the radical profeminist end of the broad men's movement spectrum. This radical profeminist stance calls not only for dismantling patriarchy but deconstructing all notions of masculine identity and behavior that rely on objectifying women. As men's movement historian Kenneth Clatterbaugh notes, the earlier radical profeminist writers of the 1970s tended to feel "tormented" with "guilt and distrust of self"; in their writings, they targeted men as the enemy and defined masculinity as an incomplete, "crippled" state.[19] Though some profeminists in the 1980s and 1990s would return to this theme, Stoltenberg's writing doesn't reveal quite that degree of self-loathing. He doesn't seek to remove manhood from sexuality, but rather wants to disentangle manhood from an aggressive, patriarchal, oppressive notion of sexuality—particularly as represented by the consumption of porn. Nonetheless, the radical profeminist notion that men must dismantle oppressive masculinities is a hard sell for most people.

Stoltenberg's influence on NOCM in the 1980s was considerable: as well as forming the Antipornography Task Group, he helped organize "Brother-Storm" in 1985, a "National Men's Call to Action to End Men's Violence against Women." According to a Brother–Storm brochure, men across the

United States were invited to share three minutes of silence at a particular time and day, organize rallies, or contribute to a local rape crisis center. The list of men's groups endorsing Brother-Storm shows that antiviolence and anti-rape issues were being taken up by profeminists across the country.[20] Brother-Storm also took the form of a march at the 10th Men & Masculinity conference. According to Clatterbaugh, Stoltenberg spoke at this demonstration, effectively calling on profeminist men to spend less time on "helpless self-hate and self-blame" or "learning to cry," and more time on practical political action, particularly against men's violence. One commentator hoped that Stoltenberg's talk was signaling a shift within NOCM toward "a greater commitment to political activism in the men's movement."[21]

A year later, Brother-Storm had become BrotherPeace, no longer merely a national event but an "International Day of Actions to End Men's Violence" organized by Stoltenberg and the NOCM Ending Men's Violence Task Group. At about this time, BrotherPeace adopted the slogan "Men Breaking Silence to End Men's Violence," used later by the White Ribbon Campaign. An August 1987 open letter from Stoltenberg (see n. 8) reported that the 1986 event "brought together groups of men in nearly forty cities across North America and in Europe" and that "[t]he momentum of BrotherPeace is growing." Even more important than that, however, was "a simple and astonishing thing: *Our taking a stand created hope for people.* . . . it was as if they had been waiting all their lives to hear the message of BrotherPeace [author's emphasis]."

The references to hope, the hint at salvation, and even the name BrotherPeace convey evangelistic undertones. Rather like the White Ribbon Campaign, a strong commitment to an intensely emotional issue motivated men to unite. For a while, this sense of unity held firm as a series of annual BrotherPeace protests took place throughout the late 1980s and early 1990s. Campus-based BrotherPeace protests were still being held as recently as 1997, possibly even later. The BrotherPeace name also currently lives on through the activities and resources offered by the Twin Cities BrotherPeace chapter, a "men's social action group" formed in 1988, "dedicated to ending the violence of men against women."[22]

In its heyday, BrotherPeace was a high profile event but only one of many projects undertaken by the Ending Men's Violence Task Group. Another initiative, the task group's *Ending Men's Violence Network Newsletter*, was first published in 1984. Until the mid-1990s, this newsletter regularly offered between twelve and twenty pages per issue of articles, speeches, reports, fact sheets, and resources related to the problem of men's violence against women and efforts to end it. Also part of the EMV's mandate was outreach to feminist groups and public acknowledgement of feminist work. Notably, the EMV's first BrotherPeace Award in 1990 was presented to Mary Koss (see chapter 6) for "her outstanding academic contributions to anti-rape activism." The *Ending Men's Violence Newsletter* described Koss's work as a "shining example of academic work that has been an indispensable tool for activists."[23]

## ENDING MEN'S VIOLENCE: SHOULD MEN FEEL GUILTY?

However, as had been the case in the late 1970s and early 1980s, tensions were constantly arising between men who felt that radical political action against sexism was top priority, and men who felt that it was more important to understand their own emotional lives and make efforts to reduce the hazards of being male. Simply put, the conflicts between antisexist men and the liberationists in the 1970s, then in turn the men's rights advocates of the 1980s, had never been resolved. One way in which these tensions played out was a difference in views about pornography—a situation similar to that within the women's movement about the value of anti-porn legislation. Clatterbaugh describes how a 1985 forum about pornography published in the profeminist magazine *Changing Men* was divided along radical and liberal lines: radicals arguing that porn is so inimical to women's freedom that it can't be conceived as free speech, and liberals countering that any censorship, even of porn, is "too blunt and dangerous an instrument."[24] Most radical of all, though, was an argument that no existing systems under patriarchy—neither courts nor laws nor ordinances—were sufficient to protect women. According to Clatterbaugh, such "assertions, from deep within radical feminism itself, were unavailable to liberalism, given its trust in the political and legal system."[25] If it did nothing else, this forum helped articulate the schism between radical antisexists and liberal profeminists. It does not appear likely that these radically opposing views were ever satisfactorily mediated.

Some radical profeminists doing antiviolence work even questioned whether men were capable of responding responsibly to the problem of male violence. In its first year, Canada's White Ribbon Campaign confidently asserted that while men have been defined as the problem, men could also be part of the solution. But the 1989 Montréal massacre had also affected anti-male–violence profeminists in the United States, prompting some writers to ask tough questions about all men's tendency toward violence and whether even well-intentioned men were really prepared to take meaningful action. In 1990, a year before the WRC was formed, EMV activist Russ Ervin Funk warned that Marc Lépine, the man who had killed the fourteen women in Montréal, was no madman: "rather than being the 'oddball' he was described to be, he was actually very 'average.' " In sympathy with what many Canadian feminists were asserting about the massacre, Funk effectively argued that all men are capable of violence and none can defend a self-righteous attitude:

Oh yes, the men did indeed respond to the concerns . . . of wimyn [*sic*] were raising. The men responded with defensiveness; with put downs and sarcasm; with attempts to shut the wimyn up, to talk over and past the wimyn; with harassment (verbal, physical and sexual) and threats; with vandalism and other forms of violence. . . . Marc Lépine's actions were nothing more than a logical extension—albeit an extreme extension, but an extension nonetheless, of the attitudes, beliefs, and yes the behavior that the men were representing all over that campus . . . the "good" men, the average men, the "normal" men. . . . [26]

Another radical response to the Montréal massacre was put forward by profeminist writer Paul B. Seidman in the magazine *Changing Men*. Reflecting the views of Andrea Dworkin, whom he quotes, as well as Marilyn French, he reminded readers that a long and systematic war against women has been waged by men. The fourteen dead women were just the latest casualties. Seidman's most powerful argument—again, echoing what many Canadian feminists were claiming—is that there was nothing extraordinary about Lépine; he was just being a good soldier:

a normal woman-hater, [he] was only unusual in that he was resourceful. In this respect he mimicked the tactics of his German brothers 50 years ago: get your enemies into a room and then kill them all at once. This event signals a change in men's approach to dealing with the woman problem. What is now acceptable, in the sense that it is socially invisible as an act of warfare against women, is mass extermination.[27]

In their slightly different ways, both Seidman and Funk take the radical (and some would say essentialist) positions that all men are prone to misogyny and violence. The argument that men are at war against women is a very difficult one for most men and even many women to swallow. At best, this argument is useful for men and women who are already feminist sympathizers; it forces them (or us) to re-view patriarchy in an appropriately ugly light and to recognize the often hidden patterns of domination that can shape even the most seemingly innocent transactions between women and men. At worst, however, the metaphor of gender warfare puts pressure on thoughtful men to demonize themselves. As John Rowan and Victor Seidler have argued, self-demonizing can induce a paralyzing guilt, which from the viewpoint of motivating men to take action seems to be a singularly unproductive strategy. As a way of conveying profeminist principles to the public, the gender wars metaphor is worse than useless, perpetuating all sorts of unfortunate gender stereotypes. Asserting that women are victims from Venus and men are monsters from Mars is hardly a productive starting point for ending violence, whether against women or against other men.

Having said that, it's only fair to add that Seidman's main suggestion is a practical one: profeminists must encourage—if not insist—that the media provide a forum for feminist discussion of violence against women. Funk, on the other hand, challenges profeminist men, the "good" guys, to look within themselves and be honest about their own inherent capability for violence:

> For all men who consider ourselves allies to wimyn [*sic*]—allies to feminists; for all men who are supportive of the revolution, the question is not how we are different from men like Marc Lépine. The true question, the question with importance—The questions we need to be asking ourselves—and each other—is [*sic*] how are we similar to Marc Lépine? . . . I must question—I must examine: how different am I truly, than Marc Lépine? . . . We were both raised to be violent, to be oppressive, and to direct that violence and oppression to wimyn and children. He did it by shooting wimyn, I have done it and continue to be sexist through a host of other and less frequently defined "violent" ways. . . . As painful and difficult and as much as I do not want to compare myself to Marc Lépine, I must—if I am truly serious about working to end men's violence, I must identify, acknowledge, and expose those similarities.[28]

This passage has been quoted at length to show how often one theme surfaces—"I and all men are inherently violent." This can't have been an easy passage to write, nor does its intensity encourage the average reader to feel that men can do profeminist work without undergoing a thorough psychological scouring.

Though it's probably fair to say that as a whole, the EMV was too radical in its views to capture a broad public following, its efforts helped raise awareness within academic and feminist activist circles about what American men can do to help end male violence. The *EMV Newsletter* is no longer published, but the "EMV–Net"—a collection of resources and activist groups—still exists and operates under the auspices of NOMAS. The EMV has clearly had a significant influence on profeminists within and beyond NOMAS: for example, there is no doubt the EMV inspired the strategies of other profeminist projects, notably the White Ribbon Campaign.

## AUSTRALIAN MEN AGAINST VIOLENCE: MARCHES, WHITE RIBBONS, AND WINE

Organized men's movements started later in Australia than in the United States or Britain, with no concerted campaign for a national men's organization and no national conferences throughout the 1970s and early 1980s. But by the early 1990s, the Australian men's movement—every bit as diverse as that in North America—was energetically sponsoring a range of events and projects. The White Ribbon Campaign was imported, but most events generated by the Australian men's movement reflected that country's distinct character. These ranged from the relatively mainstream, like the annual Sydney Men's Festival and a wine bottle labeling event, to more radical efforts, like men's participation in women's anti-violence marches and the decade-long life of the strongly profeminist men's magazine *XY*—one of the world's very few international profeminist publications, along with *Achilles Heel* and *Changing Men*. As in North America, Australian men interested in change were often more comfortable with a liberationist stance—understanding how masculinity and men's lives can be reconfigured. Fewer men adhered to an activist profeminism. But given the strong and often radical stance Australian feminists have traditionally taken on redressing violence against women, it's not surprising that a great deal of Australian profeminist energy would be channeled into educating men about this issue.

### Men against Sexual Assault

It proved to be no easier for Australian profeminists than for their North American counterparts to sustain a national profeminist effort against men's violence. However, Men against Sexual Assault, or MASA, came closest to this goal. MASA is rooted in the late 1970s, when at least one antisexist group had formed and established men's work against male violence to women as a significant part of a large and diverse men's antisexist agenda. By 1985, this group—Men against Sexism (MAS)—had roughly 200 members and/or sympathizers. Based in Melbourne, MAS had established the Australasian Men's Network, which was sponsoring monthly forums on a number of gender- and feminist-related subjects, and was doing some creative outreach work, such as distributing stickers on ANZAC Day[29] and protesting sexist advertising.

In the spirit that antisexist reform is inseparable from a larger agenda of social transformation, MAS also cultivated a close relationship with the political left. One of MAS's organizers, Ian Bell, who spoke about men's responses to gender issues at the Broad Left Conference in 1986, argued that though men on the left "have learnt new rhetoric and (generally) changed our world view to incorporate feminist analysis we haven't significantly changed our behavior." In his notes for this talk, Bell listed a number of causes men on the left had "failed to support," such as working against pornography, rape, and domestic violence.[30] At the same time, Bell's talk emphasized that men need to understand the obstacles and hazards posed by dominant masculinity and to rethink what it means to be a man.

Working within this social context, a significant number of MAS activities appear to have focused on violence against women. By the mid-1980s, these projects included but weren't limited to domestic violence, the problem of sex tours in the Phillipines, men's sexuality and pornography, and rape culture.[31] This focus on male violence became even sharper in

1989–1990, when MAS was superceded by a new profeminist group, Men against Sexual Assault (MASA; also see chapter 4). According to brochures and ephemera, this new group retained some of MAS's members but adopted the three major principles of the U.S.-based National Organization for Men against Sexism: to be pro-feminist, gay-affirmative, and male-positive. MASA was prepared to retain its predecessor's emphasis on understanding and resisting hegemonic masculinity, and strongly rejected the extreme radical stance of "condemn[ing] ourselves and other men." However, there is no doubt MASA's primary goal as a group was to "work towards the elimination of patriarchy and its attendant horrors, specifically sexual assault." For MASA, "taking the lead of women" was also a primary goal, part and parcel of its concept of what it meant to be profeminist.

MASA members were optimistic that they would be able to inspire men on a national level, and for several years their efforts were fruitful. Among the activities and projects MASA undertook in 1992 was organizing a national gathering of MASA groups: "a gigantic step towards the building of MASA into a thriving, active and enduring organization throughout the nation." In truth, the gathering was attended by only about eighteen men and two feminist monitors. Reporting about this gathering, MASA's newsletter emphasized that this small number still represented five major cities whose different profeminist groups had formed "quite independently of each other over the past 2–3 years."[32] The optimistic tone of this report suggests that MASA enjoyed or wished to convey a positive self-identity and a conviction that men could unite as profeminists. It's interesting that at a time when NOMAS was experiencing crises (see chapter 8), Australian profeminist and men's groups were finding new energy and hope. Indeed, also in 1992, MASA was engaged in the following varied activities:

- planning a second men's national gathering for 1993[33]
- encouraging MASA chapters to form in each Australian state
- investigating whether to establish a national day to remember victims of violence (more on this below)
- strategizing men's participation in a National Day of Action against violence to women (the plan was for men to learn to listen to women by observing a minute of silence before the marches).

## "March of the Caring Men"

September 1, 1990, "witnessed Melbourne's first ever march against rape and sexual violence by men,"[34] an event organized by the revivified core group of profeminists which had given birth to MASA the previous year. Like the BrotherPeace protests in the United States, Australian men's marches against sexual assault were the most highly visible forms of profeminist activism besides their white ribbon campaigns. The "Men Can Stop Rape" march received considerable local news coverage, and according to at least two newspaper articles, no fewer than 300 and possibly up to 400 men participated.[35] Quoted in the Melbourne newspaper *The Age*, Bob Pease—a MASA co-founder and march organizer—said he felt very optimistic about the high turnout. Pease hoped it could mean men were more willing to be progressive about issues like violence, or at least, that men might be starting to see the benefits of recognizing and dismantling macho forms of masculinity.[36] Rather than being "paralysed . . . by guilt and passivity," profeminist men were, according to Pease, better off "shar[ing] the vision of a feminism that aims to eliminate gender hierarchy" by engaging in positive individual and collective action.

After this fairly encouraging start, indications are that the success level became more difficult to sustain. MASA organized two more "Men Can Stop Rape" marches in Melbourne in 1991 and 1992, but it's unclear how many men attended. One newspaper article implies that the second march drew up to 500 men and the third, in 1992, attracted a disappointing 200. Another source puts the number of men in 1991 at no more than 200. Either way, fewer men came back a second or third time.

Part of the reason for this decline in participation may be related to the fact that these Men Can Stop Rape marches attracted lively criticism. Indeed, given that country's history of tense gender relations, the organizers almost should have expected to generate controversy. Some radical feminists expressed distrust that men, who in their analysis were inherently prone to rape, apparently were trying to subvert that analysis. Reflecting much later on this event, Pease felt that profeminist men at least should be able to understand, if not necessarily agree with, feminist women's reasoning:

> while that [criticism] was on one level hurtful and on another level not a particularly wise intervention . . . I also acknowledge too that some women's experience of men has been of incredible abuse and that they have very few if any positive experiences of men. So I also think that when some women express hostility that I kind of take as a given that that is grounded in some sort of lived experience of men in their own lives . . . [37]

Indeed, the Women's Research Officer for LaTrobe University admitted in an article that women "are so used to seeing men as the enemy that we are not really sure about what to do with them as allies." While guardedly positive about the 1990 Men Can Stop Rape march, she nonetheless raised the often asked question of whether such activism is "just another example of men trying to be in control." Like the early 1990s critics who wondered whether Canada's White Ribbon Campaign was just thinly disguised chivalry—men charging in like white knights to rescue helpless women—this writer wondered too whether such men's marches were a patronizing example of "the boys . . . still looking after us." As well, given that men have historically had much greater access to information sources and distribution than women, feminist sceptics can reasonably ask whether an issue like sexual violence attracts more public notice because men "give it a sense of worth—it becomes validated merely because men choose to recognise [*sic*] it."[38]

Tomlins' article also inquired how useful it was for men to "focus on 'the streets,' " implying that profeminist men are limited by a belief that "the half-crazed, sexually obsessed pervert" poses the greatest risk for women. It might have been better, Tomlins suggests, for these well-intentioned men to adopt a strategy for change that more directly challenges deeply rooted attitudes and addresses "your average, everyday, working guy; husband, father, brother, uncle, grandfather who abuses the women to whom he is closest because he has the power to do so."

This is a valid argument, but it ignores the fact that groups like MASA were adopting several different awareness and education strategies in an attempt to focus attention on male violence to women. The "Men Can Stop Rape" march, albeit conspicuous and well-publicized, was only one of several projects implemented over a period of years, a fact not mentioned in Tomlin's article. Another problem with this criticism is that while it questions the effectiveness of men hitting the streets, it doesn't make the same point about women's street marches, such as the annual Reclaim the Night. Marches and street protests have been a traditional Second Wave strategy for raising public awareness about feminist issues. Criticizing profeminist men for adopting a feminist strategy is warranted only if there are legitimate concerns about how men exercise power and use resources, *and*, I argue, only if the men are given the opportunity to engage in dialogue with feminists about these power concerns.

But if I had been a profeminist involved in those marches, I might have found it most hurtful to be criticized for believing that violence to women impinges on men who have mothers, sisters, daughters, and female co-workers—in other words, basically all men. Tomlins' article suggests that some Melbourne feminists found this motive not only traditional but patriarchal: "Once again there is a feeling that traditional structures, in this case the family, are being invoked and lauded—a man must look after his wife/mother/sister etc. Inherent in this however, is the historical notion of ownership and possession, the desire of men to protect what's theirs."[39] I cannot imagine such a criticism being leveled at women who march to protect other women. But the main assumption underlying this criticism again concerns male power and men's perceived collusion with patriarchy. Given that men have historically controlled women's lives, and in many respects and locations still do, then even an apparently positive and innocent motive like the desire to protect female loved ones will be difficult for some feminists to disentangle from a more sinister objective. These concerns are unfortunate but by no means unusual or isolated; as chapter 4 discussed, very similar comments have been made about profeminist initiatives worldwide in an ongoing struggle to articulate and strategize men's roles in feminism.

Perhaps not surprisingly, a number of criticisms about the "Men Can Stop Rape" marches came from other men.[40] These criticisms tend to fall into two general and almost completely opposite categories: profeminists are overreacting and guilting men out, or profeminists are not doing enough. Critics in the first category insist that rape and sexual assault statistics are exaggerated and that rape is "a disgusting pursuit of sexual gratification by a psychopathic . . . few"; only "extremists" who have a "sour obsession with 'patriarchy' " would claim that rape is a tool of power potentially available to all men.[41] The implication is that profeminists are a puritannical breed doing their best to make all men feel guilty, and intelligent people should dismiss such marginal tactics and arguments. But the other, opposite argument condemns men in general for not taking enough of an antiviolence stance. One article noted how defensive men can become when asked to "think about all the sexual crimes they have committed": "this is what seems to stop many men from taking that first step and deciding to take a stand against rape. They resent the *mea culpa* of collective responsibility. Instead, they feel personally accused—and personally outraged."[42] Quoted in this article, MASA spokesman Stephen Foley said that MASA's challenge was to educate men to see sexual assault as a collective, societal problem, not as an individual crime committed by a particular man. But at least one other male critic was unsure about whether a march against rape would effectively drive home the notion that "while all men may not be rapists, all rapists are men." Jonathan Green (see n. 40) wrote that the mood of the 1991 "Men Can Stop Rape" march was "closer to self-congratulation; 200 little cones of male silence warmed by the inner glow of righteousness." Perhaps, he implies, many men would see the fact they showed up on a Saturday morning as a good enough gesture. While a very similar concern came to the foreground during the White Ribbon Campaign in Canada, when some wondered whether wearing a white ribbon was an empty gesture, Green gave his criticism a purely Australian context: the cartoon accompanying the article shows three men in a pub. One says to the other—"Your shout!" The second yells, "Men can stop rape!" The third looks shocked. In Australia, "Your shout" means—"Your turn to buy the next round." Shouting is a male social ritual; if you leave the pub before everyone has "shouted," your masculinity is in question.

This cartoon says volumes about trying to be profeminist in a culture in which masculinity is so heavily bound up with macho display. While not trying to provide undecided men with excuses to opt out, it's a difficult challenge in this macho social context for most men to give even lip service to ending rape and fighting sexism, let alone take action. The fact that groups like MASA have made even a small imprint on Australia's sociopolitical landscape represents a great deal of determination and commitment.

### MASA's White Ribbon Campaign

MASA's plans to establish a national day of remembrance for victims of male violence came to fruition in 1993 with the first of several national white ribbon campaigns. This was Bob Pease's initiative; he had heard about the Canadian campaign and mentioned it as a possibility at the 1992 MASA national gathering. That December, the campaign had limited runs in Melbourne and in Canberra, the national capital. There, MASA men distributed 3,000 white ribbons in stores, movie theaters, offices, and outdoor stalls from December 1 through 6.[43]

However, about half-way through this campaign, an editorial in the *Canberra Times* noted the MASA men's "failure . . . to draw a crowd." One significant problem was that MASA's choice of December 1 to launch the campaign clashed with International AIDS Day, which according to Bob Pease "was a real stumbling block for us."[44] The editorial also speculated that one reason for this failure was the fact that the WRC's catalyst—the murder of fourteen women at a Montréal university half a world away—"was an import, virtually unknown here."[45] This comment says volumes about motive in any profeminist project. The WRC in Canada could count on the fact that most Canadian men were horrifed by the Montréal massacre and that some would channel their horror and outrage into positive action.[46]

Nonetheless, MASA felt that a White Ribbon Campaign could work in Australia, and December 1993 saw a much more highly publicized campaign taking place in several cities. The Brisbane chapter of MASA launched a week-long series on events from December 6 through 11 featuring a raft of speakers, a community theater presentation; a seminar on men, violence, and the media, and a planned visit to the Queensland State Parliament where ribbons were to be distributed to members of the legislative assembly (MLAs). Supporters included the Lord Mayor of Brisbane along with several other politicians and a number of academics and activists.[47] Pease, who also helped organize the Melbourne MASA group's White Ribbon Campaign, told a local newspaper that this year's WRC hoped to sell 10,000 ribbons. In the spirit of the Canadian campaign, a man did not have to be a card-carrying profeminist activist to wear a white ribbon: "The only thing you need, to be able to wear a white ribbon, is to be opposed to violence against women."[48]

The Melbourne and Brisbane campaigns were careful to forefront Australian research on violence against women in their fact sheets and to define the problem as local and national, not an import. The first page of a 1992 WRC information sheet states, among other facts, that 62 percent of women surveyed in an Adelaide study had been raped (citing the *Australian Journal of Sex, Marriage and Community* as the source); and also that out of 2,334 complaints handled by the Anti-Discrimination Board and the Equal Opportunity Tribunal, 34 percent were sexual harassment cases.

Australian public figures were also enlisted to support the campaign. In December 1993, the Melbourne WRC invited Democrat Sid Spindler, Senator for the state of Victoria, to speak at the campaign launch. Spindler publicly called on Australian men to wear white ribbons "as a sign of their opposition to violence against women." Given the long history of male violence and its inseparability from the tradition of "mateship" in Australia, it's significant that Spindler insisted so strongly that men's violence against women is no longer an acceptable aspect of Australian society:

> Recent statistics illustrate that 25 per cent of all Australians believe that it is okay for a man to bash his wife under certain circumstances. This is a disturbing reality which the White Ribbon Campaign goes some way to addressing. . . . I encourage all Australian men to take responsibility for violence against women and get behind this campaign of community education and action.[49]

Fact sheets for the 1993 WRC in Brisbane also tried to show the relevance of the white ribbon campaign for Australian men by listing Australian statistics and quoting several Queensland public figures. Among the notables urging men to support the campaign were the Minister for Family Services and Aboriginal and Islander Affairs, a Supreme Court judge, and the Lord Mayor of Brisbane. Even so, the publicity materials for the Australian WRC's first two years still bear the stamp: imported. Beginning with the story of the Montréal massacre and defining this event as the campaign's catalyst, the materials closely resemble their Canadian sources, right down to the formatting, some of the artwork, and the simple, white-on-black white ribbon logo.

Starting in 1994, the Australian WRC went national, with campaigns in several major cities, and began to develop its own unique character. The most significant difference from 1993 was moving White Ribbon Week back four months so that it took place in early September. The WRC also connected itself with the International Year of the Family, and did not forefront the Montréal massacre. As Pease later stated, no Australian symbol existed that was able to represent the horror of violence against women as powerfully as the December 6 massacre, but that event was too far removed from most Australians' experience. So "we decided to use more issues focused around our local context." Indeed, the fact sheets for the

1994 WRC define the problem of male violence in strictly Australian terms, quote local public figures, and even feature some artwork that is clearly homegrown.

Australia's White Ribbon Campaign lasted for several years and enjoyed some success in raising awareness of men's violence against women: a notable accomplishment in a country where "the physically and sexually violent history of the early . . . colonies"[50] has been invoked to justify and sanction antiwoman behavior. But the state of MASA today is uncertain; all but one chapter has folded since the mid-1990s. Only the Melbourne group continues to meet and stay involved in profeminist projects, and these—like an educational package the group was working on in 1999—tend to be relatively low profile efforts. Pease still coordinates the Melbourne meetings, and also continues to write and publish profeminist books as well as teach courses in men's issues and gender relations. Other MASA men are turning their efforts now toward integrating, in a fairly low profile manner, profeminist principles and practices into their professional lives. Except for their continuing willingness to support the women's Reclaim the Night events each year, MASA men no longer march.

## BRITISH WORK AGAINST VIOLENCE TO WOMEN: AN "EVERYMAN" APPROACH

Partly because of a history of political splits and occasional misunderstandings when trying to get involved in feminist projects, British men wanting to end sexism have adopted a somewhat less "political" stance than their North American or Australian counterparts, who tend to rely on public campaigns and education to teach men about the consequences of violence against women. In the view of men involved with *Achilles Heel* and doing other radical men's work, a first priority is to improve relationships among men and change the individual behaviors engendering violence. British men against sexism believe violent men need to be seen and treated as individuals, not merely as products of a patriarchal system.[51] Thus therapy and co-counseling, often provided through small, supportive centers, are important tools for British men working to end violence. Often equally vital is the principle that men and women can, up to a point, work together to end violence.

A notable example of these principles is the Ahimsa[52] Centre (formerly The Everyman Centre) in Plymouth. Established in 1989, the center retains some female staff and acknowledges accountability to feminist principles and women in treating male violence. In practical terms, this means the center provides a reciprocal women's service for partners of men referred to the center's program, delivered jointly with staff from the Plymouth Women's Refuge. An essay by center director Calvin Bell explains why it is so important to remain accountable to the female partners of violent men:

> We recognize that the very offer of a service to her partner is likely to be the most significant factor in a woman's decision to stay in a violent relationship or to return when she might have otherwise stayed away. . . . Apart from providing information about legal and support services, regular contact with partners also enables us to gauge the man's minimisation, assess risk, emphasise that the man's violence is entirely his responsibility (many of the women have been convinced that they are wholly or partly to blame) and dispel any expectations she may have about the prospects of him changing being rapid or guaranteed. It also allows a woman to verify her partner's attendance and his level of commitment to the programme.[53]

As well as this service to female partners, Ahimsa puts male clients through a rigorous core program. According to Ahimsa's website, referred men first undergo comprehensive screening, including "safety planning sessions" to determine how dangerous they are, before being allowed to explore the underlying factors grounding their violent behavior. Ahimsa stresses that "men's violence to women is an abuse of power . . . an exertion of control." Clients then work with an individual counsellor, followed by group therapy. After satisfactorily completing this core program, clients are "invited" to join "an open weekly support group." Some clients volunteer for training as co-counselors.

One member of the counseling staff at Ahimsa, Paul Wolf-Light, is also part of the *Achilles Heel* editorial collective. When I talked with him, he revealed he is uncomfortable with a tendency for profeminist men to talk about themselves disparagingly in relation to women. Wolf-Light believes it is essential for men to come to terms with gender equality by respecting their own experiences rather than relying too heavily on feminist thought. When undergoing therapy, men are indeed exposing aspects of themselves that are uncertain and less strong than the gender role norm dictates; in the sense that men are dehumanized in many ways, male privilege doesn't necessarily grant power. Wolf-Light maintains that faced with what they perceive as women's growing power—with physical power becoming less relevant in the context of new economies—some men project their own fears in the form of violence.

Yet Wolf-Light acknowledges that men aren't oppressed in the same ways as many women. Women are oppressed by "institutions that encourage men to oppress women," experiencing a double layer of control. While feminism alone shouldn't be men's only guiding principle, it is "part of a much bigger frame of egalitarian change," part of the "general . . . awareness taking place" about social transformation.[54]

Wolf-Light's strong interest in relations among men, power, and social change ties in with Ahimsa's practice of combining the treatment of individual behaviors with involvement in the larger community. The center's activities range from participating in domestic violence forums to endorsing more political events like International Women's Week.[55] As director, Bell has published numerous articles, and Center researchers have provided educational and training packages for a variety of institutions: notably the United Nations European Institute of Crime Prevention and Control in 1998. Overall, the Center's program is considered unique and effective enough to have been the subject of several British TV documentaries and other media coverage.[56]

It's possible to debate whether profeminists should adopt a more overtly political stance—taking their arguments against male violence loudly and proudly to the streets and schools—or whether it's just as effective to do antiviolence work more quietly, putting individuals before groups. The efforts and projects outlined in this chapter illustrate that profeminists can remain open and transparent to feminist concerns while still designing a variety of culturally specific projects "by men, for men" to help end men's violence against women. But it's also clear how difficult it can be for profeminist work to sustain its momentum. Like their feminist counterparts, profeminist groups have faced not only external obstacles and criticisms, but internal political crises: some so acute that a group's very existence is jeopardized.

## NOTES

"Breaking Men's Silence to End Men's Violence" was the title of the White Ribbon Campaign's press statement for its inaugural White Ribbon Week, December 1–6, 1991.

1. Editorial (1991, December 6), p. A28.

2. The White Ribbon Campaign's inaugural press statement, "Breaking Men's Silence to End Men's Violence: December 1–6, 1991," was released in November 1991.

3. Chris Watson (1998, June 1). (The WRC homepage may no longer have this article archived.)

4. The claim that the White Ribbon Campaign was the first national men's antiviolence protest is cited in two Toronto-based articles: Susan Cole (1991, December 5–11), pp. 14, 17 and an editorial (1991, December 6), p. A28).

5. I am grateful to White Ribbon Campaign co-founders Michael Kaufman, Jack Layton, Ron Sluser, and other WRC staff and volunteers for granting me permission to look through and use materials from campaign minutes and internal reports.

6. University of Toronto *Varsity* newspaper writer Mary Boite (1992, December 3) wrote this scathing critique of former Prime Minister Brian Mulroney's endorsement of the White Ribbon Campaign:

"On December 6 of last year [1991], Prime Minister Brian Mulroney and his cabinet ministers suddenly broke out in a flurry of white ribbons, announcing to the world (including Canadian women) that they were opposed to violence against women. This gesture, understandably, caused some confusion. . . . Obviously, if Mulroney is against it, violence must not include: poverty caused and exacerbated by an unfair taxation system, the GST, unemployment due to the [Free Trade Agreement] . . . or cuts in transfer payments to provinces leading to cutbacks in social programs and benefits. . . . These acts must not constitute violence against women in Brian Mulroney's view." (p. 5, 7)

7. Michael Kaufman (1992, December 3–9).
8. The White Ribbon Campaign's home page is <http://www.whiteribbon.ca>.
9. White Ribbon Campaign (1993). Quote is from p. 2.
10. The White Ribbon Campaign website (see n.8) provides information about educational materials the campaign has produced over the past several years. Among other things, the site allows visitors to link to a gender and violence awareness package designed for high schools.
11. Not all antiviolence and antisexist men agree that public awareness and group education are the best tools for helping men "unlearn" violent behavior. For example, the Ahimsa Centre in Devon, UK, believes that an important first step is to address individual behaviors and psychological influences. Reinforcing the view that educational initiatives based on wholly sociopolitical models can't be effective on their own is Chris Bullock (2000), who argues that "what is missing from feminist sociopolitical theory is attention to the inner life of the batterer. . . . The inadequacy of socialization theory by itself . . . should lead us to pay attention to inner life, however contested that term has become. . . ." (p. 50).
12. According to a 1983 information-sheet about Rape and Violence End Now (RAVEN), by September 1978 approximately 400 men had come to RAVEN. This service offered men an initial "intake" session, individual or group counseling, and the "pairing" of new men with "those who have been with us a while." Its reputation—and also perhaps the depth of untapped need—was apparent by the fact that in 1979, courts in the St. Louis area began referring male offenders to RAVEN. "Who is RAVEN?" (1983).
13. One of the most recent activities of the Oakland Men's Project was the development of "Making the Peace: A 15-Session Violence Prevention Program for Young People," by Allan Creighton and Paul Kivel (1998), which was selected by the Kentucky Domestic Violence Association as a school pilot project in 1998. Kivel, an educator and activist, has written a number of books focused on educating boys and men about male violence.
14. Tim Wernette, Craig Scherfenberg, Tom Mosmiller, Bryan Coleman, Alan Acacia (1980), pp. 7–8.
15. While the California Anti-Sexist Men's Political Caucus no longer exists as such, its original statement of men against rape still inspires a variety of organizations. Students Concerned About Rape Education (SCARED) at Rensselaer Polytechnic Institute; the Minnesota Center Against Violence and Abuse; the California Coalition Against Sexual Assault; and the Oklahoma Coalition against Domestic Violence and Sexual Assault all refer to "the men's pledge" and credit the CAMP Caucus for its creation.
16. From a draft of an article by Tom Mosmiller (1992).
17. John Stoltenberg wrote to Don Long, Co-Chair of the National Organization for Changing Men (May 3, 1984), 2 pp. In August 1987, Stoltenberg wrote again

to NOCM's executive to report the success of the 1986 BrotherPeace Event. Both in the Changing Men Collection, Michigan State University Library.

18. From John Stoltenberg (1984, May).

19. Kenneth Clatterbaugh (1997), p. 50.

20. Men's groups endorsing "Brother-Storm" included RAVEN (Rape and Violence Stop Now) of St. Louis, Men Stopping Rape of Madison, Men against Rape of Seattle, and of course the group Stoltenberg, Brannon, and Kimmel helped form: Men Against Pornography of New York. Men Stopping Rape, founded in 1983, was still active as of 2001; its mandate is to unite men at the University of Wisconsin-Madison with men in the Madison community to talk with men about rape and sexual violence, network with local domestic violence organizations, and sponsor workshops. Their homepage is <http://www.men-stopping-rape/org>.

21. Clatterbaugh (1997) includes more of Stoltenberg's talk as well as reactions from NOCM members, pp. 53–54.

22. The BrotherPeace Twin Cities Chapter homepage is <http://freenet.msp.mn.us/org/bptc>.

23. First Annual BrotherPeace Award! (1990), 9.

24. From an article in the *Changing Men* Forum, 1985. Quoted in Clatterbaugh (1997), p. 55.

25. Clatterbaugh (1997), p. 55.

26. Russ Ervin Funk (1990), pp. 8–9.

27. Paul B. Seidman (1991, winter/spring), p. 11.

28. Funk (1990), pp. 8–9.

29. ANZAC was the name given to the Australian and New Zealand Army Corp soldiers who landed at Gallipoli on April 25, 1915. Equivalent to Memorial Day in the United States and Remembrance Day in Canada (both on November 11), ANZAC Day is celebrated annually on April 25.

30. Ian Bell, 1986, Men's responses to gender issues. From an unpublished outline of his talk at the Broad Left Conference, Australia. I am very grateful to Bob Pease and Michael Flood, who each own a number of unpublished, miscellaneous documents and hard-to-find newsletters concerning Australian profeminism and who generously allowed me to go through these materials in May 1999.

31. From a one-page information sheet about Men Against Sexism, 1985, in Bob Pease's personal collection.

32. MASA National Gathering (1992), pp. 1–2.

33. MASA organized a total of five national gatherings from 1992 through 1995.

34. Jenny Brown (1990, October 3), p. 3.

35. Ibid., and Jacqui Tomlins (1990, October 12), p. 6.

36. Pease is quoted in Brown (1990, October 3).

37. Bob Pease (1999, May 6).

38. Tomlins (1990).

39. Ibid.

40. Local newspaper articles in Bob Pease's collection containing men's criticisms include Michael Barnard, 1990, Why I'm still not marching, *The Age* (Sept. 11); Jonathan Green, 1991, Men begin a long march, *The Age* (Sept. 4); and Men drag their feet over call to march against rape, 1992, *The Age* (Sept. 11). To be fair, a number of articles expressed women's and men's support of the marches, among them: Deborah Stone, 1991, Men's talk, *The Sunday Age Agenda* (Feb. 10), p. 5;

and Jane Cafarella, 1990, Why I didn't march against rape, either, *The Age* (date unknown but likely after Sept. 4; this is a satirical response to Michael Barnard's first anti-march article "Why I didn't march on rape," Sept. 4 1990). (These articles are not included in the References.)

41. Barnard, 1990 (see n.40). Among the many letters to editors Bob Pease wrote in the 1990s to describe MASA or respond to sexist articles, at least one letter was addressed to the editor of *The Age* countering some of Barnard's arguments.

42. See n.40, Men drag their feet over call to march against rape, 1992.

43. Claire Tedeschi (1992), Non-violent men recognising that they must speak up. *Canberra Times* (Dec. 12), p. C4.

44. Pease (1999, May 6).

45. Editorial (1992, December 3).

46. Using the Montréal massacre as a catalyst created a different "stumbling block" in Canada. After establishing December 1–6 as White Ribbon Week, the WRC faced criticisms that men were trying to appropriate the symbolic power of the anniversary of the Montréal massacre. Far from clashing with December 6, the WRC was accused of being too close to a day that many women and some men felt belonged to women. In the discourses of those arguing that December 6 should be preserved for women, terms like "vigil," "exclusive," "safe space," "share," and the uses of visual symbols associated with women, convey an emphasis on women's shared mourning and experiences with male violence: rhetorical territory that many believed men had no right to enter. Ultimately, the Canadian WRC moved its White Ribbon Week to late November, symbolizing profeminist men's willingness to "step back" and "remain silent" on a day women had designated as their own.

47. From various publicity materials about Brisbane's 1993 White Ribbon Campaign, supplied by Bob Pease.

48. Linda Kane (1993, December 3).

49. More action on men's violence: Democrats (1993, December 5). Media release, Parliament of Australia—The Senate, 1p.

50. Gail Mason (1998), pp. 337–344. Quote is from p. 337.

51. Amanda Goldrick-Jones (1998, summer/ autumn), pp. 32–34.

52. "Ahimsa" is the Sanskrit word used by Gandhi to describe his campaign for nonviolence.

53. Calvin Bell (1999, September).

54. Paul Wolf-Light (1998, January).

55. Sources: The Everyman Centre Newsletter (August 1997); a personal interview with the center's director Calvin Bell (January 29, 1998); a personal inteview with Center counselor Paul Wolf-Light (January 30, 1998), and the homepage of the Ahimsa Centre, at <htp://www.ahimsa.org.uk/>. Retrieved May 6, 2001.

56. Bell (1999).

# 8

# Politics and "the" Antisexist Male

For profeminists, being antisexist and doing feminist work has had its rewards. There were moments of solidarity, when it seemed as if diverse men could work together; moments when it seemed possible that profeminist men might make a difference. There was triumph in conveying a profeminist message to a larger public, and satisfaction in helping feminist groups campaign for legislation or policies to improve women's lives. But the potential for internal conflict always has characterized men's groups and gatherings, just as for feminist groups. At times, the conflicts arising out of ideological differences have been severe enough to split entire organizations asunder—a sombre end to the initial excitement, joy, and sense of solidarity motivating liberated men in their early Second Wave days. This chapter describes some crisis points experienced by British and Australian profeminists as well as by the National Organization for Men against Sexism. The focus here is on conflicts prompted by the challenges of radical feminism, differing attitudes about male guilt, and tensions between straight and gay profeminists.

## LIBERATED, ANTISEXIST, OR RADICAL? CONFLICTS IN THE BRITISH MEN'S MOVEMENT

Of all the conflicts punctuating profeminist activism since the early 1970s, one of the most contentious has been between men focusing on liberating themselves from the "rites of man"[1] and men taking an active stance against sexism. The idea of men taking an antisexist stance has been riddled with struggle, not the least because, from a radical feminist standpoint, men are implicated in and inseparable from patriarchy. Why should they try to change something that benefits them? How can men be trusted? Indeed, for many men, it was easier and perhaps more personally rewarding to embrace a liberal feminist notion that men are not the problem; instead, women and men are both oppressed by social stereotypes and injustices. Some liberationist men sympathetic to feminist ideals suspected "a rigid and moralistic tendency within anti-sexism which involved a rejection of men and masculinity."[2]

As Kenneth Clatterbaugh explains, "Very early . . . the radical wing came to reserve the term *anti-sexist* as a label for men who accepted radical feminism and the term *liberationist* for those who followed liberal feminism."[3] In the United States, liberationists—who later split into men's rights, warrior, and mythopoetic groups—have operated separately from profeminists, forming their own organizations and creating their own publications. While profeminist men have made attempts to bridge this communications gap,[4] profeminist reaction to men's rights antifeminism is, understandably, not positive. At least one Australian profeminist sees the need to defend feminism against conservative forces and to "take up men's rights issues, but differently." In general, profeminists see any opportunity for dialogue with men's rights groups as a chance to "assert a feminist-supportive and male-positive perspective."[5]

In Britain, however, the split between antisexist and liberationist men occurred earlier, in the 1970s. Along with other sharp political differences, this split dramatically reshaped the direction of the men's movement in that country. British men wanting to be part of the excitement of men's liberation were, at first, dealing with some of the same issues as their North American counterparts. British profeminists were tremendously interested in aspects of feminism that would help them liberate themselves as men. But for those British feminists who were willing to work with men, it wasn't enough that men were willing to liberate themselves from restraining sex roles. Men also needed to accept the feminist socialist analysis—rooted deep in British feminist thought—implicating capitalism and traditional marriage as primary causes of women's oppression. Profeminist men had to be prepared to do antisexist work that would help dismantle or undermine those structures. This double challenge—to change not only themselves but the very structures that benefited significantly more men than women—would prove to be incredibly daunting.

## Struggle and Paralysis

"Tuttle's *Feminist Encyclopaedia* suggests that the first men's group in Britain started in Brighton in 1971."[6] Not long after, two distinct types of men's movements emerged. One was decidedly antisexist and consisted of men whose female partners or friends were active in the Women's Liberation Movement.[7] Writer-theorist John Rowan records that one antisexist group—Men against Sexism—favored a Marxist theoretical framework motivated by the principle "No women's liberation without revolution: No revolution without women's liberation."[8] A minority wing of this antisexist movement was a radical stream exemplified by a group called Unbecoming Men, who attempted "to relate directly to . . . the strongest and most militant wing of the women's liberation movement" through "a radical questioning of everything to do with masculinity."[9] As will become clear, this radical outlook would pose enormous challenges to British profeminism.

As Rowan puts it, even the less radical antisexist men's groups "could be uncomfortable places."[10] Many members "had been told by their friends or wives in the women's liberation movement that they should go and work things out with other men."[11] Indeed, according to Mick Cooper, a writer, activist and chronicler of British profeminism, some of these men were initially "pushed . . . by their feminist colleagues" and "were unsure of their role in the feminist struggle and were thus indecisive about what action they could take."[12]

Like their American counterparts, these British antisexist groups adopted models of consciousness-raising (CR) inspired by feminism. But many took the slightly different approach of trying to integrate a variety of personal and political perspectives in CR sessions: therapeutic, antisexist, and socialist. Some of these group members, including Rowan and Victor Seidler, were concerned enough about the relation between personal therapy and politics that they created the Red Therapy group, which functioned from 1974 to 1977. According to Rowan, this "leaderless therapy group" also created "a political critique of . . . therapy, personal growth, counseling."[13] Rowan notes that one positive outcome of this group, which had male and female participants, was stronger relations with feminism. At about the same time, a more liberationist movement emerged, partly the result of a conflict between those who favored what Cooper calls "a high degree of theoretical self-consciousness" about anti-sexism and those who wanted a more CR-oriented approach that would help them understand themselves as men.[14] By and large, liberationist men were less interested in antisexist activism and Marxism, and more intent on understanding masculinity, working toward self-improvement, and forging better relationships with other men.

Initially British antisexist and liberationist men tried to work together, attempting unity through their common concern with understanding men's lives. But secondhand reports of antisexist activism (see esp. Rowan, Cooper, and Rutherford) describe divisions among antisexist and liberationist men as well as growing tensions around gay issues. Cooper's description and critique of a 1973 Men against Sexism conference, which had about thirty attendees, indicates that British men were willing to discuss such topics as "liberation from the disadvantages of masculinity" and "liberation from sexism as a counter-revolutionary ideology" as long as they could focus mainly on masculinity and men's lives.[15] Rowan's take on this conference is that it "was a start in bringing together the scattered groups and getting more of a feeling of being some kind of movement."[16] Cooper argues that the few records of the 1974 conference send strong signals of "a conflict . . . developing between the 'men's liberationists' and the 'antisexist men.' "[17] This argument is supported by Jonathan Rutherford, who has examined some of the antisexism versus liberationism writings coming out of the Men against Sexism group. "[D]iscussion and debate tended to polarize around a "men's liberation" position, concerned with "men's issues" and a pro-feminist politics that eschewed discussions and activities solely addressing masculine identities and sensibilities."[18]

## "The Ten Commitments"

After two conferences in 1974, no other British men's conferences would take place until 1978. At that time, as Rowan describes it, "there was a resurgence of the men's movement" in Britain.[19] That year and the next saw the emergence of the magazine *Achilles Heel*, a series of meetings about men's politics, the establishment of the London Men's Centre, and the first ever national men's conference in Manchester, attracting about 300 attendees.[20] Cooper notes that with the passage of time and the fading of earlier conflicts, the atmosphere of the 1978 conference "returned to the cosiness [*sic*] of the men's liberation groups," but the 1979 Manchester conference carried a stronger antisexist agenda.[21]

Partly because of its more political agenda, this conference sowed fresh seeds for discord between liberationist and antisexist men. Tensions came dramatically to a head in 1980 at a conference in Bristol, when some antisexist men put forward a proposal they had drafted the previous year in Manchester. This proposal asked delegates to endorse a set of "Ten Commitments" representing men's willingness to adopt feminist principles in their daily lives. To the antisexists, the Commitments[22] represented an endorsement of the women's movement as well as a call for men to change themselves and take responsibility for their actions. These commitments included sharing childcare, learning from gay and feminist culture, linking up with other men's antisexist groups, renouncing violence, and supporting the Women's Liberation Movement.[23]

Cooper implies that while these notions shouldn't have presented much of a challenge, "the emphasis on supporting women and practical action was alien to many men."[24] But according to Rowan, many of the delegates felt that adopting the Commitments would amount to an admission of male guilt. Rowan says he found the admonishing (and it must be admitted, occasionally self-righteous) tone of the Commitments very off-putting, comparing it to "a giant superego sitting on my shoulders shouting in my ear all the time 'you're not living up to it, you're not living up to it!' "[25] A similar reaction to heavy-handed feminist arguments comes up in Harry Christian's *The Making of Anti-Sexist Men*, in which one subject says "Feminist influence might get my hair up on end if it wasn't delivered properly . . . I'd think 'Somebody's standing on a soapbox shouting.' If it's not being hammered down your throat it's more acceptable."[26] Although no one wants to be shouted at, one difficulty with this position is that whatever constitutes shouting depends on which man you're talking to. It is also a common complaint among feminists that any mention, however small, of women's or feminist issues tends to get men's backs up. As expressed by David Bouchier, who has compared British and American women's liberation movements in the 1970s, "Men are powerfully attached to their own view of the world and their place in it. . . . Any movement for women's liberation will therefore produce defensive and aggressive responses from men."[27] This is a useful reminder: what seem to be fairly common sense propositions for profeminists are, for other men, quite threatening.

Thus, criticisms about the heavy-handedness of the radical men's arguments are important even for profeminists to recognize. The failure of the Ten Commitments may indeed represent a failure to recognize a diverse audience and adapt arguments strategically to a range of backgrounds and attitudes to feminism. What happened instead was that a compromise was put forward in the form of a "Minimum Definition of the Anti-Sexist Men's Movement," which, according to Cooper, included statements about the importance of therapy and gaining support from other men but which "did not compel the men in the movement to do anything."[28] While perhaps exaggerated, this statement by Cooper reflects antisexist men's frustration that the men's movement was providing little motivation for men to do much more than make token gestures toward ending sexism.

## The Politics of Guilt

According to Cooper's strong antisexist perspective, after the Manchester conference and the defeat of the Ten Commitments, the British antisexist/profeminist movement once again lost enthusiasm and clout, going into a steep decline, while the liberationist movement gained momentum. Rowan believes that the Ten Commitments event did some damage to the movement, but he argues that a more serious clash occurred in 1983 over a seventeen-page article in an antisexist newsletter as to whether and how antisexist men should explicitly hold themselves accountable to feminism (see chapter 4 for more perspectives about accountability). In Rowan's view, "this major word Accountability turned out to be the Commitments writ large," basically another "guilt-provoking attack" thinly disguised.

Rowan believes that this incident played a larger role than the 1979–1980 Commitments conflict in pushing British profeminism to the margins of the men's movement during the 1980s.[29]

Male guilt has been a significant obstacle to productive antisexist action in the antisexist men's movement. Particularly difficult to get past is the principle that men are guilty because of their sex—an argument put forth by some, though by no means all, feminist women as well as profeminist men. As antisexist writer and theorist Victor Seidler puts it, "we can easily end up feeling guilty for being men, since we cannot escape our situation as 'oppressors.' We can feel we have got no right to exist."[30] Feminist women can be leery of men's wish to be involved in antisexist projects, and profeminist men may be reluctant to take action in case they do the wrong thing or are seen as tainted by patriarchy. As Rutherford explains, from the earliest days of groups like Men against Sexism, "[men's] attempts at self-comprehension which did not directly address the power men wielded in patriarchal relations, were met with suspicion and accusations of self-indulgence."[31]

Conflicting arguments about male guilt, and especially men's role in perpetuating women's oppression, also reflected and deepened the schism between liberationist and antisexist men. Antisexist men tended to argue strongly that men were oppressors, as evident in a special issue of a newsletter published in 1976 by one of the very first Australian anti-sexist men's groups, "Men against Sexism" (MAS). Entitled "Why We Are an Oppressor's Club," this issue argued that the main problem of integrating antisexist and liberationist men in the same men's group was that work would focus on "the male role" and not on "feminism." Described by the antisexist writers are the political struggles to produce a manifesto arguing that the group must remain profeminist or die: "The producers of this newsletter, which is the manifesto group, believe that MAS must adopt the major thrusts of the manifesto or eventually dissolve. . . . The manifesto group strongly reject that men are oppressed by sexism, and even more forcibly that men are oppressed by women."[32]

This MAS manifesto defines sexism as "the oppression of women by men. . . . Those in power cannot be oppressed; hence men, although restricted by their sex roles, cannot be oppressed." The prospects of men relinquishing their position as oppressors are bleak, according to these writers. The reason is that while men's support of "the oppressed" can effect changes in power structures, men will never stop being oppressors "because they retain the power at any time to withdraw their support." The only hope is for anti-sexist men to confront other men about their sexism "as well as challenging their own [sexism]."

Although it's easy to criticize such arguments after almost thirty years and within the context of enormous changes in feminism, it must be said that the tone is aggressive and strongly redolent of political correctness.

The MAS manifesto is also undermined by the early Second Wave feminist assumption that all women and all men share sex-class characteristics. While the arguments are well meaning, it's not hard to imagine that few men outside the hard-core antisexist cadre would accept them. The political struggles motivating the creation of this Australian manifesto not only reflect the splits occurring in Britain at the time, but also graphically illustrate that men's attempts to deal with guilt were not confined to any one country or area.

Victor Seidler has also discussed the guilt resulting when men define masculinity primarily in terms their own oppressive power over women. They then try to make up for the guilt by trying too hard to make themselves accountable to feminism:

> We are left with the guilt that arises from the recognition that we belong to an oppressive group and are therefore part of the oppression of women [despite] whatever efforts we make on our own behalf. At least this involves taking the demands and politics of the women's movement seriously, but this can create its own politics of guilt. . . . [33]

One result of dwelling on guilt can be a paralysis that ultimately sabotages attempts at practical action to help end sexism. While it's impossible to say for certain that all profeminist failures to act have been caused by guilt and paralysis, two cases of failed British profeminist projects are very suggestive.

These projects, "Crèches against Sexism" and "Cash against Sexism," were both established in 1980 and quickly came into conflict with the women's movement over a question of funding. According to Mick Cooper, the men withdrew funds and volunteer childcare they had been willing to donate to a feminist conference when the women said they preferred to use paid childcare workers. "This move infuriated many women who felt that the men were using the money to control the women's movement. . . ."[34] Stung by this criticism, both Crèches and Cash against Sexism fell apart. It isn't clear who was blaming whom, but it is reasonable to suspect that lack of an open and respectful communications process played a part here. It may also be that the men were unwilling to recognize and find ways to work through the conundrum of being well-intentioned oppressors.

Similar forms of paralysis descended several times on the British men's movement in the 1970s and early 1980s when the question of accountability to feminism was raised[35]—by early antisexist groups and conferences, by the Ten Commitments issue, by the antisexist newsletter's 1983 article, and once again in the mid- to late 1980s by the members of the *Achilles Heel* editorial collective. In all cases, men backed off from an explicit commitment or plan to make themselves accountable to the feminist movement, and generally turned their activism more toward a men's liberation agenda:

working on themselves and their relations with other men. Indeed, when some men within *Achilles Heel* have tried to propose a more explicit statement of accountability to feminism, conflicts have resulted about how to escape the trap of equating men's accountability with men's guilt. It is perhaps not difficult to see why former *Achilles Heel* co-editor John Rowan, among others, is very leery of accountability, calling it a "dead end, more liable to halt men than to lead them on."[36] *Achilles Heel* editors told me that the magazine at one point explicitly stated its accountability to feminism on the masthead. But the editorial collective agreed to drop this statement in the early 1990s in favor of the less contentious "We recognize the importance of dialogue with women, and welcome any contributions and comment from women . . . we will not publish anything we consider to be sexist." Most members of the editorial collective I interviewed in 1998 generally agreed that encouraging dialogue between women and men, as well as publishing work that interrogates traditional masculinity and gender relations, is a legitimate form of profeminist political action. They believe this strategy is less likely to generate the sharp conflicts repeatedly plaguing the British men's movement of the 1970s and 1980s.

Another response to the question of whether profeminist men are doing enough or doing the right things has been to devise ways of making profeminist men accountable to feminist women (see chapter 4). In the context of male guilt, a relevant question is—can even clear mechanisms for accountability allow men to get past guilt? As Rowan has pointed out, accountability in some contexts can be highly charged with negative implications—Big Sister is watching, men are not good enough, men are guilty. Rowan argues that calls by antisexist men to "confront, challenge and . . . criticise [*sic*] other men" are intended to be motivating, but can have the opposite effect: "whatever the truth of this position, and whatever its acceptability to feminist women, it simply paralyses [*sic*] men. They are not energised and made more potent in their anti-sexism by this kind of message."[37] Rowan's use of the word "potent," I think, deliberately challenges some radical antisexist men's paralyzing rejection of masculinity. While "potent" may not sit well with some feminists, the term highlights some very tangible differences between extreme radical antisexism and a more male-positive position.

Rowan believes that men must integrate a positive self-image with antisexist work—a conviction shared later by the National Organization of Men against Sexism and the White Ribbon Campaign. Seidler offers another suggestion for avoiding the dangerous possibilities of guilt-induced paralysis and failure to act against sexism. Men do need to work on themselves, but they must also understand how the personal intersects with the political. Men need to be aware of the extent to which masculinity, men's roles, and sexism are inseparable from the social and economic conditions—and power relations—that oppress women and men:

one of the most concrete ways men can support the women's movement is through being ready to change ourselves, rather than thinking the issue has nothing to do with us. . . . Rather than simply withdrawing into a painful silence, we are finding a new kind of strength and a new weakness in asking basic questions that directly challenge the prevailing definitions of masculinity in society. . . . [38]

## GAY PERSPECTIVES AND RADICAL CHALLENGES I: BRITAIN

Another site of continual struggle for the men's movement within and outside North America is sexual politics. In Britain during the 1970s, gay men, inspired by the American Black liberation movement, "had quite suddenly discovered their energy, their voice, their ability to fight back against the oppression which they felt they had for so long endured."[39] Not surprisingly, a number of gay men who considered themselves antisexist took a much more radical stance toward masculinity than their straight "brothers," including calling into question whether any straight man could truly be antisexist.

In November 1974, tensions over sexual politics boiled over into a conflict between gay and straight antisexist men following the publication of an article in the British newsletter *Brothers against Sexism* entitled "Coming Out Is the Only Way Forward." The basic argument was that men could successfully fight sexism only by "sacrific[ing] the privileges they obtain from women and relat[ing] on a sexual level exclusively with men."[40]

If men are serious about being antisexist, then they must sacrifice the privileges they obtain from women and relate on a sexual level exclusively with men. . . . Only when men are prepared to risk their masculinity to the extent of becoming homosexual can a men's movement challenge sexism in the way gay liberation has.[41]

Mick Cooper reports that conflicts over this article dominated a 1974 conference; eventually, several gay men walked out "after accusing the 'straights' of homophobia."[42] Yet in Cooper's analysis, the gay men's criticisms were not far off and revealed growing weaknesses in profeminism: "The belief that in changing ourselves through consciousness-raising [men] were liberating women was delegitimized [sic] through an intense attack from an oppressed group."[43] The Coming Out conflict not only exposed the schisms between the radical and more moderate antisexist camps, but also exacerbated the growing antisexist/liberationist split. According to Cooper and John Rowan respectively, the November 1974 schism over the Coming Out article "devastated"[44] and "virtually shattered"[45] the men's movement in Britain; indeed, for several years very little public profeminist activity took place. As Rowan interprets this period, radical and gay men in both Britain and the United States were focusing so much on the sexual politics of dismantling masculinity that they alienated less radical men and, in some cases, the feminists with whom they were hoping to ally. Cooper takes a different perspective, arguing that the 1974 conference had "made salient the fact that the men's movement *was not challenging sexism*"[author's emphasis] and that the gay men's critique had exposed the extent to which men's interests, rather than antisexism, were dominating the agenda. Argues Cooper, "men could have responded to this critique by an intensifying of antisexism and pro-feminist activity. It is a significant fact that rather than reacting in a positive manner, their only answer was self-criticism and disintegration."[46]

Nor, since this disintegration, have British profeminists revamped and attempted to form larger groups with profeminist agendas. Yet the *Achilles Heel* men generally agree that publishing a "radical men's magazine" is a political act. To use the language on the masthead, the magazine challenges "traditional forms of masculinity and male power." Articles thoughout the 1980s and 1990s have, among many other topics, focused on such diversity issues as male sexuality (gay and straight), homophobia, gay culture, and class politics. Though the magazine masthead "especially welcome[s]" articles from gay and black men, most issues between 1985 and the late 1990s have not focused as obviously on the politics of race as on the politics of sexuality or class. Providing an outlet for male-positive and antisexist arguments, the magazine also acts as a kind of a political safety valve, allowing expression of significant differences in British men's attitudes toward sexual orientation, class, and accountability to feminism. After the conflicts of the 1970s and 1980s, perhaps *Achilles Heel* represents a "middle road" for British men's movements.

## GAY PERSPECTIVES AND RADICAL CHALLENGES II: THE UNITED STATES

By the end of the 1970s, the U.S. men's movement was becoming more diverse in terms of sexual orientation. Profeminist writer Tom Mosmiller describes the demographics at this time:

> Although nearly all the men involved are white, their class and sexual orientations are much more varied. Most men express middle-class values, regardless of their class background, but recently some working-class men have begun strongly articulating their differences with these values. Furthermore, at least on the national level, there are about equal numbers of heterosexual and homosexual men, and a significant representation of bisexual men.[47]

In Britain, the radical challenge leveled by the Coming Out gay men was too much for the rest of the men's movement to assimilate. But in the United States during the 1970s, relations between gay and straight men were more positive. Arising from mass radical activity in the 1960s, the gay movement was still gaining energy, according to the Berkeley-based *Brother: A Forum for Men against Sexism.* Writing in 1974, the editors claimed "[T]here are more groups that are specifically gay than men's groups. . . . In the gay male movement we see a resurgence of radical activity. . . ."[48]

That same year, the *Brother* editorial collective described itself as "made up predominantly of faggots" (that term co-opted by the editors for an empowering purpose) who hoped an antisexist message would appeal to political men of all sexual persuasions. Accordingly, *Brother*'s summer 1974 theme issue—"Men in Love: A Dialogue on Bisexual, Straight and Gay Male Sexual Politics"—was followed by an issue devoted to gauging "the current state of male non-sexist activity." As the editors noted, "*Brother* is something of an oddity because gay men and straight men are working together on it. It is supposed to reflect some consciousness about men having a stake in the struggle against sexism that gay men and straight men can share."[49] In other words, the editors shared a strong sense that overcoming not only sexism but heterosexism was a task open to all interested and sympathetic men. This magazine was outspoken about the importance of gay perspectives to the men's movement, but did not radically challenge straight men's sexual choices.

Discussion of gay issues was also enthusiastically supported at the annual Men & Masculinity conferences in the United States. In 1975, the first year of these conferences, session topics included "The Black Male Experience" and "The Gay Male." The following year, M & M ran into trouble for openly supporting gay men. The conference was to be held at Pennsylvania State University, but the university administration withdrew its support when it learned that gay-positive topics would be in the program. In solidarity, the entire conference moved across the street to a Holiday Inn.[50] By 1978, the M & M Gay Task Force had assumed a high profile. Guided by the themes "Men Overcoming Sexism" and "Men and Sexism," many gay issues were discussed and a number of gay speakers and workshops featured. Among the resolutions passed at this conference was one promising to continue this pro-gay work at future conferences and fight discrimination against gays.[51]

For a while, this momentum in support of gay issues was sustained. At the M & M conference in 1979 a three-hour workshop was held on "The Common Fight for Gender Justice—Toward an Integration of Straight Male, Gay Male, and Female Objectives." The eighth M & M conference in 1983, whose double-entendre theme was "Men Cooperating for a Change," featured a major presentation focused on "Cooperation between

Gay and Straight Men."[52] The M & M conference topics convey the apparent willingness of straight men to learn from the experiences and perspectives offered by gays, and offer numerous sessions targeted to gays and men comfortable with a variety of sexualities. As well, some sessions were clearly designed to make slightly nervous straight men feel more comfortable with gay perspectives. A few titles include "Understanding Gay Men" (1976), "Everything You've Always Wanted to Ask about Being Gay," (1985), and "Why Are Men Wearing Dresses at the 10th M & M?" (1985).

The language of these titles reflects the well-intentioned goal of encouraging straight men to doff their homophobia. But in doing so, the risk again rears its head that heterosexuality is implicitly defined as the norm and being gay as the "other," the one to be "understood." Even some of the gay-positive titles exaggerate differences between gays and straights, though usually for the purpose of celebrating gay culture and often in a spirit of fun; the write-up for the "Why Are Men Wearing Dresses" part of the 1985 M & M program cleverly subverts traditional masculine notions of dress and makes me wonder—*why* don't more men wear skirts . . . ? It may seem easy to critique such language from a distant vantage point, after years of often bitter debate about representation. But these titles stand as a good reminder of how easy it is to define white, straight, middle-class as the basic operating default mode. It's not difficult to imagine that the effect on some gay men, at least—and perhaps even some straight men—was exclusionary.

Adding to this problem, I think, is that some of these discourses integrating gay perspectives and the men's movement assume a single, total, essential state of gay being (notably "The Gay Male").[53] As sociologist Michael Messner notes, the 1970s ideal of one particular gay experience "was a key to the development of a successful and empowering gay politics of identity." The universalization of the gay experience helped forge the sense of community that would allow gays to fight such challenges as homophobia and AIDS.[54] But as Messner argues "this normalized gay identity was based on a falsely universalized white, upper-middle-class, and highly masculine gay male experience, thus tending to render invisible the experiences of lesbians, gay men of color, poor and working-class gay men, and effeminate gay men. . . ."[55]

Indeed, very early in the U.S. men's movement, some gay antisexist men recognized that buying into a universal gay experience was no more helpful than buying into traditional masculine roles as a way of ending women's and gay men's oppression. The radical 1973 Effeminist Manifesto, signed by three men and eventually circulated to various men's resource centers, locates sexism not only within traditional patriarchy but leftist politics, Men's Liberation, and Gay Liberation. For the Manifesto writers, these movements are not only incomplete analyses of oppression but "are all tactics for preserving power in men's hands by pretending to struggle for change." Masculinist standards are strongly criticized, but aspects of gay culture, notably transvestitism and the "combination of anti-woman mimicry and self-mockery known as camp," are not spared. The Manifesto writers uncompromisingly critique camp as an offering "by the patriarchy which is designed to keep us oppressed and also increase the oppression of women."[56] The Manifesto argues that effeminacy in men—the "Female Principle"—must be sought after and valued, and can take many forms.

In some ways similar to the British Coming Out article, the Effeminist Manifesto called on men to support feminism and condemned any actions that would "conflict with the goals of feminists. . . ." Like many radical men, the writers were excited by the possibilities offered by feminism for social transformation: "That is why we are gynarchists; that is, we are among those who believe that women will seize power from the patriarchy and, thereby, totally change life on this planet as we know it." In the spirit of radical action, the Manifesto exhorted effeminate men to "prepare for all forms of sabotage and rebellion which women might ask of us." But unlike the Coming Out article, these writers did not demand that men relate only to men:

> we do not automatically support or condemn faggots or effeminists who live alone, who live together as couples, who live together in all-male collectives, who live with women, or who live in any other way—since all of these modes of living in and of themselves can be sexist but can also conceivably come to function as bases for anti-sexist struggle.[57]

Yet by the 1980s, the Gay Liberation condemned by the Effeminist Manifesto was the dominant voice of gay men and, according to Michael Messner, had come "largely to define itself in the liberal language of individual equal rights and assimilation into a commercial, capitalist order."[58] By then, a schism had also developed between gay male liberationists, who focused mainly on their own sexual freedom, and lesbians, who tended to identify with feminist views about such issues as pornography. According to Messner, the increasing prevalence of a "radical feminist women's gender focus" concerning pornography made profeminism an increasingly uncomfortable fit for gay men to whom pornography represented "their first positive affirmation of same-sex desire."[59]

## "SO MUCH SLIME . . .": NOMAS'S CRISIS OF COMMITMENT

In 1992, a public affirmation of same-sex desire become the catalyst for a shattering crisis within the National Organization for Men against Sexism (NOMAS). Ironically, this crisis illustrated Messner's view that gay perspectives on male sexual freedom indeed can conflict with profeminist and feminist struggles to eliminate pornography. The largest profeminist organization in the world had painstakingly built an identity as a group committed to balancing antisexism with being male-positive and gay-positive. But the degree of NOMAS's commitment to antisexism was severely challenged in the fall of 1992, after the profeminist magazine *Changing Men* (*CM*) published several articles (issue 24, summer/fall) about sexuality. One, Duane Allen's "An Invitation to Transgressive Sex," proposed that women and men, including profeminists, should de-politicize sex, focusing less on power relations and more on pleasure. To this end, fetish objects and even porn could be involved. Another article, "First Loves," was penned by a NOMAS co-founder and executive member, Jeff Beane, and described his experiences as a gay male teen in the late 1950s and early 1960s. When he was seventeen, one of these experiences included a sexual encounter with a boy of twelve. Coincidentally in that same issue of *Changing Men* appeared a discreet ad for the North American Man-Boy Love Association (NAMBLA), as well as an ad for an exotic magazine.

Reactions to this issue were swift and overwhelmingly critical.[60] A number of these criticisms were printed in the letters-to-the-editor pages of *CM*'s next issue (winter/spring 1993), a move probably intended to create a forum for discussion. However, the views are so oppositional, the attacks and defenses so pointed, that real dialogue is difficult to discern. Expressing her anger and disappointment at Allen's article, anti-porn activist Melissa Farley argued that Allen was effectively betraying years of feminist activism against pornography and, among other things, ignoring the consequences of transgressive sex, such as "the issue of physical violence as a real danger to those who are oppressed." By not engaging those issues, Allen was "transparently exhibit[ing] middle class, white male privilege."[61] Allen's response, printed on the same page as Farley's, expressed shock at the implication that he "has wandered from the feminist fold and become a danger to women." His position, he wrote, was that profeminists should embrace more than the "one brand of feminist thought . . . shaped largely by the so-called anti-pornography feminists." Such thinking about sex is "*little different from a right wing/fundamentalist policing of gender and sexual binaries. . . . They both harm women*" (author's emphasis).[62] This conflict is rooted in a history of contested feminist and profeminist viewpoints about pornography, a history briefly outlined in chapter 6.

The bitterest criticisms, though, targeted Beane's article, particularly his apparent seduction of a 12-year-old boy. Of the several letters to the editor published in *CM* reacting to Beane's piece, most expressed hurt and anger. It's notable that at least one of these criticisms was written by a member of the NOMAS leadership collective. But perhaps the angriest reaction came from anti-pedophile activist Nikki Craft in an article written in 1992 and published in the winter/spring 1993 issue of *Changing Men*. Craft questioned how NOMAS could ever again claim to be committed to feminist principles. In her view, not only had "a big wheel" in the organization like Beane effectively advocated child pornography, but the entire editorial collective of the magazine—a publication closely associated with NOMAS—had approved material like the ad for NAMBLA.[63] Craft argued that such materials and *CM*'s sanctioning of them illustrated the extent to which "the pedophile movement is a contradiction and a threat to the profeminist, and indeed to any progressive, egalitarian agenda."[64]

Craft's entire article is bluntly worded, and a section called "Pro-Feminists! Shit or Get Off the Pot" is a direct challenge to NOMAS: "Are 'enlightened' men such easy marks that they fall for the pedophile's bullshit about justice, egalitarianism, oppression, and consensuality? . . . Are many of you just so apathetic that you can't bring yourself to care much one way or the other?"[65] Craft also listed a number of remedies NOMAS, *Changing Men*, and other profeminists should undertake, including identifying and exposing pedophile organizations and their leaders and establishing editorial guidelines that would clarify what male-positive means. Only then, she argued, would profeminists—and by extension NOMAS—be able to claim honestly that they are "allies with women who are working to end sexual exploitation."[66]

The published materials around this incident show that with a few exceptions, NOMAS leaders and members of *CM*'s editorial panel felt that issue 24 should be disavowed. In "A Statement from the Editors and Publishers" published in winter/spring 1993, *CM*'s editors acknowledged they had made "serious errors" and that "lax review procedures" had gone uncorrected. They also distanced themselves from Beane's article:

> we now understand [Beane's article] to be a first degree sexual assault of a child by an older adolescent male (according to our state's . . . and other states' laws). . . . We are very sorry that these materials in our last issue hurt or betrayed some of our readers, especially those who are survivors of sexual assault. . . . We commit to never letting mistakes like these happen again, and are taking pro-active measures to support our commitment.[67]

Of *CM*'s regular contributors, only one appears to have defended Beane's right to express his views. Poetry editor Bob Vance argued that

> The strength of any movement is in its diversity. . . . In any group process, cohesiveness is born out of acceptance of inter-group differences. . . . Can we afford to be disunited . . . even if our focuses and methods differ? . . . Whose ends do we serve by withdrawing support and dialog from those whose goals are clearly similar to ours?[68]

*CM*'s book review editor Michael Kimmel was another defender, even though he "personally . . . didn't especially like [Beane's] story." For Kimmel, the principle wasn't merely freedom of expression. As he put it, how would he know, as a straight man, what it's like to be gay and to "struggle against the brutality of heterosexism, to search for a sexual identity in the absence of any role models"?[69] For his part, Beane responded to the critical letters to the editor in *CM*'s issue 25 by politicizing the "attacks against my character and behavior." He defined such attacks as incompatible to a "pro-feminist, gay affirmative . . . men's movement." Instead of "righteous, punative . . . responses," he wrote, "We need constructive and cooperative discussion on the issues of child abuse, gay adolescent sexuality and the way we talk about this and other sensitive issues."[70]

The NOMAS leadership collective was faced with a quandary: unwilling (one assumes) to let a colleague and friend swing in the wind, yet unable to ignore the fact that Beane's article and the NAMBLA ad had deeply offended many profeminists and their feminist allies. In January 1993, the collective met and discussed the problem for more than 7 hours. The published account of this meeting indicates that the NOMAS leadership wanted to acknowledge that harm had been done, but not only to those offended by Beane's article. Thus, while the leadership expressed their opposition to "tolerating or romanticizing pedophilia" and asked Beane to "acknowledge, more clearly and publicly, his adult awareness of the issues raised," the leadership also recorded their objections to the "dehumanizing and isolating manner" in which NOMAS and the editors of *Changing Men* had been treated by critics.[71]

But too much damage had been done to the credibility of NOMAS and *Changing Men*, at least in the eyes of the Beane controversy critics. Overly optimistically, as it turned out, *CM*'s "Statement from the Editors and Publisher" predicted that "*Changing Men* will emerge stronger for having accepted the challenge to change our practices—in order to become more fully responsible to . . . the pro-feminist movement that sustains us and that we in turn hopefully nurture."[72] But without strong signals of a renewed profeminist commitment beyond apologies or editorials, the ability of not only *Changing Men* but NOMAS to represent profeminist interests was called into question. This perceived lack of commitment was considered a sufficient cause for many feminist and profeminist supporters to start abandoning the organization. By 1994, unable to raise sufficient funds from NOMAS members, *Changing Men* had ceased publication. Effective 1996, delegates to the yearly Men & Masculinities conference, which NOMAS had sponsored, were given the option of not having to join NOMAS. While it continued to be associated with the Men & Masculinity conferences during the rest of the 1990s, NOMAS appeared, in many respects, to be a national organization in name only (but see Appendix A for signs that NOMAS may be returning to life).

## SHOULD PROFEMINISTS GATHER IN LARGE GROUPS?

Kenneth Clatterbaugh strongly implies that NOMAS's crisis of commitment has served to undermine the unity of American profeminism. In his view, the organization's apparent collapse also indicates "a weakening of the profeminist movement" overall.[73] For entirely different reasons, including burn-out, other established profeminist groups also folded in the mid- to late 1990s: among them Men's Network for Change in Ontario, Canada and Men against Sexual Assault in Australia, except for the Melbourne chapter. At about the same time, events like the evangelical Promise Keepers gatherings and the Million Man March of 1995 were exercising far more drawing power than any profeminist march or rally.

Indirectly supporting a pessimistic view of the strength and influence of American profeminism is Clatterbaugh's 1994 survey of men's publications and their circulation figures in *Serials Review*[74]. Among the American profeminist publications still extant that year was *The Activist Men's Journal* (Seattle), a newsletter of the radical profeminist wing, featuring John Stoltenberg as a frequent contributor. Focusing on violence against women and the need for men to do work in that area, this newsletter was highly critical of NOMAS's stance on the Jeff Beane affair. Its circulation was 50. The academic journal *masculinities* (formerly the *Men's Studies Review*), began in 1993 with a circulation of 400. When *Changing Men* ceased publication, it had a respectable circulation of around 6,000. By comparison, *The Liberator*, the official newsletter of the Men's Rights Association, had 2,000 readers in 1994. But the *Seattle M.E.N. Newsletter*, featuring articles about men's rights, mythopoetics, and occasionally profeminism, circulated 5,000 copies. The *Men's Council Journal*, on male spirituality, distributed 10,000 copies, and *Wingspan: Journal of the Male Spirit* reached 150,000 readers.

To put these publications into perspective, consider that the *Men's Journal*—with its "no problems" attitude, "hard bodies," liquor ads, and pictures of sexy women—had a circulation of 160,000, according to Clatterbaugh's research. But outgrossing them all is *Maxim*,[75] the general interest men's magazine starting up in 1997. While it occasionally shows flashes of irony and self-mockery, *Maxim* goes out of its way to insult men's intelligence and keep misogyny alive and well with features like "girls of *Maxim*," "stupid fun," "world o' sex," and "beer and chow." Depressing as this is to think about, by 1999 the magazine had a "guaranteed" circulation of 2 million. The earnest, academic, "no fun" rhetoric of profeminism stands little chance against these blandishments—and around that fact, profeminist men should do some serious strategizing.

Given profeminism's current lack of popularity, along with the fairly recent fragmentation or burn-out of profeminist organizations, it's tempting to be pessimistic about the future of men who believe in feminism. But perhaps it's a problem of method rather than principle: profeminists may have been overly ambitious in expecting to change the attitudes of men across nations by creating elaborate executive structures and expending energy on intra-organizational political conflicts. In fact, as Bob Connell has argued, perhaps antisexist or profeminist work should not be channeled through large, centrally organized groups. Instead of a mass men's movement, Connell sees more promise in what he calls "alliance politics," in which "the project of social justice depends on the overlapping of interests between different groups (rather than mobilization of one group around its common interest)."[76] Bob Pease, who co-founded MASA, also thinks that "proposing a profeminist political strategy will not in itself politicize men." Instead, he suggests profeminist men need to "talk to 'ordinary' men" and locate moral and ethical reasons for being profeminist within men's "enlightened self-interests."[77] In other words, it's essential for men to locate profeminism within men's daily experiences as well as within feminist frameworks.

What it comes down to is this: men need to know and see concretely how they, their partners, and their children will benefit when men are willing to work for gender justice. This is a very tall order, and it might be a while before two million average men start throwing their copies of *Maxim* into trashcans for burning. But in their drive to create unified structures and work through ideological differences, profeminists may have lost sight of the excitement, positive energy, sense of humor and play, and the sheer hope igniting men's imaginations across places and times, from the 1840s to the 1990s. Without necessarily working within organizations, profeminists are engaging in other creative ways to convey the basic message that it's good for men to believe in feminism. You will find some of these efforts—large and small—documented in Appendix A, "The Current State of Profeminism Online."

## NOTES

1. Rosalind Miles (1991).
2. Victor J. Seidler (1991b), p. x.
3. Kenneth Clatterbaugh (1997), p. 43.
4. Some attempts to create dialogue between profeminist and men's rights groups are described in Michael Flood (1997, spring), pp. 37–39; Bob Pease (2000), and Michael S. Kimmel (1995).
5. Flood (1997), p. 38.
6. Mick Cooper (1991), p. 6.
7. Ibid.; Derek Shiel (1990, autumn). Unpublished report. 4 pp. Obtained from Achilles Heel Editorial Collective.
8. John Rowan (1987), p. 17.
9. Ibid.
10. Ibid.

11. Ibid.
12. Cooper (1991), p. 6.
13. Rowan (1987), p. 21.
14. Cooper (1991), p. 6.
15. Ibid.
16. Rowan (1987), p. 19.
17. Cooper (1991), p. 6.
18. Jonathan Rutherford (1992), p. 6.
19. Rowan (1987), p. 48.
20. Ibid.
21. Cooper (1991), p. 8.
22. "Notes and riders" forming the Ten Commitments can be found in Rowan (1987), p. 49.
23. Rowan (1987), p. 49 and Cooper (1991), p. 8.
24. Cooper (1991), p. 8.
25. Cited in ibid., p. 9; also see Rowan (1987), pp. 48–53.
26. Quoted in Harry Christian (1994), p. 31.
27. David Bouchier (1984), p. 102.
28. Cooper (1991), p. 9.
29. Rowan (1987), pp. 50–53.
30. Seidler (1991), p. 40.
31. Rutherford (1992), p. 5.
32. Why We Are an Oppressor's Club (1976, January).
33. Seidler (1991), p. 40.
34. Cooper (1991), p. 9.
35. Also see ibid., p. 5, and Seidler (1991), pp. 39–40.
36. John Rowan (1994, autumn), p. 6.
37. Rowan (1987), pp. 52–53.
38. Seidler (1991), pp. 41, 47.
39. Derek Shiel (1990, autumn).
40. Quoted Cooper (1991), p. 7.
41. Ibid.
42. Ibid.
43. Ibid.
44. Ibid.
45. Rowan (1987), p. 24.
46. Cooper (1991), pp. 7–8.
47. Tom Mosmiller, Mike Bradley, and Michael Biernbaum (1980, fall/winter), p. 3.
48. Berkeley Brother (1974).
49. Berkeley Brother (1973), p. 2.
50. Men Supporting Men (1976).
51. From a summary of resolutions dated December 29, 1978, taken at the 5th National Conference on Men & Masculinity, Los Angeles. From Changing Men Collection, Michigan State University Library.
52. Ironically, one of the presenters was Jeff Beane, a co-founder of the National Organization of Men (later National Organization of Changing Men, then National Organization of Men Against Sexism). Beane's article "First Loves" *(Changing Men*

issue 24 Aug. 1992) celebrating his sexual experiences as a gay teenager (discussed later in this chapter) would precipitate a bitter debate about the organization's commitment to antisexism.

53. Defining ideal communities, signaled by a totalizing "the" or singular noun, was common in women's and black liberation movements as well.

54. Michael A. Messner (1997), pp. 86–87.

55. Ibid., p. 87.

56. Steven Dansky, John Knoebel, and Kenneth Pitchford (1973).

57. Ibid.

58. Messner (1997), p. 81.

59. Ibid., p. 84.

60. Nikki Craft (1993, winter/spring), pp. 18–23.

61. Melissa Farley (1993, winter/spring), p. 3.

62. Duane Allen (1993, winter/spring), p. 3.

63. Craft (1993), pp. 18–23.

64. Ibid., p. 18.

65. Ibid., p. 21.

66. Ibid., p. 22.

67. A statement from the editors and publisher, 1993 (winter/spring). p. 7.

68. Bob Vance (1993, summer/fall), p. 4.

69. Michael Kimmel (1993a), p. 3.

70. Jeff Beane (1993, winter/spring), p. 5.

71. NOMAS Leadership Collective (1995, January), pp. 7, 23.

72. A statement from the editors and publisher (1993, winter/spring), p. 8.

73. Clatterbaugh (1997), p. 56.

74. Kenneth Clatterbaugh (1994, spring), pp. 25–30.

75. "Maxim's guaranteed rate base will be two million for the second half of this year, representing a boost of 1,050,000 copies, or 111% over the second-half 1999 figure of 950,000. Maxim's circulation is more than double that of its closest rival. Maxim debuted in April 1997 and is now the largest general interest men's magazine in America." Maxim Online Pressroom (1999, April). We're kings of the hill! . . . <http://www.maximonline.com/press room/press detail.asp?press id=36>. Retrieved May 23, 2001.

76. Robert W. Connell (1995), p. 238.

77. Bob Pease (1996), p. 306.

# Appendix A: Profeminism on the World Wide Web

Many profeminist men's organizations and projects have come into being since the early 1970s—notably in the United States, Britain, Canada, Australia, and Europe. Some of these organizations disbanded quickly; others flourished for a while; still others faced crises and challenges that became the catalysts, if not the root causes, for dissolution and extinction. While many profeminist groups that formed in the 1970s and 1980s no longer exist, this appendix emphasizes that profeminism itself is far from defunct. The fact that profeminist or related men's sites have a distinct presence on the World Wide Web indicates that—even in an age when the masters of the world are intent on rebuilding the machineries of war and domination—some men continue to be interested in ending gender oppression. In many respects, the profeminist websites available today represent the accomplishments and determination of antisexist men worldwide.

These sites are a bit reminiscent of the original men's gatherings in basements and community halls or the mimeographed newsletters some groups produced. Unlike the little publications of the 1970s, though, these websites are instantly available to researchers and activists worldwide. While computer access is still mainly the province of middle-class, educated English-speakers, the Web offers some potential for new forms of grassroots profeminism.

This appendix has been divided into two major sections: (1) organizations and campaigns and (2) databases, discussion groups, and selected publications. Within each section, entries are listed alphabetically. However, these lists are far from exhaustive mainly because I have chosen to focus on profeminist groups working on a national or international scale (though I have included one or two smaller groups notable for their longevity). A few sites—such as the National Organization for Men Against Sexism, the White Ribbon Campaign, and Men Against Sexual Assault—represent organizations I have described elsewhere in this book.

Since websites can change location frequently or disappear altogether, some of the URLs listed here may no longer be accurate by the time you are reading this book. But as of February 2002, all home pages and other URLs listed here were current and correct. Many of these home pages also offer links to a variety of local groups not listed here (though bear in mind that not all website managers update their links regularly).

## PROFEMINIST ORGANIZATIONS AND CAMPAIGNS

**The American Men's Studies Association (AMSA)—United States**
Home page: *http://www.vix.com/men/orgs/writeups/amsa.html*

An academic organization, AMSA includes both women and men "dedicated to teaching, research and clinical practice in the field of men's studies. Our goal as an association is to provide a forum for teachers, researchers and therapists to exchange information and gain support for their work with men." AMSA organizes a yearly conference.

**The European Profeminist Men's Network—Toulouse and Brussels**
Home page: *http://www.europrofem.org/*

This site serves as a nexus-point for European men's efforts to promote gender equality and end violence against women. News, notices about White Ribbon campaigns, articles in several languages, and calls for papers on gender or violence issues are available here.

**The International Association for Studies of Men (IASOM)—Norway**
Home page: *http://www.rolstad.no/iasom/*

IASOM's "Platform" page articulates the goals of this organization: "The goal of The International Association for Studies of Men (IASOM) is to promote international cooperation and development of studies of men, based on profeminist, gay affirmative and antiracist principles, and to enhance the critical depth, variety and methodological and theoretical development of this field." The most recent newsletter was published on this site in 1999, so it is unclear how active this organization is currently.

**Men Against Sexual Assault (MASA)—Victoria, Australia**
Home page: *http://www.borderlands.org.au/MASA/*

While only the Melbourne chapter of MASA is still active, this organization achieved national status in the 1990s. Its goals include "ending the sexism in society that leads to sexual assault. We recognise, along with feminists, that men must take responsibility for changing a dominant male culture that harms women."

**Men Can Stop Rape—United States**
Home page: *http://www.mencanstoprape.org/index.htm*

This active organization articulates the following goals: "Men Can Stop Rape empowers male youth and the institutions that serve them to work as allies with women in preventing rape and other forms of men's violence. Through awareness-to-action education and community organizing, we promote gender equity and build men's capacity to be strong without being violent." The "Calendar" page <http://www.mencanstoprape.org/calendar2702/calendar.htm>. lists events up to and including February 2002.

**Men for Change—Halifax, Canada**
Home page: *http://www.chebucto.ns.ca/CommunitySupport/Men4Change/index.htm*

Men for Change first formed as a male response to the massacre of fourteen young women in Montréal in 1989 by a man who claimed he hated feminists. The organization's brochure states that one of its main purposes is to combine "political accountability" to feminism with "consciousness raising amongst members about the dynamics of traditional 'male culture.' " Members share their feelings and reflect on their experiences as men in small supportive groups and on retreats. At the same time, members hold public meetings, speak at schools and community centers, and have created a Healthy Relationships Violence-Prevention Curriculum package, now being piloted in some Canadian high schools.

For this group's vision statement, mission statement, and core values, go to <http://www.chebucto.ns.ca/CommunitySupport/Men4Change/vision.htm>. A related page features interviews with participants/leaders of Men 4 Change about the way the group works, as well as its history and struggles. The site also includes observations by these men on their relationships with feminist women. *http://www.chebucto.ns.ca/CommunitySupport/Men4Change/research.html*

**Men Stopping Violence—Atlanta, Ga., United States**
Home page: *http://www.menstoppingviolence.org/*

This very active group focuses mainly on violence prevention training. The group also takes a strong profeminist position, including insisting on maintaining close ties to the battered women's movement to help keep the group accountable. The summer 2001 issue of the newsletter "Uptake" can be found at <http://www.menstoppingviolence.org/uptake.html>.

**Meninist—United States**
Home page: *http://www.feminist.com/resources/links/men.html*

Meninist is "a new global organization of men that believes in a woman's right for equality in society including political, social and especially in the workplace [*sic*]." Based in New York state and linked with feminist.com, this site appears to serve as both the base of an organization and as a web resource.

**Men's Network for Change (MNC)—Ontario, Canada**
Home page: *http://www.magi.com/~mensnet/*

This group (not related to the Halifax Men for Change) was formed at a gathering in Orangeville, Ontario, in the spring of 1989 and was formally dissolved in 1997. To quote from <http://www.magi.com/~mensnet/MNC arc.html/>, "The MNC has played an important role in the lives of a great many people in Canada and beyond. To mention one example, Michael Kaufman spoke of some of the links between the MNC (and the Kingston and Grindstone Island Men's Conferences) in the development of the White Ribbon Campaign, which is quickly becoming international in scope." However, "Men's Net" website (last updated in 1998) is still maintained and contains some interesting archival material. For example, the "Mission Statement" can be found at <http://infoweb.magi.com/~mensnet/mission.htm>. Also on this site, a Men's Network for Change newsletter editor provides some insight as to why the MNC folded; see <http://www.magi.com/~mensnet/news.htm>.

**Men's Resource Center of Western Massachusetts (MRC)—United States**
Home page: *http://www.mensresourcecenter.org*

This long-lived group celebrated its fifteenth anniversary in 1998 and is still extant. Founded in 1983, the MRC sought to raise men's awareness of male violence and related issues through consciousness-raising and political events. While not as overtly political as Canada's Men for Change, the MRC continues to work against violence with a combination of men's support groups and community events—including a youth education program designed to raise awareness of gender stereotyping and encourage mutual respect. An introduction to their vision and organization is at: <http://www.valinet.com/~mrc/vision.html>. Another page stresses the emphasis on diversity; groups for African American, Latino, and other visible-minority men have been created over the seventeen years that the center has been in operation.

**National Organization for Men Against Sexism (NOMAS)—United States**
Home page: *http://www.nomas.org*

While NOMAS has experienced upheavals and was all but defunct during the late 1990s, the organization has an active web presence and is still involved in organizing the annual Men and Masculinities conferences. NOMAS is—to quote from the home page—"an activist organization of men and women supporting positive changes for men. NOMAS advocates a perspective that is pro-feminist, gay-affirmative, anti-racist, and committed to justice on a broad range of social issues including class, age, religion, and physical abilities. We affirm that working to make this nation's ideals of equality for all people a reality is the finest expression of what it means to be men." Other useful links provide information about the history of NOMAS: <http://www.nomas.org/history/>; the statement of principles <http://www.nomas.org/principles/>; and NOMAS's relationship with feminism <http://www.nomas.org/tenets/index.html>.

**Oh! Brother—United States**
Home page: *http://www.nostatusquo.com/ACLU/ohBROTHER/index.html*

This site, created by Nikki Craft, features scathing critiques of NOMAS (also see chapter 8). I have included it in this appendix because the male contributors are former NOMAS members as well as radical profeminists. The critiques focus not only on the scandal surrounding the 1992 Jeff Beane article, "First Loves," but on other decisions by NOMAS that seem sexist, antifeminist, or racist. Contributors include Geov Parrish and John Stoltenberg.

**White Ribbon Campaign—Canada and International**
Home page: *http://www.whiteribbon.ca*

This Canadian-based men's group was formed in 1991 initially as a response to the December 6, 1989, Montréal massacre. To quote from the WRC's "About Us" page, it is now "the largest effort in the world of men working to end men's violence against women. . . . We decided that wearing a white ribbon would be a symbol of men's opposition to men's violence against women." As the link "Related Sites" outlines <http://www.whiteribbon.ca/related sites/>, the campaign has expanded from Canada. Several states in the United States, as well as other countries worldwide, organize yearly White Ribbon Campaigns.

## DATABASES, DISCUSSION GROUPS, AND PUBLICATIONS

### Databases

**Ending Men's Violence Citebase—United States**
Located at: *http://www.europrofem.org/02.info/22contri/2.04.en/4en.viol/31en vio.htm*

This list was compiled by Jack C. Straton, an anti-rape activist who formed a Men Against Rape group in 1985. "This citation database (CitebaseTM) and accompanying files are designed to provide phrasing and reference information to increase the credibility of ending men's violence activists with news media and public officials." The latest cites were updated as of 1999. (I am grateful to Mr. Straton for his permission to include the Citebase here.)

**Feminist.com's listing of profeminist men's resources—United States and International**
Home page: *http://www.feminist.com/resources/links/links men.html*

This Internet clearing-house for feminist activism and resources provides a comprehensive listing of topics related to profeminist men's work.

**The Men's Bibliography—Australia**
Home page: *http://www.anu.edu.au/~a112465/mensbiblio/mensbibliomenu.html*

This comprehensive bibliography of writing on men, masculinities, and sexuality is compiled and regularly updated by Michael Flood, a long-time profeminist activist in Australia who also founded *XY* magazine. The bibliography also provides a search engine.

**Men's Issues/Masculinity/Fatherhood—The Netherlands**
Home page: *http://www.pscw.uva.nl/sociosite/TOPICS/men.html*

Maintained by the Social Science Information System at the University of Amsterdam, this site provides a list of web resources related to the topics above.

**The Men's Studies Press Homepage—United States**
Home page: *http://www.mensstudies.com/*

The Men's Studies Press publishes the *Journal of Men's Studies*, the *International Journal of Men's Health*, and a variety of books focusing on men's issues. Topics of interest include profeminism and men's activism.

**Profeminist.org—United States and International**
Home page: *http://www.profeminist.org/*

Profeminist.org provides links to a variety of profeminist organizations, including NOMAS, Men for Change, and others listed in this appendix. This site is also part of the "Men Against Violence Webring," a series of linked sites all focusing on one related topic.

## Discussion Groups

**MenAgainstSexism@onelist.com—United States**
Home page: *http://www.geocities.com/CapitolHill/Parliament/4774/*

MenAgainstSexism@onelist.com is an electronic discussion forum for "(pro)-feminist men who want support, inspiration, and educational dialogue from one another, in an attempt to foster a sense of community while engaging in our everyday struggles to confront our place and roles in a patriarchal society." A link to subscription information is provided on the home page.

**PRO-FEM E-mail list—Australia**

This unmoderated list, administered by profeminist writer and academic Michael Flood, is an international electronic discussion group focused on profeminist issues. Its goal is to promote healthy and respectful discussion about men, masculinities, and gender relations from profeminist perspectives. Subscribers may also choose to receive postings in digest form. For information about this list and how to join, go to <http://www.anu.edu.au/~a112465/profem.html>.

## Publications: Magazines and Selected Articles

**Achilles Heel: The Radical Men's Magazine—Britain**
Home page: *http://www.achillesheel.freeuk.com/*

Please see chapter 2 for more details about this publication, which as of 2002 was the only extant men's magazine (in print and online) focusing on a variety of men's issues from radical and/or profeminist perspectives.

**Gender Policy Review—Europe**
Home page: *http://gender-policy.tripod.com/journal/index.html*

*Gender Policy Review* is a monthly magazine for policy professionals and individuals interested in gender and international, development and domestic politics. The site features an article by profeminist writer and theorist Michael Kimmel about masculinities in global contexts, located at <http://gender-policy.tripod.com/journal/index.html>.

**"Men for Change Gets Personal"—Canada**
Located at: *http://www1.minn.net/~hmm/men for change story.htm*

This 1997 synopsis by Dave Redwood of Men for Change conveys a positive feeling for the group. Redwood talks at one point about the fact that feminist women's groups were uncomfortable with the men speaking at events, so the men agreed to do hosting and catering instead.

**"Men, Women, and Myth": A Critique of Michael Kimmel and Profeminism—United States**
Located at: *http://privat.ub.uib.no/bubsy/CAPP.HTM*

This anti-profeminist paper by Professor David Kubiak of Wabash University, is somewhat inflammatory in tone. Kubiak argues, among other things, that "profeminists are wimps, and pro-feminism is tolerated by academics but nowhere else because academics are sorely out of touch with reality."

**"Profeminist men and profeminist politics"—Australia**

Profeminist writer and theorist Michael Flood produced a number of articles for the profeminist magazine *XY: men, sex, politics* (see below). His "FAQ about profeminist men," among other articles, defines many basic profeminist principles and is cited often: <http://www.anu.edu.au/~a112465/pffaq.html>.

**XY: men, masculinities, and gender politics—Australia**
Home page: *http://www.xyonline.net/index.shtml*

Formerly *XY: men, sex, politics*, this magazine sought to promote "the belief that many of our society's attitudes about masculinity are harmful to men and boys in a variety of ways, as well as being oppressive to women and children. *XY* is a forum for men who are seeking to build life-affirming, joyful, and non-oppressive ways of being." The introductory page to this site also notes that "*XY* began life as a printed magazine, published in Canberra (Australia) four times a year from 1990 to 1998. The magazine was titled *XY: men, sex, politics*. We published 397 feature articles in 26 editions of the magazine." The magazine experienced a hiatus after 1998, but has now returned as a web-based archive for *XY*'s print articles as well as a resource center. The *XY* web resource is overseen by Michael Flood, a former editor of *XY*.

# Appendix B: A Method of Analyzing Profeminist Men's Motives

The ideals of unity and solidarity usually do not account for diversity, and thus are seldom achieved in real life and almost never within social movements, including feminism. Still, profeminists wanting to form a national profeminist organization have been motivated by a desire to achieve unity and solidarity. An open letter circulated to Men and Masculinity Conference delegates in 1981 eloquently summarizes these ideals: "to help anti-sexist men find and communicate with one another, to form new men's centers and consciousness-raising groups, to disseminate our ideas and values to the general public, to speak with a strong and unified voice, and to take effective action on a range of issues. . . ."[1] One of these goals—a strong and unified voice—suggests a desire for solidarity and strength in numbers. Strength and unity with others are fundamental motives for joining a group, motives vitally important to the women's movement as well as to the Left. Organizations able to convince the public that its members are acting in solidarity, even if the groups are internally in shambles, have more credibility and a much better chance of achieving a goal than a group that appears publicly fractured.

This emphasis on solidarity also reflects a deep desire to achieve a sense of identification with others. According to Kenneth Burke, a critic and philosopher of language, the only way we can achieve identification is through language; words and other symbols are the only means we have to achieve closeness or to merge with others. Indeed, the heart of all human communication—its prime motive—is our human need for unity and identification with others. But Burke also believes that identification with some is achieved only at the price of division from others.[2] This portrait of human discourse constantly shifting between identification and division is a powerful one; for one thing, it helps explain the conflicts, mixed feelings, and dilemmas experienced by profeminist men. Should they be trying to identify with as many men as possible? Should they try to achieve closeness with feminist groups? Should they make a major effort to identify themselves as separate from other, non-profeminist, men's groups?

Profeminists have had to walk a fine line between closely identifying with feminist principles and keeping a respectful distance from feminist territory to diminish the threat of appropriation. Such movements between closeness and distance exemplify Burke's concept that persuasion is a process of creating identification with one person/group, and simultaneously distance or division from another person/group. Indeed, Burke warns that our desire for closeness and our fear of estrangement inevitably sow the seeds of division, for in desiring closeness to one person or group, we separate ourselves from another person or group. Indeed, group unity is often achieved only at the cost of division, through excluding others, or even creating scapegoats. Such division creates a sense of autonomy and solidarity within a particular group, but also gives rise to conflict, misunderstanding, and estrangement in relation to other groups.[3] Burke clearly stesses that "there is division. Identification is compensatory to division. If men [*sic*] were not apart from one another, there would be no need for the rhetorician to proclaim their unity."[4]

A desire for division or separation might seem to describe the discourses produced by men. According to some feminist theorists, men are schooled to autonomy rather than cooperation; to conflict and debate—even territorialism—rather than consensus, whereas women speak and write in ways that stress connection and aim to consolidate relationships. To use Carol Gilligan's famous metaphor, women use a "different voice" than men—and she also argues that men can and do also use this voice.[5] Increasing numbers of feminist critics, philosophers, and educators began to adopt this different voice theory throughout the mid- to late 1980s.[6] These theorists argue that women's discourses are more likely than men's to stress the following characteristics: a sense of care or empathy for others; a sense that discourse is mutually constructed—it's a dialogue rather than adversarial argument; an interest in process over product, especially in regard to collaboration and cooperation; and a willingness to share rather than hoard knowledge.

Is this an entirely realistic picture of women's discourse? Most people's real life experiences suggest not. Indeed, the concept of the scapegoat—that ultimate symbol of division or "the Other"—looms over any group's attempt to persuade others to come on side.[7] The Scapegoat is generally innocent, but becomes the symbolic repository of evil or harm. Nor is scapegoating unique to discourses created by men. Critic Marsha Vanderford has noted a general tendency in social movements, including feminist movements, to "vilify opponents in order to encourage, shape, and sustain activism. If so, alienation and motivation are inseparable. If division is inherent in motivation . . . what price in social division will be paid [?]."[8]

While a feminist ideal—and one well worth pursuing—is to emphasize strategies to achieve identification, it must be acknowledged that creating identification with one group or person gives rise to exclusions and, thus, conflicts. Indeed, Burke sees this state of always being divided from others as an essential human tragedy, integral to our lives. Feminist women have, in their discourses, traditionally and strategically tried to create solidarity with women and simultaneously divide themselves from patriarchy. Sometimes these strategies end up dividing women from men—which has at times proven to be a politically productive move. At other times, attempts to create identification and solidarity—the sisterhood—have exacerbated rifts between straight women and lesbians, white women and women of color, or middle-class and working-class women.

Yet Burke's emphasis on division and opposition may not sit well with some feminist critics, who may prefer to view feminist discourse within a framework of women's ability to make connections. The idea of discourse as a kind of struggle seems much more suited to the trench warfare of patriarchal organization building. Yet the ineluctable fact that almost all organization building—feminist or not—involves shifts between identification and division is a major reason why a Burkeian approach to analyzing motives and conflicts can be more effective and broad based than an analytical framework that privileges making connections. To gain insights into the challenges faced by groups trying to do feminist or other transformative work, we need methods for understanding the workings of conflict. Yet, because Burke's critical stance sees division as inseparable from identification, some feminist rhetoricians have logically created a link between the way Burke equates identification with closeness and the way some feminists theorize women's discourse as focusing on relationships.[9] In other words, a Burkeian analysis is also a feminist relational analysis.

Burke is no cynic, but has no illusions about humans. With wry humor, he argues that engaging in public discourse inevitably takes us into "the Scramble, the Wrangle of the Market Place, the flurries and flare-ups of the Human Barnyard. . . ." Burke's analytical framework is valuable for reminding us that we must "scrutinize the concept of 'identification' very sharply to see, implied in its every turn, its ironic counterpart: division. Rhetoric is concerned with the state of Babel after the Fall."[10]

In feminist and profeminist groups, identifying with a principle that creates solidarity is often inseparable from division: whether from patriarchy or violence, or from people within the group who may not share certain sets of values. Profeminist men have—whether they've known it or not—been pioneers in a unique attempt to balance identification with division. Under certain circumstances, the prospect of division can help open up a respectful dialogue about gender differences and power inequities. Under other circumstances, the divisions can be so sharp and bitter as to fragment groups, indicating that perhaps the grounds for solidarity were unstable to begin with.

## NOTES

1. Bob Morgan (1981).

2. Kenneth Burke (1962), p. 21. Burke also thinks of identification in almost mystical terms as "consubstantiation," by which he means closeness or merging with others. For an excellent introduction to a related Burkeian method of discovering motives—exploring interrelationships among "clusters" of terms—see Sonja K. Foss (1996), pp. 63–120.

3. Burke (1962), p. 23.

4. Ibid., p. 22.

5. See Carol Gilligan (1982); Gilligan, Ward, and Taylor (1988); and Gilligan, Lyons, and Hanmer (1990). Very briefly, Gilligan established that "two moral voices" exist, one emphasizing care and responsibility to others as well as one emphasizing justice and individual rights. Gilligan's concept of the caring voice

centralizes connectivity between the self and others, recognizes a universal need for compassion, and encourages a sense of responsibility to others. Gilligan did not originally equate the voice of care with femininity, but rather saw women's emphasis on care as a much-needed addition to concepts of ethics (see M. J. Larrabee [1993], pp. 4–5). Nonetheless, Gilligan's "ethic of care" has been interpreted as a "mode of moral concern [which] typically dominates the moral reasoning of women" (5). This claim has been taken up by a number of feminists in many disciplines, to the extent that Gilligan's "ethic of care" has become equated with women's ethical values, morals, ways of reasoning, and even ways of writing and speaking—their "voices."

6. A few exemplars of the many books and articles in the 1980s and early 1990s applying Gilligan's concept of the "caring voice" to women's thinking and writing are: M. F. Belenky et al., (1986); L. Ede and A. Lunsford (1990); E. Flynn (1988), pp. 423–435; and Larrabee (1993).

7. For Kenneth Burke (1969), the scapegoat "represents the principle of division in that its persecutors would alienate from themselves to it their own uncleanliness." Members of a group are "those whose purified identity is defined in dialectical opposition to the sacrificial offering" (p. 406).

8. Marsha Vanderford (1989), 166–182. Quote is from p. 179.

9. Among the feminist rhetorical critics who have connected Burkeian identification/division with feminist epistemology are Sonja K. Foss (1996); Cindy L. Griffin (1992), pp. 330–349; Jan Swearingen (1991); and Heather Brodie Graves (1993, April), pp. 139–163.

10. Burke (1962), p. 23.

# References

For this book, I've referred to a variety of unpublished documents or materials that aren't available publicly, such as minutes, memos, brochures, leaflets, letters, drafts, now-defunct publications, or localized news articles. My main sources for these materials are the Changing Men Collections at the University of Michigan, the private collections of Bob Pease and Michael Flood in Australia, and the informal archives of the *Achilles Heel* Editorial Collective in Britain. All unpublished or now-defunct materials from these sources are cited in the chapter endnotes but not included in the References.


About NCADV. (2000). Welcome to the National Coalition Against Violence web site. Available <http://www.ncadv.org/index.htm>. Retrieved Nov. 7, 2000.

Achilles Heel: The Radical Men's Magazine. (1991, autumn). Masthead, (9), p. 3.

Achilles Heel Collective. What future for men? (1990, autumn). *Achilles Heel: The Radical Men's Magazine.* Available <http://www.achillesheel.freeuk.com/issue10.html>. 23 paragraphs.

Adamson, N., Briskin, L., & McPhail, M. (Eds.). (1988). *Feminist organizing for change: The contemporary women's movement.* Toronto: Oxford University Press.

Allen, D. (1980, spring). An interview with Marilyn French. In *M.: Gentle Men for Gender Justice*, pp. 6–7, 24–25.

Allen, D. (1993, winter/spring). [Letter to the Editor]. Re: "Transgressive sex. *Changing Men, 25*, p. 3.

A men's group. (1974, July). *Milwaukee Men's Gathering Newsletter*, 3 pp.

Anti-Sexist Men's Forum: Success! (1983, summer). *Brother: The newsquarterly of the National Organization for Men, 1*, pp. 1–2.

A statement from the editors and publisher. (1993, winter/spring). *Changing Men, 25*, p. 7.

Astrachan, A. (1984, August). Men: A movement on their own. What men haven't said to women. *Ms. Special Issue, 13*, pp. 91–93.

Assembly of First Nations. (1992, June 24). Canadian Panel on Violence Against Women (Aboriginal Circle). Available <http://www.afn.ca./resolutions/1992/aga/res29htm>. Retrieved June 7, 2001.

Atwood, M. (2000). Pornography. In Sarah Norton & Nell Waldman (Eds.), *Canadian content* (4th ed) (pp. 347–353). Toronto: Harcourt Brace Canada. (Original work published in 1983)

Backhouse, C., and Flaherty, D. H. (1992a). Violence against women. In C. Backhouse & D. H. Flaherty (Eds.), *Challenging times: The women's movement in Canada and the United States* (pp. 183–185). Montreal and Kingston: McGill-Queen's University Press.

Backhouse, C., & Flaherty, D. H. (Eds.). (1992b). *Challenging times: The women's movement in Canada and the United States*. Montreal and Kingston: McGill-Queen's University Press.

Bartky, S. (1998). Foreword. In *Men doing feminism* (p. xiii). New York: Routledge.

Barton, E. R. (2000a). Parallels between mythopoetic men's work/men's peer support groups and selected feminist theories. In E. R. Barton (Ed.), *Mythopoetic perspectives of men's healing work: An anthology for therapists and others* (pp. 3–20). Westport, CT: Bergin & Garvey.

Barton, E. R. (2000b). Preface. In E. R. Barton (Ed.), *Mythopoetic perspectives of men's healing work: An anthology for therapists and others* (pp. xi–xiii). Westport, CT: Bergin & Garvey.

Beane, J. (1993, winter/spring). Beane responds. *Changing Men, 25*, p. 5.

Belenky, M. F. et al. (1986). *Women's ways of knowing*. New York: Basic Books.

Bell, C. (1999, September). Ahimsa. Ahimsa—The Everyman Centre. Available <http://www.europrofem.org/02.info/22contri/2.04.en/4en.viol/2en vio.htm>. Retrieved May 6, 2001.

Bergman, B. et al. (1991, November 11). Women in fear. *Maclean's*, 26–30.

Berkeley Brother. (1973). About us. *Brother: A forum for men against sexism*, p. 2.

Berkeley Brother. (1974). About this issue. *Brother: A forum for men against sexism.*

Biden, J. S. (1992). Introduction. In Majority Staff of the Senate Judiciary Committee, *Violence against women: A week in the life of America*. Senate Judiciary Report. Available <http://www.inform.umd.edu/EdRes/Topic/WomenStudies/GenderIssues/Violence;+Women/WeekInAmerica/introduction>. Retrieved November 12, 2000.

Boite, M. (1992, December 3). The March to de-ribbon Mulroney. *The Varsity University of Toronto*, pp. 5, 7.

Bolan, Kim. (1992, December 2). Women angry over money spent by men's White Ribbon Campaign. *The Vancouver Sun*, p. A1.

Bouchier, D. (1984). *The feminist challenge: The movement for women's liberation in Britain and the USA*. New York: Schocken Books.

Brannon, R. et al. (1981, fall). A national anti-sexist men's organization. *M.*, pp. 6–7.

Brannon, R. (1983, summer). Press conference statement. *Brother: The Newsquarterly of the National Organization for Men, 1*, p. 5.

Brillantes, M. (1984, May 9). Barry Shapiro takes on a man-sized job: Sexual harassment in the workplace. *Santa Barbara News-Press*.

Bristow, Joseph. (1992). Men after feminism: Sexual politics twenty years on (pp. 57–79). In D. Porter (Ed.), *Between men and feminism*. London: Routledge.

Brod, H. (1998). To be a man, or not to be a man—that is the feminist question. In T. Digby (Ed.), *Men doing feminism* (pp. 197–212). New York: Routledge.

Brookmire, P. (1979, October 25). Conference says liberation not just for women. *The Milwaukee Journal*, p. 10.

Brookmire, P. (1984, winter). Together at the 8th National Conference. *M: Gentle Men for Gender Justice, 11*, 3–6.

Brother Collective. (1974, fall). About this issue. *Brother: A Forum for Men Against Sexism*, pp. 1–2.

Brown, J. (1990, October 3). March of the caring men a first. *The [Melbourne] Age*, p. 3.

"Bruce." (1974). Why a men's movement? *Morning Due, 1(1)*, 2 pp.

Bullock, C. (2000). Warriors and fathers: Once were warriors and the mythopoetic understanding of men's violence. In E. R. Barton (Ed.), *Mythopoetic perspectives of men's healing work: An anthology for therapists and others* (pp. 46–58). Westport, CT: Bergin & Garvey.

Burke, K. (1962). *A rhetoric of motives*. Berkeley: University of California Press.

Burke, K. (1969). *A grammar of motives*. Berkeley: University of California Press. (Original work published 1945)

Califia, P. (1994). Among us, against us: Right wing feminism. *Public Sex*. Quoted in Pornography the debate, *World Association for Christian Communication*. Available <http://www.wacc.org.uk/womedia/porn.htm>. Retrieved March 15, 2001.

Came, B. (1989, December 18). Montreal massacre. *Maclean's*, pp. 14–17.

Canaan, J. E., & Griffin, C. (1990). The new men's studies: Part of the problem or part of the solution? In J. Hearn & D. Morgan (Eds.), *Men masculinites and social theory* (pp. 206–214). Critical Studies on Men and Masculinity Series (J. Hearn, Ed.). London: Unwin Hyman.

Caplan, P. J. (1994). *Lifting a tone of feathers: A women's guide to surviving in the academic world*. Toronto: University of Toronto Press.

Cassidy, B., Lord, R., & Mandell, N. (1995). Silenced and forgotten women: Race, poverty, and disability. In N. Mandell (Ed.), *Feminist issues: Race, class, and sexuality* (2nd ed.) (pp. 26–54). Scarborough, ON: Prentice Hall Allyn & Bacon Canada.

*Chicago Men's Gathering Newsletter*. (1973, June). *1*(1).

*Chicago Men's Gathering Newsletter*. (1974). *2*(3).

Christian, H. (1994). *The making of anti-sexist men*. London: Routledge.

Clatterbaugh, K. (1994, spring). Men's movement publications. *Serials Review*, pp. 25–30.

Clatterbaugh, K. (1997). *Contemporary perspectives on masculinity: Men, women and politics in modern society* (2nd ed.). Boulder, CO: Westview.

Cole, Susan. (1991, December 5–11). Remembering Montreal. *Now Magazine*, pp. 14, 17.

Collective statement. (1974). *Morning Due: Voices of Changing Men, 1*(1). Seattle: Men's Resource Center, 10 pp.

Collective Statement. (1977). *Morning Due: A Decent Men's Journal, 3*(1). Seattle: Men's Resources Center, n.p.

Collins, L., & Walton, P. (1996, spring/summer). Flexible work patterns for men. *Achilles Heel: The Radical Men's Magazine, 20*, pp. 28–30.

Collins, P. H. (1990). *Black feminist thought: Knowledge, consciousness, and the politics of empowerment*. London: HarperCollins.

Connell, B. (1995). Men at bay: The "men's movement" and its newest best-sellers. In M. S. Kimmel (Ed.), *The politics of manhood: Profeminist men respond to the mythopoetic men's movement (and the mythopoetic leaders answer)* (pp. 75–88). Philadelphia: Temple University Press.

Connell, R. W. (1987). *Gender and power*. Stanford: Stanford University Press.

Connell, R. W. (1995). *Masculinities*. Berkeley: University of California Press.

Cooper, M. (1991). *Searching for the anti-sexist man: An Achilles Heel publication*. London: Achilles Heel Publications.

Craft, N. (1993, winter/spring). So much slime, so little time: The transgression of profeminism. *Changing Men, 25*, pp. 18–25.

Creighten, A., and Kivel, P. (1998). Making the peace: A 15-session Violence Prevention Program for Young People. Available <http://www.kdva.org>. Retrieved November 15, 2000.

Crowe, C., and Montgomery, C. (1992, November 27). Putting on a ribbon isn't nearly enough. *The Globe and Mail*, p. A25.

Daly, M. (1973). For and against us: Antichauvinist males and women's liberation. *Social Policy, 4*(3), pp. 32–33.

Dansky, S., Knoebel, J., Pitchford, K. (1973). *The effeminist manifesto*. New York: Templar.

Daphne, M. (1999, May 9). Personal interview.

Daphne, M., & Murdolo, A. (1992, spring). A weekend away with the boys. *XY: men, sex, politics, 2*(3), p. 28.

Davis-Barron, S. (1992, November 24). Ribbon drive leads to tangle. *The Ottawa Citizen*, p. B1.

Delmar, R. (1986). What is feminism? A Re-examination. In *What is feminism?* (pp. 8–33). New York: Pantheon Books.

Denborough, D. (1994). A model of hope: Men against sexual assault—accountability structures. *Dulwich Centre Newsletter*, nos. 2&3, pp. 45, 47, 50–54.

Digby, T. (1998). Introduction. In *Men doing feminism* (p. 1). New York: Routledge.

Domanick, J. (1986, May 9). The men's movement today. *Utne Reader*.

Dworkin, A., & MacKinnon, C. (1988). *Pornography and civil rights: A new day for women's equality*. Minneapolis: Organizing Against Pornography.

Ede, L., & Lunsford, A. (1990). *Singular texts/Plural authors*. Carbondale: Southern Illinois University Press.

Editorial. (1975, July). *Brother: A Forum for Men against Sexism, 13*.

Editorial. (1980, spring). *M.: Gentle Men for Gender Justice, 2.*

Editorial. (1981, fall). *M.: Gentle Men for Gender Justice, 6.*

Editorial. (1990, April). *Achilles Heel: For Changing Men, 9*, p. 3.

Editorial. (1991, December 6). Ending violence against women. *Toronto Star*, p. A28.

Editorial. (1992, December 3). Raising men's consciousness. *Canberra Times.*

Edwalds, L., and Stocker, M. (Eds). (1995). *The woman-centered economy: Ideals, reality, and the space in between.* Chicago: Third Side Press.

Ehrenreich, B. (1983). *The hearts of men: American dreams and the flight from commitment.* New York: Anchor Books.

Elliot, P., & Mandell, N. (1995). Feminist theories. In N. Mandell (Ed.), *Feminist issues: Race, class, and sexuality* (2nd ed.) (pp. 2–25). Scarborough, ON: Prentice Hall Allyn & Bacon Canada.

Engels, F. (1993). Origin of the family, private property, and the state. Excerpt in A. M. Jaggar & P. S. Rothenberg (Eds.), *Feminist frameworks: Alternative theoretical accounts of the relations between women and men* (3rd ed.) (pp. 160–170). New York: McGraw-Hill. (Original work published in 1884)

Etkin, M. (1991, January/February). The men's movement. *Canadian Dimension, 25*(2), pp. 35–37.

Evans, R. (2000, March 29). Australian feminism: From "protection" to liberation. Review of *The history of Australian feminism: Getting equal. Green Left Weekly, 399.* Available <http://www.greenleft.org.au/back/2000/399/index.htm>. Retrieved March 15, 2001.

Faludi, S. (1995, March/April). I'm not a feminist but I play one on TV. In *Ms.*, pp. 31–39.

Faludi, S. (1999). *Stiffed: The betrayal of the American man.* New York: William Morrow and Co.

Farley, M. (1993, winter/spring). [Letter to the Editor]. Re:"Transgressive sex." *Changing Men, 25*, p. 1.

Farrell, W. (1973, February). Men: Guidelines for consciousness-raising. *Ms. 8*(1), pp. 12–13, 15, 116–117.

Fasteau, M. F. (1975). *The male machine.* New York: Dell.

Finan, C. M., & Castro, A. F. (1996). Catherine A. MacKinnon: The rise of a feminist censor 1983–1993. MIT Safe Archives. Available <http://www.mit.edu/activities/safe/writing>. Retrieved February 20, 2001.

First Annual BrotherPeace Award! (1990). *Ending Men's Violence Newsletter, 7*(1), p. 9.

Fisher, K. (1993, March/April). Men's groups: Accountable to whom? For what? *Canadian Dimension*, pp. 41–44.

Flood, M. (1993/94, summer). Three principles for men. *XY: men, sex, politics, 3*(4). Available (1995) <http://www.anu.edu.au/~a112465/XY/3princip.htm>. Retrieved June 7, 2001.

Flood, M. (1997, spring). Responding to men's rights. *XY: men, sex, politics, 7*(2), pp. 37–39.

Flynn, E. (1988). Composing as a woman. *College Composition and Communication, 39*, pp. 423–435.

Foss, S. K. (1996). *Rhetorical criticism: Exploration and practice* (2nd ed.). Prospect Heights, IL: Waveland Press.

Foucault, M. (1984). Truth and power. In Paul Rabinow (Ed.), *The Foucault reader* (pp. 51–75.) New York: Pantheon Books.

Foucault, M. (1990). *The history of sexuality. Vol. 1: An introduction.* R. Hurley, (English trans. pub. 1978, Trans.). New York: Vintage Books.

Fremont-Smith, K. (1985, June). On being allies: An analysis of the men's network. *Brother, 1*, pp. 8–9.

From the Majority Staff of the Senate Judiciary Committee. (1990). *Facts about violence against women.* University of Maryland, InforM. Women's Studies Database: Gender Issues. Available <http://www.inform.umd.edu/EdRes/Topic/WomensStudies/GenderIssues/Violence+Women/facts>. Retrieved November 12, 2000.

Funk, R. E. (1990). Montreal Massacre: One year hence. *Ending Men's Violence Newsletter, 7*(1), pp. 8–9.

Gilligan, C. (1982). *In a different voice: Psychological theory and women's development.* Cambridge: Harvard University Press.

Gilligan, C., Lyon, N. P., & Hanmer, T. J. (Eds.). (1990). *Making connections: The relational worlds of adolescent girls at Emma Willard School.* Cambridge: Harvard University Press.

Gilligan, C., Ward, J. Y. and Taylor, J. M. (Eds.). (1988). *Mapping the moral domain.* Cambridge: Harvard University Press.

Goldrick-Jones, A. (1998, summer/autumn). Politics and profeminism across the pond—a personal view. *Achilles Heel: The Radical Men's Magazine, 23*, pp. 32–34.

Goldrick-Jones, A. (2000). Justice, joy, and an end to the gender wars. In E. R. Barton (Ed.), *Mythopoetic perspectives of men's healing work: An anthology for therapists and others* (pp. 246–251). Westport, CT: Bergin & Garvey.

Gordon, M.-D. (1993, summer/fall). Why is this men's movement so white? *Changing Men: Issues in Gender, Sex and Politics, 26*, pp. 15–17.

Graves, H. B. (1993, April). Regrinding the lends of gender: Problematizing "writing as a woman." *Written Communication, 10*, pp. 139–163.

Griffin, C. L. (1992). A feminist perspective on rhetorical theory: Toward a clarification of boundaries. *Western Journal of Communication, 56*, pp. 330–349.

Hagan, K. L. (Ed). 1992. *Women respond to the men's movement: A feminist collection.* San Francisco: Pandora.

Harding, S. (1998). Can men be subjects of feminist thought? In T. Digby (Ed.), *Men doing feminism* (pp. 171–196). New York: Routledge.

Heath, S. (1987). Men in feminism: Men and feminist theory (pp. 41–46). In A. Jardine & P. Smith (Eds.), *Men in feminism.* New York: Routledge.

History of the National Organization for Women. (1998). *National Organization for Women.* Available <http://www.now.org/hisotry/history.html>.

hooks, b. (1992). Men in feminist struggle: The necessary movement. In K. L. Hagan (Ed.), *Women respond to the men's movement: A feminist collection* (pp. 111–117). San Francisco: Pandora.

Hopkins, P. D. (1998). How feminism made a man out of me: The proper subject of feminism and the problem of men. In T. Digby (Ed.), *Men doing feminism* (pp. 51–52). New York: Routledge.

Hughes, A. (1992, autumn). If we are a movement . . . *XY: men, sex, politics,* 2(1), pp. 12–13.

Hughes, J. O., and Sandler, B. R. (1987). "Friends" raping friends—could it happen to you? Project on the Status and Education of Women, Association of Women Colleges. Available <http://www.cs.utk.edu/~bartley/acquaint/acquantRape.html>. Retrieved November 12, 2000.

Hughes, K.P. (Ed.). (1994). *Contemporary Australian feminism* 1. Melbourne: Longman Cheshire.

Hughes, K. P. (1997). Feminism for beginners. In K. P. Hughes (Ed.), *Contemporary Australian feminism 2* (pp. 1–29). South Melbourne: Longman.

Hughes, R. (1987). *The fatal shore: The epic of Australia's founding.* New York: Alfred A. Knopf.

Hunter, A. (1993). The story behind Fem-MEN-IN-ism. Available <WMST-L@umdd.umd.edu>. Retrieved July 6, 1993.

Interrante, J. (1982, summer/fall). Dancing along the precipice: The men's movement in the '80s. *M.,* pp. 3–6, 20–21.

Interrante, J. (1983, spring). Dancing along the precipice: The men's movement in the '80s *M.,* pp. 3–6, 32.

Jardine, A. (1987). Men in feminism: Odordi uomo or compagnons de route? In A. Jardine & P. Smith (Eds.), *Men in feminism* (pp. 54–61). New York: Routledge.

Jones, A., & Camille, G. (1992). Radical feminism in New Zealand: From Piha to Newton. In R. Du Plessis (Ed.), *Feminist voices: Women's studies texts for Aotearoa/New Zealand* (pp. 300–316). Auckland: Oxford University Press.

Jones, Craig. (1992, winter). Kingston report: White Ribbon reflections. *Men's Network News, 3*(1), p. 7.

Jourard, S. M. (1974). Some lethal aspects of the male role. In J. M. Pleck & J. Sawyer (Eds.), *Men and masculinity* (pp. 21–29). Englewood Cliffs, NJ: Prentice-Hall.

Kamuf, P. (1987). Femmenism. In A. Jardine & P. Smith (Eds.), *Men in feminism* (pp. 78–84). New York: Routledge.

Kane, L. (1993, December 3). Taking a stand on violence. *The [Melbourne] Age.*

Kaufman, M. (1991, December 17). The future of the White Ribbon campaign. Unpublished report, 9 pp.

Kaufman, M. (1992, December 3–9). The White Ribbon's meaning. *NOW.*

Kaufman, M. (1993, December 4). Personal interview.

Kaufman, M. (1993). *Cracking the armour: Power, pain, and the lives of men.* Toronto: Viking Canada.

Kilic, S. (1997). Who is an Australian woman? In K. P. Hughes (Ed.), *Contemporary Australian feminism 2* (pp. 30–51). South Melbourne: Longman.

Kimmel, M. (1993a). The politics of accountability. *Changing Men, 26,* p. 3.

Kimmel, M. (1993b). Strength through diversity. *Changing Men, 26,* p. 4.

Kimmel, M. S. (Ed.). (1995). *The politics of manhood: Profeminist men respond to the mythopoetic men's movement (and the mythopoetic leaders answer)* (pp. 1–11). Philadelphia: Temple University Press.

Kimmel, M. S., and Mosmiller, T. (Eds.). (1992). *Against the tide: Pro-feminist men in the United States, 1776–1990: A documentary history.* Boston: Beacon Press.

King, M. (Ed.). (1988). *One of the boys? Changing views of masculinity in New Zealand*. Auckland, NZ: Heinemann.

Kleiman, C. (1978, April). Good-bye, John Wayne? *Ms.*, *6*(10), pp. 45–47, 77.

Koss, M. P., & Fitzgerald, L. (1993, June 14) To the editor. [Letter to the editor]. New York Times. Available <http://www.inform.umd.edu/EdRes/Topic/WomensStudies/GenderIssues/Violence+Women/koss-letter>. Retrieved March 15, 2001.

Koss, M. P., Woodruff, W. J. and Koss, P. G. (1991, August). *1990 statistics on sexual violence against women—a criminological study*. In U.S. Department of Justice, Bureau of Justice Statistics, *Female victims of violent crime*. University of Maryland, InfoM, Women's Studies Database: Gender Issues, violence and women. Available <http://www.inform.umd.edu./EdRes/Topic/WomensStudies/GenderIssues/Violence+Women/statistics>. Retrieved November 12, 2000.

Kramarae, C., & Treichler, P. A. (Eds.). (1985). *A feminist dictionary*. London: Pandora.

Laird, Gordon. (1993, May). Direct male marketing. *This Magazine*, pp. 16–18.

Lakeman, L. (1992). *99 federal steps toward an end to violence against women*. Toronto: National Action Committee on the Status of Women.

Landsberg, M. (1992, November/December). Canada: Will ribbons keep men's violence under wraps? *Ms.*, pp. 16–17.

Larbalestier, J. (1998). Black feminism. In B. Caine (Gen. Ed.), *Australian feminism: A companion* (pp. 390–391). Melbourne: Oxford University Press.

Larrabee, M. J. (Ed). (1993). *An ethic of care*. New York: Routledge.

Laurie, A. J. (1992). Speaking the unspeakable: A background to teaching lesbian studies. In R. Du Plessis (Ed.), *Feminist voices: Women's studies texts for Aotearoa/New Zealand* (pp. 49–50). Auckland: Oxford University Press.

Layton, J. (1993, August 31). Personal interview.

Leach, M. (1993, spring). Hard yakkin'. *XY: men, sex, politics 3*(3), pp. 14–17.

LeGates, M. (1996). *Making waves: A history of feminism in Western society*. Toronto: Copp-Clark.

Levine, S. (1973, February). One man's experience. *Ms.*, *8*(1), p. 14.

Lips, Hilary. (1991). *Women, men, and power*. Mountain View, CA: Mayfield.

Lorde, A. (1981). The master's tools will never dismantle the master's house. In C. Moraga & G. Anzaldúa (Eds.), *This bridge called my back: Writings by radical women of color* (pp. 98–101). Watertown, MA: Persephone Press.

Lovell, T. (1990). Introduction. In T. Lovell (Ed.), *British feminist thought: A reader* (pp. 3–10). London: Basil Blackwell.

Lovenduski, J., & Randall, V. (1993). *Contemporary feminist politics: Women and power in Britain*. Oxford: Oxford University Press.

MacKinnon, C. A. (1987). *Feminism unmodified: Discourses on life and law*. Cambridge: Harvard University Press.

MacKinnon, C. A. (1992). Feminist approaches to sexual assault in Canada and the United States: A brief retrospective. In C. Backhouse & D. H. Flaherty (Eds.), *Challenging times: The women's movement in Canada and the United States* (pp. 186–192). Montreal and Kingston: McGill-Queen's University Press.

MacLeod, L. (1987). *Battered but not beaten: Preventing Wife Battering in Canada.* Ottawa: Canadian Advisory Council on the Status of Women.

Majority Staff of the Senate Judiciary Committee. (1990). *Facts about violence against women.* University of Maryland, InforM. Women's Studies Database: Gender Issues. Available <http://www.inform.umd.edu/EdRes/Topic/WomenStudies/GenderIssues/Violence+Women/facts>. Retrieved November 12, 2000.

Making a difference: A brief history of NOMAS and the National M & M Conferences. (1995, January). *Brother: The Newsletter of the National Organization for Men against sexism, 12*(2), pp. 15, 23.

Malette, L., & Chalouh, M. (Eds.). (1991). *The Montreal massacre.* (M. Wildeman, Trans.). Charlottetown, Prince Edward Island Gynergy Books.

Marable, M. (1997). The black male: Searching beyond stereotypes. In M. B. Zinn et al. (Eds.), *Through the prism of difference: Readings on sex and gender* (pp. 443–449). Toronto: Allyn & Bacon.

Marcus, J. (1988). Australian women and feminist men. *Hecate: An Interdisciplinary Journal of Women's Liberation*, 16(2) pp. 98–106.

MASA national gathering. (1992). *Men Against Sexual Assault Newsletter, 1*, pp. 1–2.

Mason, G. (1998). Violence. In B. Caine (Gen. Ed.), *Australian feminism: A companion* (pp. 337–344). Melbourne: Oxford University Press.

Men Against Sexist Shit. (1993, spring). Sexism, class and bullshit. *XY: men, sex, politics, 3*(3), p. 19.

Men's liberation: Responding to the women's movement. (1971). *Brother: A Forum for Men Against Sexism*, 12 pp.

Men supporting men. (1976). 2nd Men & Masculinity Conference Program. State College, Pennsylvania.

Messner, M. A. (1997). *Politics of masculinities: Men in movements.* Thousand Oaks, CA: Sage.

Miles, R. (1991). *The rites of man: Love, sex and death in the making of the male.* London: Paladin.

Mill J. S. (1970). The subjection of women. Excerpt in A. M. Jaggar & P. S. Rothenberg (Eds.), *Feminist frameworks: Alternative theoretical accounts of the relations between women and men* (3rd ed.) (pp. 150–158). New York: McGraw-Hill. (Original work published in 1869)

Modleski, T. (1991). *Feminism without women: Culture and criticism in a postfeminist age.* New York: Routledge.

Monture-Okanee, P. (1992). The violence we women do: A First Nations view. In C. Backhouse & D. H. Flaherty (Eds.), *Challenging times: The women's movement in Canada and the United States* (pp. 193–200). Montreal and Kingston: McGill-Queen's University Press.

Morgan, R. (Ed). (1970). Introduction. In *Sisterhood is powerful: An anthology of writings from the women's liberation movement* (pp. xxiii–xxiv). New York: Vintage.

Morgan, R. (Ed.). (1970). *Sisterhood is powerful: An anthology of writings from the women's liberation movement.* New York: Vintage.

Mosmiller, T. (1984a, fall). Dear council members. *Brother, 3*, pp. 1, 8.

Mosmiller, T. (1984b, fall). Looking forward and back. *Brother, 3*, pp. 1, 8–9.

Mosmiller, T., Bradley, M., and Biernbaum, M. (1980, fall/winter). Are we the first? A call for feminist men's history. *M.*, pp. 3–4, 21.

Mott, G. (1992). Following a wife's move. In M. S. Kimmel and T. Mosmiller (Eds.), *Against the tide; Pro-feminist men in the United States, 1776–1990: A documentary history*. Boston: Beacon Press.

Moyer, B., & Tuttle, A. (1977, November 10). Overcoming masculine oppression in mixed groups. *WIN Magazine*, 4 pp.

Mudge, B. (1997). *Sexism and Stoicism: Theorizing Profeminist Strategies*. Unpublished thesis, Flinders University of South Australia. Available <http://www.europrofem.org/02.info/22contri/2.04.en/5en.sex/02en sex.htm>. Retrieved May 22, 2001.

NOMAS Leadership Collective. (1995, January). Report on Changing Men Issues. *Brother, 12*, pp. 7, 23.

NOMAS (The National Organization of Men Against Sexism). (2000, July). A brief history of the M & Ms and NOMAS. Available <http://www.nomas.org/history//>. Retrieved May 22, 2001. 6 paragraphs.

Norberg-Bohm. (1987, June). Confronting NOCM organization process: The members have no voice, neither are we asked. *Brother, 5*(3), p. 4.

Oakley, Ann. (1988). *The men's room*. London: Virago.

Ohmann, R. (1987). In, with (pp. 182–188). In A. Jardine & P. Smith (Eds.), *Men in feminism*. New York: Routledge.

Paglia, C. (1995). Rape and the modern sex war. In A. M. Stan (Ed.), *Debating sexual correctness: Pornography, sexual harassment, date rape, and the politics of sexual equality* (pp. 21–25). New York: Dell.

Paisley, F. (1998). Interwar feminists and aboriginal policy. In B. Caine (Gen. Ed.), *Australian feminism: A companion* (pp. 168–173). Melbourne: Oxford University Press.

Parliament of Australia, The Senate. (1993, December 5). *More action on men's violence: Democrats* [media release], 1p.

Parrish, Geov. (1992). Male Supremacy and the Men's Pro-feminist Movement: The Dubious Legacy of the National Organization for Men Against Sexism. Available <http://www.igc.apc.org/nemesis/ACLU/oh!Brother/>. Retrieved January 26, 1998.

Pease, B. (1996). *Reforming Men: Masculine Subjectivities and the Politics and Practices of Profeminism*. Unpublished diss., La Trebe University, Bundoora, Australia.

Pease, B. (1997). *Men & sexual politics: Towards a profeminist practice*. Adelaide: Dulwich Centre Publications.

Pease, B. (1999, May 6). Personal interview.

Pease, B. (2000). *Recreating men: Postmodern masculinity politics*. London: Sage.

Pleck, J. (1976). The male sex role: Definitions, problems, and sources of change. *Journal of Social Issues, 32*, 155–164.

Pleck, J., & Sawyer, J. (Eds.). (1974). *Men and masculinity*. Englewood Cliffs, NJ: Prentice-Hall.

*Pornography: Does women's equality depend on what we do about it?* (1994, January/February). *Ms.*, pp. 42–45.

Porter, D. (Ed.). (1992). *Between men and feminism*. London: Routledge.

Portland Men's Resource Center. (1980, March–April). Principles of unity. *Forum for Changing Men*, p. 3.

Pratt, S., & Tuddenham, R. (1997, summer/autumn). Masculinity and power. *Achilles Heel, 22*, pp. 23–25.

Reade, K. (1994). "Struggling to be heard": Tension between different voices in the Australian women's liberation movement in the 1970s and 1980s. In K. P. Hughes (Ed.), *Contemporary Australian feminism 1* (pp. 198–221). Melbourne: Longman Cheshire.

Roberts, Y. (1992). *Mad about women: Can there ever be fair play between the sexes?* London: Virago.

Ross, L. (1998–99). A brief chronology of the women's liberation movement in the UK (1969–1979), The women's liberation movement: history and resources. Available <http://www.geocities.com/Wellesley/Garden/3971/chronlgy.html>. Retrieved May 6, 2001.

Rowan, J. (1987). *The horned god: Feminism and men as wounding and healing.* London: Routledge.

Rowan, J. (1994, autumn). Recounting accountability. *Achilles Heel*, p. 6.

Rowe, M. (1982). Introduction. In M. Rowe (Ed.). *Spare rib reader* (pp. 13–22). Harmondsworth, Middlesex: Penguin.

Rubin, J. C. (1999, November). Insults and injuries: Feminism in Australia. *WIN Magazine,* 26. Available <http://winmagazine.org/issues/issue26/win26d.htm>. Retrieved March 15, 2001.

Rutherford, J. (1992). *Men's silences: Predicaments in masculinity*. London: Routledge.

Ryan, B. (1992). *Feminism and the women's movement: Dynamics of change in social movement, ideology and activism.* New York: Routledge.

Saltman, D. (1997). Feminism and the health care movement. In K. P. Hughes (Ed.), *Contemporary Australian feminism 2* (pp. 216–241). South Melbourne: Longman.

Sarachild, K. (1978). Consciousness-raising: A radical weapon. In *Feminist revolution*. New York: Random House. Documents from the Women's Liberation Movement: An Online Archival Collection. Special Collections Library, Duke University. Available <http://scriptorium.lib.duke.edu/wlm/organizations.html>. Retrieved February 20, 2001.

Scanlon, J. (1994). Educating the living, remembering the dead: The Montreal massacre as metaphor. *Feminist Teacher, 8*(2), pp. 75–79.

Schacht, S. P., & Ewing, D. (1997, summer/autumn). Sharing power: Entering women's space. *Achilles Heel: The Radical Men's Magazine, 22*, pp. 34–36.

Segal, L. (1997). *Slow motion: Changing masculinities, changing men* (rev. ed.). London: Virago.

Seidler, V. J. (1991a). *Recreating sexual politics: Men, feminism and politics.* London: Routledge.

Seidler, V. J. (Ed.). (1991b). *The Achilles Heel reader: Men, sexual politics and socialism.* London: Routledge.

Seidman, P. B. (1991, winter/spring). The Montreal massacre and the war against women: The means to an end get meaner. *Changing Men, 22*, p. 11.

Shapiro, B. (1982, October). *Council meets in San Francisco, adopts new structure.* Bulletin. National Men's Organization. n.p.

Show Your Respect for African American Women: Councilwoman Fields' Statement at the Candlelight Vigil for Black Women Who Have Been Victims of Violence. (1995, June 19). Sistahspace Kwanzaa Information Center. Available <http://www.sistahspace.com/nommo/mv30.html>. Retrieved June 7, 2001.

Sluser, Ron. (1992, December 2). Personal interview.

Smart, B. (1985). *Michel Foucault*. London: Tavistock Publications.

Smith, V. (1993, July 30). Equality called key to ending violence. *The Globe and Mail*, pp. A1. A3.

Sommers, C. H. (1999). The real issue: researching the "rape culture" of America. An investigation of feminist claims about rape. Leadership U: Telling the truth project. Available <http://www.leaderu.com/real/ri9502/sommers.html>. Retrieved November 12, 2000.

Stan, A. M. (Ed.). (1995). *Debating sexual correctness: Pornography, sexual harassment, date rape, and the politics of sexual equality*. New York: Bantam Doubleday Dell.

Stanko, E. (1985). *Intimate intrusions: Women's experience of male violence*. London: Routledge.

Staples, R. (1997). Anita Hill, sexual harassment, and gender politics in the black community. In M. B. Zinn et al. (Eds.), *Through the prism of difference: Readings on sex and gender* (pp. 191–192). Toronto: Allyn & Bacon.

Steinem, G. (1970, June 7). "Women's liberation" aims to free men, too. *The Washington Post*. Available <wysiwyg://190/http://geocities.com/Yosemite/Rapids/4668/gloriasteinem.html>. Retrieved February 28, 2001.

Steinem, G. (1984, August). Men tell the truth. *Ms. Special Issue, 13*, p. 41.

Steinem, G. (1992). Forward. In K. L. Hagan (Ed.) *Women respond to the men's movement: A feminist collection* (pp. v–ix). San Francisco: Pandora.

Stevens, M. (1987, January). "This stuff is great, I think": Women's reactions to men's movement work. *Men & Women Today*, pp. 8–9.

Stoltenberg, J. (1984, May). Sex & justice. In *Antipornography Task Group of the National Organization for Changing Men Newsletter*, 1, 7 pp.

Stoltenberg, J. (1997, March 2). Male Supremacy and the Men's Pro-feminist Movement. Online posting to pro-feml@postbox.anu.edu.au.

Sullivan, B. (1995). Rethinking prostitution. In B. Caine & R. Pringle (Eds.), *Transitions: New Australian feminisms* (pp. 184–197). St. Leonards, NSW: Allen & Unwin.

Swearingen, J. (1991). *Rhetoric and irony: Western literacy and Western lies*. New York: Oxford University Press.

Sweet, E. (1995). Date rape. The story of an epidemic and those who deny it. In A. M. Stan (Ed.), *Debating sexual correctness: Pornography, sexual harassment, date rape, and the politics of sexual equality* (pp. 10–20). New York: Bantam Doubleday Dell. (Original work published in *Ms.*, October 1985, p. 56)

Task force on Men's Movement: National, Regional and Local Organizations. (1981). Resolutions presented at the National Conference on Men & Masculinity, June 12–16, 1981. St. Louis, Missouri.

Tavris, C. (1978, April). Is this the year of the man? *Ms., 6*(10), pp. 51, 78.

Tedeschi, C. (1992, December 12). Non-violent men recognising that they must speak up. *Canberra Times*, C4.

Thorne-Finch, R. (1992). *Ending the silence: The origins and treatment of male violence against women*. Toronto: University of Toronto Press.

Tolson, A. (1977). *The limits of masculinity: Male identity and women's liberation*. New York: Harper & Row.

Tomlins, J. (1990, October 12). Men against sexual assault? *The Rabelais [Melbourne: LaTrobe University]*, p. 6.

Trigiani, K. (1999). Those Martian Women! *Out of the cave: Exploring Gray's anatomy*. Available <http://web2.airmail.net/krtrig246/out__of__cave/-martian.html>. Retrieved February 15, 2001.

Vance, B. (1993, summer/fall). Strength through diversity. *Changing Men, 26*, p. 3.

Vanderford, M. (1989). Vilification and social movements: A case study of pro-life and pro-choice rhetoric. *Quarterly Journal of Speech, 75*, pp. 166–182.

Van Der Voght, Susan. (1995, January 5). Telephone interview.

Vickers, J., Rarkin, P., & Appelle, C. (1993). *Politics as if women mattered: A political analysis of the National Action Committee on the Status of Women*. Toronto: University of Toronto Press.

Voumvakis, S. E., & Ericson, R. V. (1984). *News accounts of attacks on women: A comparison of three Toronto newspapers*. Toronto: Oxford University Press.

Waterloo Men's Conference. (1975). Program. University of Waterloo, Ontario.

Watson, C. (1988, June 1). The White Ribbon Campaign: Men working to help end violence against women. In *Newsletter of Education Wife Assault*. <http://www.whiteribbon.ca/eindex.html>. Document no longer available at new site <http://www.whiteribbon.ca/>. Retrieved November 16, 2000.

What are some good men's movement books? (1997). The Men's Issues Page. Available <http//www.vix.com/men/books/reviews.html>. Retrieved June 5, 2001.

What should the relationship be between pro-feminist men and feminism? (1989, June) Conference handout. 14th Annual M & M Conference (1–4 June, 1989). From Changing Men Collection, Michigan State University Library.

White Ribbon Campaign. (1991, November). Breaking men's silence to end men's violence. Press release. Toronto: White Ribbon Campaign.

White Ribbon Campaign. (1991, December 1–6). *Breaking men's silence to end men's violence: December 1–6, 1991* [public campaign statement]. Toronto, Ontario.

White Ribbon Campaign. (1992). *How to organize the WHC in your community, school, group, or workplace: White Ribbon Campaign Organizer's Kit*. Toronto, Ontario.

White Ribbon Campaign. (1993). *Frequently asked questions about the White Ribbon Campaign*. Toronto: White Ribbon Campaign. Available <http://www.whiteribbon.ca/aboutus/>. Retrieved April 27, 2001.

White Ribbon Campaign. (1993). *White Ribbon Campaign educational development strategy*. Toronto, Ontario. 5 pp.

White Ribbon Campaign. (2000, March 23). *Frequently asked questions about the White Ribbon Campaign*. Available <http://www.whiteribbon.ca/faq.htm>. Retrieved September 19, 2000.

White Ribbon Campaign. (2000). About us. Available <http://www.whiteribbon.ca/aboutus>. Retrieved May 24, 2001.

Who is RAVEN? (1983). From Changing Men Collection, Michigan State University Library. 2 pp.

Why are we an oppressor's club? (1976, January). *Men Against Sexism Newsletter, 25.*

Williams, L. (1990, April). Men in feminism. *Women: A cultural review, 1*(1), pp. 63–65.

Williams, S. (2000, February 25). A singular history of black women. Indiana University Home Pages. Available <http://www.iuinfo.indiana.edu/homepages/2-25-2000/text/women.htm>. Retrieved June 7, 2001.

Willis, E. (1995). Feminism, moralism, and pornography. In A. M. Stan (Ed.), *Debating sexual correctness: Pornography, sexual harassment, date rape, and the politics of sexual equality* (pp. 41–49). New York: Dell. (Original work published 1979)

Wolf-Light, P. (1998, January). Personal interview. Plymouth, UK.

Women's Studies Group. (1978). Women's studies group trying to do feminist intellectual work. In Women's Studies Group (Ed.), *Women take issue: Aspects of women's subordination* (pp. 7–17, 123). Centre for Contemporary Cultural Studies, University of Birmingham. London: Hutchinson.

# Index

Aboriginal women, 12, 15, 114, 120, 124–26. *See also* First Nations women
Abortion. *See* Reproductive choice
Accountability to feminism, 6, 7, 45, 67, 77, 79, 137, 151; Australian profeminists, 75–77; definitions, 68–69, 75, 76, 161, 163–64, 179; White Ribbon Campaign, 69–75. *See also* Coalitions, feminists and profeminists; Profeminist relations with feminism
*Achilles Heel: the radical men's magazine*, 44–45, 68, 101, 143, 150–51, 160, 163–64, 166, 183. *See also* British men's movement; British profeminism
*Against Our Will* (Brownmiller), 116, 123, 136
Ahimsa (Everyman) Centre, 150–52
American feminism: anti-male violence, 115–21; anti-porn, 118–19; conferences, 23; liberal, 22–23; nineteenth-century, 13–14; radical, 14, 23, 26–27; Second Wave, 15, 22–24. *See also* National Organization for Women (NOW); Race/racism; Second Wave feminism
American liberationist men, 35, 52, 54–55
American men's movement. *See* Men's movement
American profeminism. *See* Profeminist activism
Antifeminism, 54–56, 89, 93, 158
Anti-Pornography Task Group, 7, 137–38
Antisexist men. *See* Profeminist activism
Antisexist men's activism. *See* Profeminist activism
Antisexist men versus liberationist men. *See* Liberationist men versus antisexist men
Antiviolence activism. *See* Violence against women: feminist activism. *See also* Profeminist activism: antiviolence
Australian feminism: aboriginal women, 15, 124–26; activism, 20–21, 123–26; gender relations, 75–77; history, 21, 123

Australian men's movement, 142. *See also* Australian profeminism
Australian profeminism, 51, 75–77, 142–50

Battered women's movement: organizations, 125, 128 n.50, 128–29 n.60; refuges, 121–22, 124–26, 128 n.50; shelters, 112, 115. *See also* Rape; Violence against women
Beane, Jeff, 170–73, 175–76 n.52, 181
Bell, Calvin, 150–51, 152
Biden, Senator Joseph, 115–16, 117
Black men. *See* Representation, groups in profeminism
Black women, 12, 106, 109 n.66, 120–21, 124
Bly, Robert, 5, 55
"Bra-burning," 26
Brannon, Robert (Bob), 33–34, 53, 59–60, 99–100, 108 n.35, 137–38
"Breaking Men's Silence to End Men's Violence," 131–32
British feminism: activism, 17, 23–24, 39, 121–22; 1960s and 1970s, 17–19, 121; socialism, 16, 18–19, 104, 158; women's studies, 19
British men's movement, 34–35, 159–61. *See also* British profeminism
British profeminism: antisexist men, 44–45, 55, 150–52, 158; conferences, 35, 159; gay men, 159, 165–66; radical, 159–60, 165–66. *See also* *Achilles Heel: the radical men's magazine*; Male guilt; "The Ten Commitments"
*Brother*, 43–44, 60, 92, 94
*Brother: A Forum for Men Against Sexism*, 36–37, 42–43, 44, 46, 103–4, 167
BrotherPeace: award, 139–40; Brother-Storm, 138–39, 154 n.20; marches, 139, 144. *See also* Ending Men's Violence Task Group (EMV); Stoltenberg, John
Brothers Against Sexism, 165

California Anti-Sexist Men's Political (CAMP) Caucus, 99–100, 136, 153 n.15
Canadian feminism, 19–20, 112–15
Canadian profeminism, 39, 62, 74. *See also* White Ribbon Campaign
*Changing Men: issues in gender, sex, and politics*, 46, 49 n.68, 141, 143, 170–72
Changing Men Collections, 49 n.52
*Changing the Landscape: Ending the Violence, Achieving Equality*, 113–14
Christian, Harry, 3, 161
Class: men, 7, 43, 75, 166, 168, 170; women, 11, 13, 16, 21–24, 124; working-class men, 100–103. *See also* Representation, groups in profeminism
Clatterbaugh, Kenneth, 35, 46, 138–40, 158, 173
Coalitions, feminists and profeminists, 69, 74, 83–84 nn.23–24, 103
Connell, R.W. (Bob), 34, 53, 101–2, 174
Consciousness-raising (CR): "bitch session cellgroup," 37–38; men's, 4, 6, 36–40, 42, 89, 159; Sarachild, Kathie, 27, 38; women's, 20, 24, 27, 37, 38–39
Cooper, Mick, 159–61, 163
Craft, Nikki, 170–71, 181

Daphne, Marnie, 75–76
Date rape, 117–18
December 6. *See* Montréal massacre
Denborough, David, 75, 76–77
Diversity. *See* Representation, groups in profeminism
Domestic violence. *See* Violence against women
Dulwich Centre, 75
Dworkin, Andrea, 79, 116, 119, 123, 137, 141

École Polytechnique (Université de Montréal). *See* Montréal massacre
"Effeminist Manifesto," 168–69

Ending Men's Violence Task Group (EMV), 105, 131, 136–37; EMV-Net, 142; *EMV Network Newsletter*, 139–40, 142. *See also* BrotherPeace; Stoltenberg, John
Enfranchisement. *See* Votes for women
Engels, Friedrich, 11, 13, 31
Equal Rights Amendment (ERA), 23–24, 28, 40, 58
Exclusion of men. *See* Separatist feminism

Faludi, Susan, 5, 127 n.30
Farrakhan, Louis, 106, 109 n.66
Farrell, Warren, 32–33, 36–38, 53
Fasteau, Marc F., 32–33
Fathers' rights. *See* Men's rights
Feminism: brief history of, 11–15; definitions of, 11, 79
Feminist activism in: Australia, 20–22, 122–26, 145; Britain, 12–13, 16–19, 121–22; Canada, 19–20, 112–15; New Zealand, 25; United States, 13–14, 22–24, 26, 112, 115–21. *See also* Feminist politics; Second Wave feminism
Feminist men. *See* Profeminism; Profeminist activism
Feminist politics: conflicts, 17–18, 20, 24–25, 27, 58, 100, 118, 121–22, 125, 145; heterosexuality, 20, 24, 26; liberal, 13–14, 17, 22, 32, 46, 58, 158; Marxism, 13, 18, 21, 26; media images, 26; radical feminism, 14, 17–18, 23–27, 145, 169; socialism, 16, 18–19, 104, 109 n.55. *See also* Accountability to feminism; Lesbian feminism; Pornography; Profeminist relations with feminism; Separatist feminism
Feminist reformers, 3, 12–15, 16
Femocrats, 21–22
First Nations women, 15, 114
First Wave of feminism, 13
Flood, Michael, 4, 46, 49 n.57
Foucault, Michel, 84 n.39
"Freedom trash can," 26
Free Men, 54–56, 58–59
French, Marilyn, 46, 141
Friedan, Betty, 17, 22
Funk, Russ Ervin, 140–42

Gay men: culture, 44, 160, 168–69; "First Loves" controversy, 7, 170–172; liberation, 17, 26, 165, 169; perspectives, 7, 46, 167–68, 169–72; profeminist support for, 7, 43, 59, 160, 167; radical views, 165–67; representation in profeminist groups, 59, 64 n.14, 103–4, 166, 168; straight men, 157, 159, 165–66, 167–68. *See also* Beane, Jeff; "Effeminist Manifesto"; Pro-gay men; Representation, groups in profeminism
Gender: oppression, 34–35, 38, 52–53, 54, 158, 162–63, 169; relations, 8, 32, 145; roles, 32–34, 151, 168; "wars," 141. *See also* Masculinity; Power: gender relations; Sex roles
Greer, Germaine, 17, 20
Guilt. *See* Male guilt

Heterosexism, 64 n.14, 104, 167, 172
Heterosexuality, 103–4, 166
Hispanic women. *See* Women of color
Homophobia, 56, 59, 168
Homosexuality. *See* Gay men; Lesbian feminism
hooks, bell, 2, 105, 120, 136

Ideological differences, 52–55, 157, 160, 174
Inclusivity. *See* Representation, groups in profeminism
International Women's Day, 112
International Women's Week, 152
*Iron John*. See Bly, Robert

Kaufman, Michael, 62–63, 65 n.39, 72–75, 79, 91, 134, 137. *See also* White Ribbon Campaign (WRC): co-founders
Kimmel, Michael S., 31, 46, 55, 64 n.15, 80, 138, 171–72
King, Martin Luther, 105
Kivel, Paul, 136, 153 n.13

Koss, Mary, 116–18, 122, 127 n.30, 139–40

Landsberg, Michele, 71–72
Layton, Jack, 62–63, 73, 80. *See also* White Ribbon Campaign (WRC): co-founders
Lépine, Marc, 61, 140–42. *See also* Montréal massacre
Lesbian feminism: American, 23, 26; international, 17–18, 20, 24–25; perspectives, 24–26, 169; radical views, 26, 81–82. *See also* Feminist politics; Separatist feminism
Liberal feminism. *See* Feminist politics: liberal feminism
Liberationist men. *See* Men's liberation
Liberationist men versus antisexist men, 34–35, 44, 46, 52–53, 140, 157–64
Lorde, Audre, 67

*M.: Gentle Men for Gender Justice*, 44–46, 58–59, 64 n.24, 90
MacKinnon, Catharine, 116, 119, 123, 137
MacKinnon-Dworkin Ordinance, 119, 138
Male guilt, 6, 7, 42, 90, 102–3, 137–38, 144–45, 147, 157, 160–65
Male-positive, 40–42, 93–94, 132, 159, 164, 166, 170–71
Male power, 6, 68, 70–72, 84 n.40, 82, 146, 151, 162. *See also* Power
Male privilege. *See* Male power
Male violence against women. *See* Violence against women
Manhood. *See* Masculinity
Marxist-Socialist feminism, 13, 159
Masculinity, 6, 32–35, 138, 143, 145, 147, 158–59, 163–65. *See also* Sex roles
Masculinity studies. *See* Men's studies
Maternal feminism, 14, 28 n.9
*Maxim*, 173–74
Men Against Sexism (Britain), 159–60, 162
Men Against Sexism (MAS, Australia), 143–44, 162–63
Men Against Sexual Assault (MASA), 4, 7, 68, 78, 143, 178; accountability models, 75–77, 82; "Men Can Stop Rape" marches, 145–47; White Ribbon campaigns, 131, 142, 148–50
Men and Masculinity/ies (M & M) conferences: activism at, 136, 139; early conferences, 39–41, 53–54, 136; feminist representation at, 90, 95; link to national men's organization, 56, 58, 172; Martin Luther King Day controversy, 105; topics, 39–41, 54, 59, 64 n.4, 104, 136–37, 167–68
"Men Can Stop Rape" marches. *See* Men Against Sexual Assault (MASA)
Men 4 (for) Change (Halifax), 45, 113, 179, 183
Men "in" feminism debate, 78–83, 107–8 n.21
Men's Alliance for Liberation and Equality (MALE), 52, 56
Men's antisexist groups (1970s), 4, 34–35, 62, 136
Men's antiviolence activism. *See* Profeminist activism: antiviolence
Men's conferences/gatherings, 35, 39–40, 54, 62, 76, 159–60, 165. *See also* Men and Masculinity/ies (M & M) conferences
Men's liberation, 4, 32–34, 42, 52–53, 158
Men's movement in: Australia, 142; Britain, 7, 34–35, 158;1970s, 32–35, 42, 135–36; United States, 32–33, 34, 35, 42, 103–4, 135–142
Men's Network for Change, 4, 62, 173
Men's rights, 35, 52–54, 93, 158
Men's studies, 2, 4
Messner, Michael A., 32–34, 105–6, 109 n.55, 169
Middle-class. *See* Class
Million Man March, 5, 106–7, 109 n.66
Morgan, Robin, 37, 38, 118
Montréal massacre: December 6, 1989, 61, 63, 73–74, 83 n.2, 131, 155

n.46; feminist responses, 113, 118
motive for White Ribbon Campaigns, 61, 131, 148; profeminist responses, 135–36, 140–41. *See also* Lépine, Marc
*Morning Due*, 91, 104
Mosmiller, Tom, 31, 46, 52, 94, 97, 137, 166
*Ms. Magazine*, 2, 3, 36, 71, 116, 127 n.30
Mythopoetic men, 5, 45, 55, 64 n.15, 158. *See also* Bly, Robert

National Abortion Campaign (NAC, Britain), 18
National Action Committee on the Status of Women (NAC, Canada), 19, 72
National Coalition Against Domestic Violence, 115, 126 n.22. *See also* Violence against women: feminist activism
National men's conferences. *See* Men & Masculinity/ies (M & M) conferences; Men's conferences/gatherings
National men's organizations. *See* National Organization for Changing Men (NOCM); National Organization for Men Against Sexism (NOMAS); Profeminist organizations; White Ribbon Campaign (WRC)
National Organization for Changing Men (NOCM): formation of, 43, 57, 88; goals of, 57–58, 87, 94; governance of, 92, 95–97, 108 n.25; motives, 58–60, 64; name change, 53, 57; as National Organization for Men, 52–53, 56; Open Forum, 60; organizational structures, 56, 59–60, 88–93, 95–98; regional representation, 95–100; task groups, 96–97, 105, 137–39. *See also* Profeminist organizations; Representation, groups in profeminism
National Organization for Men Against Sexism (NOMAS): Beane-NAMBLA "crisis of commitment," 7, 169–73; current status, 7, 172; Men & Masculinity/ies conferences, 40, 172; history, 53–54, 56; principles, 144; race, 104–7; relations with *Changing Men*, 49 n.68, 171–72; task groups, 142. *See also* National Organization for Changing Men (NOCM)
National Organization for Women (NOW): history of, 3, 20, 22–23; model for profeminist organizations, 53, 57–59, 90; relations with profeminism, 36, 60
National women's conferences, 17, 20, 21, 25, 90
New Zealand feminism, 25, 28 n.16
North American Man-Boy Love Association (NAMBLA), 170–71

Oakland Men's Project of California, 136, 153 n.13
Oppression. *See* Gender: oppression; Power: gender relations

Patriarchal structures/systems, 71, 91–92, 99, 124, 146
Patriarchy: definitions, 5, 23; "the master's tools," 67; men dismantling, 6, 24, 67, 91, 94, 138, 144, 169
Pease, Bob, 145, 148, 149–50, 174
"Pedophile movement," 171, 172
Pleck, Joseph, 32, 33
Pornography: anti-porn activism, 118, 120, 135, 143, 170; censorship, 119–20, 127 n.33, 128 n.36, 140; conflicting views about, 127–28 n.35, 137, 140, 169–71; definitions, 118–19; MacKinnon-Dworkin Ordinance, 119, 138. *See also* Profeminist activism: anti-porn; Sexual: freedom of expression
Power: definitions, 78, 84 n.39; gender relations, 7, 77–78, 84 n.40, 90, 165, 168; male domination, 68, 71–72, 75–77, 82, 89, 100–101; race, 106. *See also* Male power

Profeminism: definitions, 4, 78, 79, 81; liberal position on, 42–43, 59, 140, 143; principles, 40, 42–45, 65 n.23, 88, 97, 144, 160, 171, 174. *See also* Radical profeminism

Profeminist activism: anti-porn, 135, 138, 143; anti-rape, 41, 135–36, 139, 143, 144–48; antisexist, 5, 35, 42–45, 62, 103, 160; antiviolence, 4, 7, 41, 59, 61–63, 69, 72–75, 131–52; demonstrations, 37, 136, 139, 144–47; publications, 4, 32–33, 37, 40–47, 103–4, 139–40, 143, 164–65, 167, 172–73, 176 n.75. *See also* Men's conferences/gatherings; Profeminist motives; Profeminist relations with feminism; White Ribbon Campaign (WRC)

Profeminist motives, 42, 51, 52, 56, 76; criticisms, 70–72, 146–47; ending violence against women, 61, 63, 139, 146, 148; feminist influences, 3, 37, 57–58, 61, 161; sex-role liberation, 32, 37; unity, 57, 60, 139. *See also* Montréal massacre

Profeminist organizations, 4, 6, 7, 135–36, 173; formation, 52, 56, 60–63, 69, 88, 94, 143–44, 160; goals, 2, 4, 47, 57, 59–62, 72, 88, 92, 94, 144, 174; internal conflicts, 43, 46, 52–53, 58, 59–60, 93, 95–98, 152, 157–72; leadership, 59, 73, 80, 91, 95–96, 98–100, 105, 108 n.35, 172; organizational structures, 57, 59–60, 64, 67–69, 72–73, 76, 88–89, 91–92, 95–100, 105, 174. *See also* National Organization for Changing Men (NOCM); National Organization for Men Against Sexism (NOMAS); Representation, groups in profeminism

Profeminist relations with feminism: alliances, 40, 61, 62, 72–73, 74–75, 76, 82, 123, 163; feminism as inspiration or motive, 6, 32, 36–37, 55, 61–62, 91–93, 95, 111, 139–40, 150, 159; inclusion of women, 40, 68–69, 73, 76, 88–91; tensions, 6, 69–72, 123, 145–47, 159, 161, 163, 170–71. *See also* Accountability to feminism; Coalitions, feminists and profeminists; Men "in" feminism debate

Pro-gay men, 35, 43, 52, 53, 59, 160, 167, 170. *See also* Gay men

Pro-male. *See* Male-positive

Promise Keepers, 5, 173

Race/racism: effects on women, 114, 120–21, 124–26; as issue for feminists, 20, 23, 25; as issue for profeminists, 104–7, 166, 168. *See also* Aboriginal women; Black women; First Nations women; Representation, groups in profeminism

Radical feminism, 17–18, 20, 23, 46, 58, 112, 118, 154, 157, 166

Radical profeminism: activism, 37, 42, 138, 167; criticisms of, 93; definitions of, 42–43, 140, 158; goals, 59, 104, 158–59, 167, 168–69. *See also* "Effeminist Manifesto"; Gay men: perspectives; radical views; Profeminist activism: anti-porn

Rape: attitudes toward, 112, 116–17, 118, 121–22, 147; awareness, 41, 112–13, 115–17, 123, 135–36, 149; date rape, 117; prevention, 124; shelters/refuges, 115, 121–22, 124–26, 128 n.50. *See also* Battered women's movement; Profeminist activism: anti-rape; Violence Against Women

Rape and Violence End Now (RAVEN), 136, 153 n.12

Rebick, Judy, 71, 72, 114

"Reclaim the Night," 123, 146, 150

Representation, groups in profeminism: black men, 7, 92, 104–7, 120–21, 165, 166; diverse men, 96, 97, 166, 171; feminist women, 87–91. *See also* Class; Gay men; Profeminist organizations

Reproductive choice, 24, 54, 58, 62

Rowan, John, 44, 90, 141, 159–62, 164

Rutherford, Jonathan, 160, 162

Second Wave feminism, 14–16, 17–22, 157, 163
Segal, Lynne, 2, 5
Seidler, Victor, 44–45, 90, 101, 141, 159, 162–65
Separatist feminism, 18, 21, 25–26, 81–82, 85 n.55, 88–90, 122, 124
Sexism, 32, 38, 41, 162–63, 165
Sex roles, 33–34, 40, 47–48 n.14, 91, 94, 162–63
Sex role theory. *See* Sex roles
Sexual: abuse, 114, 145; assault, 115–18, 122, 144, 171; freedom of expression, 16, 119–20, 128 n.36, 169, 170, 172; harassment, 118, 149; politics, 165, 167, 169–72
Slavery, 12–13, 120
Sluser, Ron, 73, 74, 137
Socialist feminism, 16, 18–19, 43, 104
Sommers, Christina Hoff, 118, 127 n.30
Steinem, Gloria, 2, 3, 5, 33
Stoltenberg, John, 105, 136, 137–39, 173, 181
Suffrage. *See* Votes for women

"Take Back the Night," 112, 123, 136, 137
"The Ten Commitments," 160–63
Tolson, Andrew, 100–101
Trust. *See* Accountability to feminism; Profeminist relations with feminism

Violence against women, 111–26, 131–52: attitudes toward, 54, 112–14, 118, 121, 124, 127 n.30, 147, 149, 150; feminist activism, 69–70, 73, 107, 112, 121–25; legislation, 7, 112–13, 115, 121, 124–25; therapy for men, 150–52, 153 n. 11; sociopolitical causes, 135, 147–48, 150, 153 n.11. *See also* Battered women's movement; Profeminist activism: antiviolence; Rape
"Violence Against Women: A Week in the Life of America," 115–16
Violence Against Women Act, 115, 126 n.22
Votes for women, 13–15

"Warrior" groups, 5, 55, 158
White Ribbon Campaign (WRC): accomplishments, 7, 69, 72, 82, 131–35, 139, 142; co-founders, 60–62, 69, 73, 145–46; criticisms of WRC, 6–7, 69–72, 83 n.13, 133–34, 152–53 n.6; finances, 69–72, 134–35; formation, 6, 51, 60–62, 69, 131–32; goals, 2, 4, 61–62, 72, 93, 113, 133–35, 140, 164; white ribbon symbolism, 61, 69, 74, 132–33, 147, 148, 181; White Ribbon Week, 69, 83 n.2, 132, 134, 149, 155 n.46. *See also* Accountability to feminism; Kaufman, Michael; Profeminist activism: antiviolence; Profeminist organizations
White women. *See* Race/racism
Wollstonecraft, Mary, 11, 12–14
Women Against Violence Against Women (WAVAW), 69–70, 112
Women of color, 25–26, 120–21, 124. *See also* Aboriginal women; Black women; First Nations women; Race/racism
Women's Electoral Lobby (WEL), 21, 24–25
Women's liberation (1960s and early 1970s), 3, 36
Women's Liberation Movement (WLM, Australia), 20–21, 24–25
Women's Liberation Movement (WLM, Britain), 121–22, 159, 160
Women's movement. *See* Feminist activism in; Feminist politics
Women's shelters. *See* Battered women's movement
Women's studies, 3, 11, 19
Women's suffrage. *See* Votes for women
Working-class. *See* Class

*XY: men, sex, politics*, 44, 46, 49 n.57, 102–3, 143

Young Women's Christian Association (YWCA), 19, 74

## ABOUT THE AUTHOR

AMANDA GOLDRICK-JONES is an Associate Professor in the Centre for Academic Writing/Women's Studies Department at the University of Winnipeg. Recent publications are "Men and Feminism: Relationships and Differences," in *Gender, Race, and Nation: A Global Perspective*, ed. V. Dhruvarajan and J. Vickers (2002) and *The Broadview Anthology of Poetry*, 2nd ed., ed. H. Rosengarten and A. Goldrick-Jones (forthcoming).